THE WONDER OF LIFE

THE WONDER OF LIFE

Follow man's ignorance of the secrets of life to the marvels of today's DNA, the genetic code and the genome of man.

JOHN DURBIN HUSHER

LitPrime Solutions
21250 Hawthorne Blvd
Suite 500, Torrance, CA 90503
www.litprime.com
Phone: 1-800-981-9893

Originally Copyrighted in 2008 and Republished in 2021 John Durbin Husher.
All rights reserved.

No part of this book may be reproduced, stored in a retrieval system, or transmitted by any means without the written permission of the author.

Published by LitPrime Solutions   11/18/2021

ISBN: 978-1-955944-41-0(sc)
ISBN: 978-1-955944-42-7(hc)
ISBN: 978-1-955944-43-4(e)

Library of Congress Control Number: 2021923292

Any people depicted in stock imagery provided by iStock are models, and such images are being used for illustrative purposes only.

Certain stock imagery © iStock.

Because of the dynamic nature of the Internet, any web addresses or links contained in this book may have changed since publication and may no longer be valid. The views expressed in this work are solely those of the author and do not necessarily reflect the views of the publisher, and the publisher hereby disclaims any responsibility for them.

CONTENTS

Prelude ix
Introduction xv

The Birth of Earth 1
    The Spread of the Sun's Energy On Earth. 12
    Water, Needed for Life 13
    The Buildup of Oxygen 22

And Then Came a Meteor. 25

And Then Came Man. 27
    Man, Communication, and Education 34
    Alexander the Great 38
    The Roman Empire 39
    The Silent Deaths 43
    Summary of Disease 55
    The Printing Press. 56

The Microscope. 64
    Pasteur 71
    Koch. 75

Other Major Impacts of the Nineteenth Century. 86
    Gregor Mendel and Genetics. 86

Charles Darwin: The Theory of Evolution 92
    The Importance of Human Hygiene. 98

The Twentieth Century and Infection. .102
    Serendipity with a Fungus: Penicillin 121
    Polio and Jonas Salk 130

The Continued Search for the Secrets of Life. 138
    Cells of Prokaryotes and Eukaryotes 140
    Sex and Mating: The Chromosomes 142

Organics, Proteins, and Nucleic Acid. .150
    Amino Acids. 157

It Isn't the Proteins 164
    DNA and RNA 165

Found, The Source of life - The Double Helix and
the Human Genome 170
    Replication 174

The Way into the Nucleus. 182
    Transcription and mRNA. 185

The Genetic Code: Translation of RNA Code into Protein 189
    Protein Synthesis. 193
    Number of Genes in the Human. 194

The Human Genome 198

HIV and AIDS. 205
    Late News on Advances on HIV. 216

Stem Cells and Research 218
    The Unique Properties of Stem Cells. 228
    Pluripotent /embryonic stem cell line 232

Adult Stem Cells 235
    Plasticity of Adult Stem Cells 236
    Exciting Late News on Adult Stem Cells 245
    Pluripotent Stem Cells from Adult Skin Cells 250

The Wonder of Life 256
    Why the Technical Entities? 266

Conclusion 271
References and Credits 275
Index 279

PRELUDE

The Wonder of Life

Life fascinates all of us in one way or another, and each of us wants to learn more about it. Life on this planet is what this book is about. It provides insights into the birth of our Earth and the many changes that have occurred since then, changes that allowed for man to make his appearance and take a foothold in Earth's history. This is a story of wars between men and the wars with the silent and unseen. Each war brought new meaning to man and each battle with the silent and unseen brought us great knowledge and closer to a basic understanding of life. This is the story of the medical learning of man bringing the reader right up to the present, past DNA, to the present day work on stem cells. It covers the crude beginnings of DNA and how it eluded the understanding of man for several thousand years as he sought the answers to the secrets of life. The history of man's struggles to learn more about himself carries you through the educational process that allows him to pass this growing knowledge from generation to generation, with each generation increasing that knowledge base to another level, right up through to the present day knowledge of the human genome.

This story primarily focuses on man's learning curve and how man went from a fairly crude and ignorant beginning searching for the secrets of life to present-day man, with his increased knowledge, his improved tools, his everyday wonders, and finally to his realization of DNA's part in the total picture.

Man's early education arrived through experiences beyond his choice; including wars that eroded his chance at life in exchange for the learning that one can gain from wars. Battles with diseases, pestilence, and ignorance were also among his teachers. Each of these difficult experiences helped to educate him and bring him closer to finding the secrets of life. Over time, man shifted from a passive to an offensive role as he created tools that allowed him to observe, in order to fight these silent enemies and engage them on terms to his liking.

On this journey, man sought to determine the nature of life and what made man tick. The problem with this journey was its length and the fact that to learn what makes a man tick; he must learn what makes them stop ticking. The learning involves losing many of his kind and learning from their deaths.

When man learned that death came from the unseen, carried by those he could see, his first proactive experience with the silent enemies was to separate those who were suffering from those who were not, through quarantines. During the nineteenth century, microscopes allowed him to observe the bacteria that caused many of the issues, and he learned of their weaknesses. By seeing them he could experiment and see what affected them. In general, the battle against bacteria was well on its way to being won when the twentieth century began. Findings during that century were the clues to genetics, but these clues were not recognized until many years later.

Along the way man discovered better ways to communicate and document his findings. In chronological order the major findings were; the development of the alphabet, the invention of the printing press, and the development of the microscope. These were instrumental in allowing man to leap across a major ignorance gap to a new world of education. What was seen through the microscope could be documented, printed in different languages and distributed around the world. The ability to now see the small unknown segments that brought life or death could be analyzed and made known to people around the world.. Man's conquest over what he could see led him to achievements in conquering various illnesses. As the story proceeds to the twentieth century, the marvels of science emanated from bright minds and began to broach the secrets of the genetic code.

Such real-life human experiences are powerful stories that cannot be matched by fiction, which is why, although much of this material is based on science, I present it in a novel form that allows the average layman to easily read and understand the basics of DNA, the genetic code, the human genome, and stem cells. *The Wonder of Life* brings to you a level of understanding that will allow you to read about the everyday advancements being made in these areas, as well as an understanding of AIDS, the retrovirus that brings HIV to mankind, and how it relates to an individual's DNA. This was, and is, a war that must be fought with the inventions that extend the life of man.

The first third of the twentieth century offered great progress on innovation but not much progress on finding the cure for infection and other illnesses caused by the silent enemies. Significant advances are achieved prior to, during, and immediately following World War II, in technology, medicine, and bioscience, that allowed man to achieve major accomplishments toward defeating the silent enemies and to learn more about the secrets of life.

By mid-century man progressed from searching the proteins that he believed controlled life to the amino acids and finally to the nucleic acids. In the nucleic acids of DNA and RNA, he discovered the four base pairs that he now focused on, believing they controlled the genetic code of life. The major clue was found in mid-century, when an American and three British scientists located the double helix, which is home for the base pairs of DNA. But how did these codes make it out of the nucleus shell of the chromosomes to provide the body with all the signals needed to maintain life? The answer came by way of the genius of many people from around the globe.

During the 1980s you will meet the HIV virus and eventually AIDS, and learn about its connection to DNA and RNA. You will see that stem cells were used to overcome blood disorders. Twenty years later embryonic stem cells made their appearance and offered promise for solving these blood disorders, as well as diseases in mice that we expected mimicked ours.

At the end of the twentieth century and the beginning of this new one, we find new methods of providing adult stem cells that can be made pluripotent. Man's knowledge has increased to the point where he is now able to program skin cells to become pluripotent, which allows man to investigate how this can provide replacement parts for failing ones in our bodies.

This terrific journey through time and advances in technology and the sciences allows us to observe life in its smallest increments.

You will see how the wonders of life coalesce in *The Wonder of Life*.

To Peg, Jay, Karen, and David: my wonders of life

INTRODUCTION

Did you ever think about life? Ever wonder about people and their differences? I have. I looked at my parents for clues and noticed some traits I share with both of them, but I am clearly different. Like a snowflake, every human is different in some way. These differences and similarities are determined by genetics, and the genetic code provides the basis for why some of your traits are like one's parents, but always with differences. Even twins are different. Fraternal twins result from two eggs that are fertilized almost simultaneously, and when they are born you can see the physical difference. Even though they are twins, they don't look alike, and one can even be a girl and the other a boy. They don't have matching DNA. I was born a fraternal twin, and my twin brother is about half a foot taller than I am. But we share many thoughts and often come to the same conclusions, because we have common genes. On the other hand, some twins are almost identical. They come from a single egg, and we now know they have the same DNA. As they grow up it is difficult to tell one from the other, but there are still differences. In fact, they may be more different than fraternal twins. They may think and act differently, and when they become adults, even though they still may look a good bit alike, you can clearly tell the difference. Why is that? Same egg, same DNA, same environment, same schools, but they are different. What's in each person to make him unique, especially in identical twins? Maybe it's one small aspect of the DNA that's slightly different. Wouldn't it be boring if the two of them were really exactly alike? And yet, they have the best chance of being alike of any pair in this world of people. Wouldn't it be boring if we were all alike?

Isn't it great that the world is made up of all different people, with different thoughts, different goals, different opportunities, different dispositions, different IQs, different personal drive, some drivable and some not, some calm, some excitable, some skillful and some not so skillful, some sad, some happy, some bright, some dull? Where do they each fit in this world of differences? Life is complex in that way. I began this book with the plan of covering the reasons for these variations in each of us. I also wanted to provide the reader with some insight into the long journey man had to experience to gain the knowledge of determining the secret of life. Here we are, the most intelligent form of life, and yet intelligence is not enough; it takes time and experience to gain most knowledge. We weren't always this intelligent and this knowledgeable. How did we gain this knowledge? How did man become the top of the food chain? I thought about this and decided to go back in time and review how man came to be and how he evolved into this more educated being.

This story is about looking back to the beginning and reviewing how man has reached this level of knowledge and the events that educated him to a level beyond his ancestors'. The past wasn't like today, when you can read a book, watch television, or read the daily newspapers and learn while sitting comfortably at home. For several thousand years, man learned the hard way. He first learned by meeting his daily needs and through struggles with others. He learned though wars that pushed him out into unknown lands and taught him the ways of different people in those lands. He learned through the Crusades that again brought him the knowledge of others. Man was born to assimilate the best qualities of others, at least in acquiring their knowledge and adding it to his. He also learned a great deal in times of disease, when he sought, in desperation, to overcome what ailed him and others, while seeking the source of this silent killer. It seems the hardships of life bring out the best in man. Maybe it's because it's during these times when many share a common problem that they work together for a solution. It seems that several brains working together gain much more than the one alone. And so, my research found that there was a significant gain in knowledge during times when man was extended to his limits. You will find it interesting and entertaining as you travel through these times with me, reviewing the solutions to man's problems and the knowledge gained by these experiences. You will witness the impact of being able to speak the "same" language and eventually to invent ways to print books to document and spread this knowledge. And you will learn how these elements increased man's ability to reach new heights as each generation passed.

From the day man began his journey on Earth, he wondered about life and its secrets. The drive for this knowledge is as old as man. He is probably the only creature on this planet that thinks about history, life, himself, his future, and the limits of life. The only one who tries to solve the riddles of life. –This quest has brought us quite far, and you will read about today's levels of understanding as you reach the end of this book.

Whereas the first part of this book is about fairly old history, the rest rapidly brings you across time to meet today - face-to-face. Where sixty years ago we were still quite ignorant about the secrets of life and the genetic code of man, today we are quite informed and have moved to map man's genome. You will be brought to the current level of understanding as you journey through this book.

Time limits most things. It has been that way since the beginning of time. But when did time begin for the people on Earth? The Earth didn't always have people; in fact it didn't have any living things that we know of when Earth began its journey. If we go back in time and look at how things began and study the evolution of plants, animals, and humans, we can find clues. Maybe we can answer the ever popular "chicken and egg" puzzle of which came first. Perhaps this will tell us something about mankind and ourselves that will help us to maintain our progress as human beings on Earth.

Travel back and see what makes us tick. It will be a long trip, but it will be worth it. It's a complex journey; it will cover everything from the magnitude of planet Earth to the microscopic inner workings of cells. It will encompass the birth of Earth and the evolution of man and animals on the way to the present hunt for solutions with the aid of stem cells. History has shown that as we discover how to conquer one set of obstacles, a new set enters the picture. But man's ability to ascend the learning curve with each of these challenges primes him for the next set.

As you travel from chapter to chapter, you'll be happy to enjoy the interesting views from a comfortable distance, rather than taking part in the early battles of life yourself. The book will carry you through to today's battles and provide insights into current issues you may find difficult to understand, such as DNA and stem cells. I hope it brings clarity to your life as well. Have a great journey.

THE BIRTH OF EARTH

There are scientists who claim the Earth began as an explosion that provided all the stars, galaxies, and planets. They named it the Big Bang, and there are estimates that it occurred fourteen billion years ago. In an instant there was a colossal eruption of what had been a rather small dot in space. It erupted and spewed matter outward in all directions into this vacuum that would be the home of Earth. Scientific study theorizes that everything was dark for several hundred million years before stars began their powerful lighting of space. In the midst of this outward thrust, Earth began as fragments of space dust that settled in what is now our universe. It is estimated that this occurred four and a half billion years ago.

As Earth traveled in space, it had a few companions: just the sun and several other planets. The energy that thrust them into space carried them outward at great speed from this center that gave birth to the myriad of stars and other objects. The outward thrust eventually gave way to another force that held them in relatively suspended space. The force of gravity from huge objects in the void of space attempted to pull them back, but the expansion of the universe continued. However, a more local force—gravity, primarily provided by the sun—kept groups of these stars and objects more or less clumped together. This became the "backyard" of our planet Earth, called our solar system.

At the time, the sun and the neighboring planets showed little similarity to the solar system as we know it today. Earth was larger than it is today and the sun was not shining. (1) There was no moon. Earth was trying to ride this energy to a place farther away. However, the sun, with its large mass and huge gravitational pull, tied Earth and several planets to an orbit around itself, the stellar center of our solar system. Like an invisible string, the sun grabbed Earth and the other planets that make up our universe. Earth tried to escape this pull, which caused it to spin and tilt at an angle, as if a rope were around the knees of a captive, causing the head to lean out farther than the rest of the body as it rotated in place. That rope is the invisible pull of gravity, which allowed Earth to spin and try to escape the pull that the sun exerted on it. Earth began to orbit around its captor, starting its swift journey around the sun, Thus ended the first battle—and the first wonder—of this book.

Earth's orbit about the sun went at a swift speed of 67,000 miles an hour, while spinning at 1,000 miles an hour around its axis, tilted relative to the plane that made up the journey around the sun. What would become of this pile of space dust that made up Earth? It was a cold journey at this time, since the sun didn't put out any light or heat in the beginning and was more an antagonist then a welcome partner in this space cloud. So, round and round it went, with other fragments from the Big Bang soaring past it. Sometimes the new planet was hit by meteors, or meteorites, and perhaps a comet. When Earth was approximately four million years old, one of these space pieces hit the side of Earth and tore off a part that would eventually be our moon. That was the birth of a "son of Earth," so to speak. (1) We were to learn later that this nearby moon would be a help to Earth.

Earth's gravity and differentiation

Meanwhile this cloud of dust began to have a change in character. Like the gravity that was holding it to an orbit around the sun, Earth had its own gravity; and this force began to change the face and internal parts of Earth. It's similar to what a baby goes through as it begins its life. It becomes accustomed to its new environment and changes accordingly.

(2) Earth began a change, called differentiation, caused by the pull of gravity. This is a phase whereby the sphere segregates into different internal layers. The heavy parts of Earth gravitate to the center of the sphere; this center core is made up of iron, some gold, and the heavy elements that make up our planet. Meanwhile lighter elements tend to move to the outer dimensions of this sphere. Many heavy elements that were pulled by Earth's growing gravitational strength would not quite make it to the center of the Earth. Many heavy elements are left out of the core's center and begin to make up what is called the outer core. These heavy elements are not compatible with those making up the core and remain just outside the core. Terrific pressure is applied to this "outer core" as it is compressed by the pull of the center core and the weight of most of Earth's mass just outside the outer core. This combination of pull and compression resulted in a great rise in temperature that melted the materials of this outer core, which remained fluid. This was to be a blessing to this planet.

As Earth begins this transformation, the sun starts to shine and pour its energy onto Earth. Light begins to shine all over the universe, which had been bathed in darkness during its beginning. Some stars began to shine before our sun and some afterwards. It's worth describing why this delay occurred in the shining of the stars, including our sun. Like Earth, but many times bigger, gravitational forces in the center of these huge space giants cause extreme pressure and temperature in the center of each. Many stars are much bigger than our sun. All stars are gaseous in nature, rather than solid like our Earth. Our sun is composed of hydrogen, and the center is under tremendous pressure, causing the temperature of the central core to be much hotter then its outer edge. This pressure and heat results in every four hydrogen atoms being compressed into one helium atom in the sun's core. However, in this transformation, the helium has less mass than the mass from four hydrogen atoms. This loss of mass results in a tremendous release of energy as defined by Einstein's equation of $E = mc^2$, where E is the energy released, m is the mass in kilograms lost as the four hydrogen atoms become one helium atom, and c^2 is the speed of light squared. The speed of light is equal to 3×10^8 meters per second (187,000 miles per hour) and c^2 is equal to 9×10^{16} meters squared per second squared. This large number times the small amount of mass lost during this new formation results in a tremendous amount of energy being emitted from the sun; somewhat like the hydrogen bombs that were developed here on Earth fifty-plus years ago.

Hydrogen is continuously converted into helium; so it's like many hydrogen bombs going off constantly. This tremendous amount of energy is released from the center of the sun's core and makes its way towards space just beyond the sun. Its path is not direct. It moves toward the outside, but in darting movements. As big as our sun is, the journey is long and made longer because of this precocious movement of energy within the sun and toward space. In fact the energy released from our sun takes sixty to sixty-five million years to finally reach the outer limits in the form of sunlight. So, in the beginning there was only darkness from our sun, but eventually the sun began to shine as energy was released in the form of light and heat. In addition to this light and heat escaping from the sun, solar wind, which was made up of electrons and protons moving away into space, began. As I mentioned, just after the Big Bang space was dark, but soon space began to be lit up with shining stars. This might be called the second birth of the universe, the bright universe, which released tremendous amounts of energy.

Earth's first atmosphere

Meanwhile, Earth went through a transformation as its gravity pulled the heavier elements towards the Earth's center due to the process of differentiation previously described. Various gases that made up the relatively void portions of early Earth were squeezed out, causing eruptions in the form of volcanoes on Earth's crusty surface. These eruptions released various gases as well as hot lava flows. The gases were hydrogen, helium, nitrogen, oxygen, carbon dioxide, methane, sulfur, water vapor, and others with much less volume. From these gases, Earth's first atmosphere was formed, made up of all of these gases, less the oxygen. Oxygen did not become a part of the atmosphere because it quickly reacted with various rocks and stones that contained iron, and the oxygen was tied up due to the reaction with the iron. Through the process of oxidation, iron oxides were formed. Rocks and anything that could be oxidized became rust. This capture by the Earth's crust prevented an oxygen atmosphere. Essentially the initial atmosphere was primarily hydrogen and helium, with very little methane, carbon dioxide, and sulfur. At the same time the squeezing out of the water vapor, plus additional water as the result of the continuous strikes on Earth by various meteors, meteorites, comets, and other space entities, began to form oceans of water.

Much like a human child goes through in its early years of growth— sort of gangly and awkward, but with some direction— as the oceans and its first atmosphere developed. This is proven by the discovery of single-cell ocean-dwelling fossils that are between 3.5 and 3.8 billion years old.

For a very relatively short time this gaseous atmosphere made up Earth's first atmosphere. Soon Earth was stripped of this first atmosphere by the solar wind, which whizzes by the Earth at approximately one million miles an hour. Being very light elements, helium and hydrogen didn't require much energy to dislodge them from their place in our atmosphere, and they were released to space. Likewise, the planets Mercury, Venus, and Mars were stripped of their atmospheres.

Meanwhile Earth continued differentiation and releasing more gases from volcanoes. But by this time, the Earth's differentiation reached a more final transformation as the spinning of Earth caused the molten outer core to spin. This spinning of metal was similar to the generators and motors we humans have invented to provide electricity, and over time the spinning of the molten metal resulted in the production of Earth's magnetic field. This was a tremendous achievement, since this magnetic field prevented the solar wind from wiping away any future atmospheres. Other planets did not fare as well, and Mercury, Venus, and Mars lost their atmospheres to the solar winds. Very little has been replaced.

Earth's second atmosphere, plants, and global warming

We now find Earth in a phase comparable to a child that has learned to walk, run, and add some strength-related accomplishments. Earth now has a magnetic field to prevent sun's solar wind from doing it harm; it has oceans to cool the Earth; or at least to establish a rather stabilized form of cooling. It has heavy rains due to the resulting evaporation from the heat of the sun upon the oceans, which led to the formation of clouds and eventual precipitation. It now began to form its second atmosphere as the volcanoes continued to belch gases. This second atmosphere was made up of nitrogen (rather inert), water vapor, and carbon dioxide as the major components, plus some methane and small amounts of other gases. Oxygen was still captive in oxidizing Earth's crust and not being released to the atmosphere. This second atmosphere now set Earth up for its next big transformation, when Earth was approximately a billion years old.

As mentioned, Earth had no oxygen in this second atmosphere. With the sun's light, carbon dioxide, and water vapor, Earth now had the perfect ingredients to provide photosynthesis, which is what is required for plant and tree growth. Earth also contained several things required to establish a major change. It had, either as part of its original makeup or as deposited by other space debris, RNA (ribonucleic acid) and DNA (deoxyribonucleic acid) plus, some scientist believe, the equivalent of seeds that would produce the vegetation that became the next step in Earth's evolution. With the combination of the Sun's light, water vapor, and carbon dioxide the stage was set for the process of photosynthesis to occur and the resultant plants to grow.

In addition it had the perfect ingredients for global warming. The sun's short ultraviolet wavelengths and sunlight passed almost uninhibited through Earths cloud cover, except for some reflection, and eventually were re-radiated back toward space in a longer infrared wavelength, the characteristic wavelength constantly radiated from Earth.

All bodies of a higher temperature radiate energy to areas of lower temperature. The sun's outside portion is approximately 5,800 degrees

Kelvin and its energy to Earth peaks at a wavelength of approximately 500 nanometers (billionths of a meter).

Since the Earth is approximately one-twentieth the temperature of the sun in degrees Kelvin, approximately 300 degrees Kelvin, it emits radiation to space that has a wavelength that is approximately twenty times longer than those of the sun, primarily in the infrared wavelengths between one to ten microns (one micron equals 1,000 nanometers). Earth's radiation is of a lower energy due to its lower temperature and is in the form of the longer infrared wavelengths that radiate outward toward the cold space outside our atmosphere. Since water vapor and carbon dioxide vibrate at a frequency in the infrared frequency range, some of Earth's radiation is absorbed by these gases in the clouds overhead instead of being released back into space. These gases heat up and then radiate in all directions, with half returning to Earth and half going to outer space. This is the global warming that you have probably read about. However, in this second atmosphere of Earth, it is much higher because of the large amount of carbon dioxide and water vapor.

These gases placed a cap on the atmosphere surrounding Earth at the time. Thus began the first major global warming experienced by Earth. This was on a big scale since there was a tremendous amount of carbon dioxide in the atmosphere, along with significant amounts of water vapor. These two major constituents are ideal for global warming. The energy bouncing between the Earth and clouds and back to Earth again was ideal for plant growth, since it increased temperature, which improved the growth of plants that need the higher temperatures. These wavelengths had no other effect on the plants, which absorb the shorter wavelengths of sunlight.

Not only were the elements for global warming abundant, but the perfect ingredients for photosynthesis—water vapor, carbon dioxide, and light—were in place. With these ingredients and probably some residue of seeds left from space events or were part of Earth's initial make up, photosynthesis brought us the greenery of Earth with its plants and trees.

Photosynthesis may simply be defined as the conversion of light energy into chemical energy. Photosynthesis occurs in plants in two stages. In the first phase light-dependent reactions capture the energy of light and use it to make high-energy molecules. During the second phase, the light-independent reactions use the high-energy molecules to capture carbon dioxide (CO_2) and form the precursors of glucose. (4)

During light-dependent reactions, one molecule of the pigment chlorophyll absorbs one photon of light and loses one electron. The chlorophyll molecule regains the lost electron by taking one from a water molecule through a process called photoysis that releases oxygen gas as a waste product (thank goodness); and this is where Earth finally gets its free oxygen: O_2.

The Earth received a miracle. The process of photosynthesis and the resulting plants whose appetite for carbon dioxide begins to reduce the carbon dioxide in the atmosphere that was causing the greenhouse effect, while producing free oxygen to begin a change in the atmosphere's contents. Plants begin to grow in the solid earth, and sea kelp begins to grow in the oceans. Algae developed in multiple forms, from multicellular organisms like kelp, to microscopic, single-celled organisms.

The ability to convert light energy to chemical energy confers a significant evolutionary advantage to living organisms, in this case the plant life on Earth. Early photosynthetic systems, such as green and purple sulfur and green and purple nonsulfur bacteria, are thought to have been anoxygenic (did not aspirate oxygen), using various molecules as electron donors. Green and purple sulfur bacteria are thought to have used hydrogen and sulfur as an electron donor. Green nonsulfur bacteria used various amino and other organic acids. Purple nonsulfur bacteria used a variety of non-specific organic molecules. The use of these molecules is consistent with the geological evidence that the atmosphere was highly reduced at that time. Fossils of what are thought to be filamentous photosynthetic organisms have been found dating from 3.4 billion years ago.

It is important to realize the other advantages of this phase of Earth's existence. Most plants are photoautotrophic, which means that they are able to synthesize food directly from inorganic compounds using light energy—for example from the sun—instead of eating other organisms or relying on nutrients derived from them. Photosynthetic bacteria do not have chloroplasts; instead photosynthesis takes place directly within the cell. This is quite different from animals or humans. Plants take these inorganic materials and turn them into organic material. This is significant, since later in the evolution of Earth, it will be occupied by man and animals that will depend on obtaining organic food for their existence.

The most important contributors of free oxygen into the Earth's atmosphere were Cyanobacteria (blue-green algae). The oldest known fossils were found in rocks in Western Australia dated 3.5 billion years old. These were also photoautotrophic, allowing, through photosynthesis, these bacteria to convert carbon dioxide directly to oxygen through a chemical reaction. Another important aspect that we will discuss later is the fact that plants take in nitrogen through their roots, which becomes part of the plant's system. Human beings (although not on Earth yet) need nitrogen, but we will find that they are not able to take nitrogen in from the air and chemically process it in their bodies. Man and animals breathe nitrogen in, but it is expelled without being assimilated. We receive our needed nitrogen by eating plants or eating other animals that eat plants. Knowing this, it is quite obvious that significant plant growth had to be present on Earth for animals or humans to eventually establish themselves. So photosynthesis brought many good aspects to the young but maturing Earth in its early existence, and still does.

Earth's Oxygen Atmosphere

While photosynthetic life reduced the carbon dioxide content of the atmosphere, it also started to produce significant amounts of freed-up oxygen. For a long period of time, the oxygen produced from volcanoes did not build up in the atmosphere, since it was taken up by rocks, as recorded in banded iron formations and continental "red bed" formations. (6) It is estimated that it was only a billion years ago that the reservoirs of oxidizable rock became saturated and the free oxygen stayed in the air. By this time, huge amounts of oxygen were being supplied from forests, oceans, and jungles throughout Earth; evolving the atmosphere towards our present atmosphere; Earth's third atmosphere.

This great increase in the oxygen in the atmosphere while the carbon dioxide was decreasing resulted in the sun's ultraviolet energy splitting the oxygen atom in Earth's atmosphere to form ozone (O_3). This was a significant event, since the ozone then attenuated most of the incoming ultraviolet light. This was significant for the entrance of animals on Earth. Before ozone was formed, the ultraviolet rays were so powerful that man and probably most animals could not endure the energy of the direct ultraviolet rays, and most forms of life could not exist.

The rest of the sun's wavelengths passed through or were reflected by the clouds. Absorption of the infrared wavelengths heated the clouds, and they eventually emitted radiation from this energy in all directions. This meant approximately half the infrared energy was sent to the Earth below and the other half to space. The surface of Earth presently receives about 51 percent of the energy that reaches the outer part of our atmosphere. (7) It was higher than this when Earth was a billion years old, since there was no means of blocking the high-energy ultraviolet rays of the sun then. Later we will discuss how this changed. Most of this energy hit the oceans and was absorbed in the surface of the waters. Some hit land, but since land was only a small percentage of Earth at that time in its evolution, it received less, with most being absorbed by the oceans. This energy heated the oceans and the land. Some was reflected and some was heat radiated or re-radiated from Earth. In addition, the sun's heat resulted in evaporation from the oceans' surfaces. Then, as now, evaporated water vapor rises to the clouds and is eventually condensed, resulting in some form of precipitation falling back onto the planet. Twenty percent of the sun's energy is devoted to winds and ocean currents that tend to spread the heat from the hot equatorial waters towards the north and south poles. They also move the clouds that contain the water vapor to places across the planet until condensation results in precipitation in one form or another. Condensation results in a transfer of heat from the clouds to the upper part of the troposphere, and this heat is distributed across the planet by winds, though some is lost to space.

Since space outside our atmosphere is almost a pure vacuum, it has no molecules to be heated by the sun, and there are very few collisions with other molecules to raise the temperature. The temperature of space can be as low as 3-degrees Kelvin (the lowest temperature feasible is zero-degrees Kelvin, which is -273 degrees Celsius). However, the space just outside our Earth is warmer than this due to some radiation from Earth. We can assume the temperature of space is approximately 40 degrees Kelvin. Since heat is radiated from a higher temperature to a lower temperature, Earth at 300 degrees Kelvin radiates its heat to the cold space that surrounds us. This is a continuous radiation. Whereas the sun radiates approximately 1,400 watts/m^2 (*0.335 Calories/m^2) on a continuous basis, (8) (3) the Earth radiates 0.061 watts per square meter (1.46 x 10-5 Calories) to cold space on a continuous basis. This radiation from Earth represents some of the daily loss of the energy supplied by the sun.

(* Please note that I am using Calories with a capital C. This is the common table Calorie used in determining the energy received from food. In order to make it easier for the reader to relate to the energies discussed, I have converted all energies to the common table Calorie. This Calorie is equal to the kilocalorie used by scientists in their calculations.)

(*Please note, as I discuss events that happened a billion or millions of years ago that continue to happen today, I discuss them in the present tense so I won't have to cover the same subjects later in this book. I hope this doesn't confuse the reader)

It is important to recognize that the 0.335 Calories per square meter received from the sun is greatly reduced when we feel it on Earth. There are several reasons. Approximately half is lost via reflections from clouds, some is absorbed by the clouds, and some is reflected from Earth's surface. Another big loss is due to the Earth spinning. The sun only shines on one-fourth of Earth at any given instant as the

Earth revolves. If you could take a snapshot of planet Earth, it would show only one-fourth of Earth. If Earth was as still as such a snapshot makes it look, then the amount of heat received by the exposed part of Earth would receive the energy as described. However, that portion of Earth that was in the snapshot for that instant continues its journey on its axis. Smaller amounts of energy are received as it spins into partial darkness, followed by the dark of night and then partial darkness as it spins back toward the area where you first took the snapshot. Therefore, on a daily basis each part of Earth receives approximately 350 watts, or 0.0835 Calories, per square meter.

The Spread of the Sun's Energy On Earth

The equator receives more of the sun's energy than the temperate zones or the polar zones because this part of Earth is like a person sticking his belly out to receive more sun. The Earth's belly is the equator. (3) However, since heat travels from a hot area towards a cold area, the heat received by the equator moves toward the colder polar areas, which are directly north or directly south. Due to Earth's spin, the wind moves from west to east. Heat is carried from the equator toward the poles by the angle formed by these winds and by the ocean currents and evaporation and subsequent precipitation. The subsequent movement of this evaporated water vapor and its condensation results in heat being released in the atmosphere just above the cloud level. The jet stream reaches down from the North Pole and up from the South Pole to the temperate zones and sets a limit of sorts to the northern vector (and southern vector) of the Earth's winds. These jet streams flow around the Earth in a sinusoidal (a sin wave is the same wave of ac energy that comes out of our ac electric plugs in our homes. If you could watch it on an oscilloscope, like all engineers do, you would see this common wave form) sort of movement that reaches the bottom of the temperate zones of the northern hemisphere on its trough and the northern part of the temperate zones on its peak. It is in the form of a wave like motion moving north and south while circling the globe. The jet stream in the southern hemisphere has the same effect on the temperate zones of the southern hemisphere. The result is that, due to the spin of the Earth and these resulting air streams, the average energy received at the equator drops to around 250 watts (0.06 Calories) per square meter. The temperate zones receive an increase to approximately 235 watts (0.055 Calories) per square meter, and the north and south poles receive approximately 180 watts (0.043 Calories) per square meter. (9) So, this energy budget is spread around Earth due to the combined efforts of several of nature's forces. If Earth did not spin and create winds, the equator would be too hot to support human life and the north and south poles would be too cold to support human life.

These energy figures relate to the present. If we go back to when the Earth was a billion years old, the amount of energy from the sun that made its way to Earth was much greater, since the ultraviolet wavelengths passed through the cloud cover directly to Earth's surface. An ultraviolet wavelength has 10,000 times the energy of an infrared wavelength. Even today, the greatly reduced ultraviolet wavelengths that pass through the ozone layer can result in skin cancer due to their higher energy content.

Water, Needed for Life

The oceans that made up the Earth several billion years ago became salty from material carried from the volcanoes and were not fit for life as we know it. However, some forms of life found this habitat very comfortable. Meanwhile the lands that projected above the oceans supported no form of animal or human life and little, if any, fresh water. That changed as the sun's energy heated the oceans and water began to evaporation. This is water without salt, which supplied the land with fresh water, able to support life forms.

Nature's big circle: The hydrologic cycle

Think of a big circle that connects the oceans to the clouds and the land back to the ocean. This circle, called the hydrologic cycle, is the path of the salt-free water that is evaporated into the air and makes its way to various parts of Earth. When it condenses, precipitation in the form of rain or snow falls on the land of Earth. Now picture this fresh water from precipitation flowing in the rivers and lakes of the world. Much of it is used presently by humans, animals, and plants to provide the necessary water requirement for life. Water flows from the mountains when the snow melts. It fills the wells in the earth that flow to the creeks and rivers. Its water that fills the underground aquifers that then flow towards other water outlets, being filtered by the Earth's filtering system as it moves on its way. Rivers fill and flow from rain or the melting of the snow. Fresh water lakes fill from precipitation while being supplemented by the flow of the rivers into and out of them. This journey of the water via the waterways of Earth provides the world it's only source of fresh water. Eventually, the rivers find their way back into the oceans; thus completing this fantastic journey and completing this circle that is required for life. Isn't Mother Nature wonderful? Just think of this circle and how unique it is. The ocean's waters are desalinated through evaporation to provide this huge cycle of fresh water, and the rivers of the world return unused water to the oceans. This is now, as it was then.

This cycle is presently called the E- P cycle (evaporation - precipitation cycle) and it is quantified. (10) It takes 585 Calories of solar energy to convert 2.2 pounds of water into a vapor. It only takes 80 Calories of solar energy to convert 2.2 pounds of ice to water at 0 degrees C (32 degrees F). Likewise, converting water vapor back into water requires the removal of 585 table Calories per 2.2 pounds during condensation (in the clouds that take up the energy of condensation). The removal of 80 Calories per 2.2 pounds of water is necessary to convert water at zero degrees C to ice. The equation for the Ocean Mass Budget is E - P = 0; Evaporation must equal Precipitation. (16) The salinity should remain constant over time in the Earth's ocean surface waters for this to hold true. This was true billions of years ago as it is today. In order to determine if this equation is presently holding true, the salinity of the ocean's surface waters must be tested. Such testing shows that this has held true for many years. The precipitation P has to be taken from observations over the world. The highest precipitation is just north of the equator and at 50 degrees + and - latitudes where the polar fronts exist. I am discussing this in the present state since this is how we get our drinking water now and this had to exist billions of years ago for plants and animals to have survived. The development of this cycle from the sun's energy was a basic need for life to ever have existed.

It is important to realize that this cycle has a delay built into it. Clouds can only hold water for eight or nine days before there is some form of precipitation. (11) It takes time for the water that is evaporated for this cycle of evaporation and precipitation to create the flow of water to the various waterways. It takes time for precipitation to flow down the rivers and other waterways to complete its journey back into the ocean. Therefore, P is not directly related to the E in this equation for a given time or day. This is not a problem as long as the cycle is a continuous one. In this case, the return of water to the ocean is from evaporation from a previous time. This equation of Ocean Mass Budget represents a snapshot that should be continuous and checked at the same time each year. As long as it is continuous and has the same results, the oceans' salinity remains constant.

In other words evaporation removes fresh water and the flow of fresh water back into the ocean. Also, the precipitation that falls directly into the oceans must be equal for the salinity to match. The fact that measurements have shown no significant change in the salinity of the oceans' surface water is proof that the water cycle is continuous in real time—and perfectly balanced. Relative to the present day and the idea that there is global warming would require that this cycle is being maintained. If it is maintained, it will result in an increase in evaporation, an increase in precipitation, an increase in fresh water provided to the animals, plants, and humans on Earth and an increase in the flow of water back into oceans. This cycle has been going on since the early years of Earth's existence and has remained fairly constant. There have been periods of ice ages, and the passing of these ice ages over time have increased or decreased the water being transferred in this cycle during these transient conditions to provide balance and keep the temperature of Earth rather constant around a temperature of 57 to 58 degrees Fahrenheit. When the temperature is such that we are out of the ice ages, it returns to this hydrologic cycle. The amount of water in the cycle has changed to meet the conditions that prevailed over time. This has kept the climate on Earth from running away in either direction, hot or cold.

This hydrologic cycle is a subject of much discussion today regarding how global warming may affect Earth and its inhabitants. Global warming might affect the oceans' rate of evaporation, the amount of water the clouds can hold, the number of days of precipitation the clouds can hold, an increase in precipitation and the additional amount that the cycle is trying to balance to keep the Earth at a constant climate. These are all the variables that result as the Earth tries to increase its temperature and the demands it places on the system that is presently in balance to remain in balance. Scientists are debating this subject. Any climate change must result in some change in accommodating this circle. Since the energy from the sun is a constant and there has been a balance such that the temperature of the earth has remained fairly constant with this energy as supplied, any increase in the temperature of Earth will result in a change in the hydrologic cycle to offset the climate change. It's possible that larger clouds could form as a result of an increase in the water being evaporated and act as reflectors against the sun's energy to prevent additional heating of the Earth, thus offsetting any change in climate. There is also the possibility that the additional water vapor and CO_2 in the atmosphere would result in the absorption of additional infrared heat coming in from the sun that would return half of it back toward space, thus offsetting any increase in global warming. The oceans of the world provide the world with a buffer for any increase in temperature and change in climate.. The huge size of the oceans means they have a high enertia (a property of matter whereby it remains at rest or continues in uniform motion unless acted upon by some outside force. The higher the mass the greater the enertia and the more difficult to change it) against changes. It is the key to preventing any additional changes in the climate. This efficient cycle by Mother Nature is probably the most difficult function on Earth to change.

The distribution of sea surface salinity mirrors the distribution of the E-P cycle over large parts of the ocean. Deviations occur from river run-off. On a global scale, the balance is: (12)

Evaporation = 440 x 10^3 km^3 year-1
Precipitation = 411 x 10^3 km^3 year-1
River run-off = 29 x 10^3 km^3 year-1

The melting and freezing of ice is balanced (except on the geological time scale). Most rivers are found in the northern hemisphere, so the proportionality between sea surface salinity and E-P is better over most of the southern hemisphere.

The average time for evaporated water to reside in the atmosphere in a cloud formation is eight to nine days. The water that is evaporated today will result in some form of precipitation in a little over a week. It is during this time that wind and other elements can move these clouds and distribute the water or snow or other form of precipitation to the Earth. If you include the time before precipitation, then it turns out that the clouds empty their precipitation an average of 45 times a year. This happens at various points across the globe, and sometimes when there is a large amount of precipitation in one area of the world, other areas suffer from drought. So, the atmosphere acts to store water for evaporation collection before precipitation occurs. Any increase in the evaporation rate due to global warming will result in a decrease in the number of days that the water is held in the atmosphere and an increase in the annual precipitation. The atmosphere can only hold so much water. It is like a sponge that can fill so much and then it gets squeezed out. This is only true if all things remain constant in these calculations. If, for example, cloud formations increase, they reflect additional energy from the sun and keep the surface water from heating.

By reviewing the amount of rainfall in the world annually scientists can determine if there is any increase. If global warming were occurring, we would expect to see an increase in the yearly rainfall and this has not been the case to date.

Precipitation may change its location, but the total amount doesn't change over a period of time. The main reason for this continuous cycle relates to a few constants. The first constant is the heat the sun supplies to Earth each and every second of the day. The other constant is the oceans of the world. Neither of these two constants has shown changes. Ice may melt more one year than the next and more water may freeze from one year compared to the next, but in general the Earth's oceans remain constant. With these two huge systems remaining constant the amount of precipitation on Earth remains a constant. Each year there are areas in the world that have abnormal rain fall, either more or less. This is obvious based on the many media stories one reads about or watches on television. There is a flood situation in Texas as I write this book. Last year there were floods in other parts of the United States and in other parts of the world. At the same time, there are media reports of the lack of rainfall in certain parts of the world each year. This year (2007) it happens to be in Australia for one. There are other places in the world suffering from drought at the same time as the floods are involved in parts of the world. In some cases, the lack of rain in a location over a period of time results in a drought and is treated as a serious situation. I live just about ten miles from San Jose, California, and this morning's San Jose Mercury News reported that San Jose only received 9.28 inches of rainfall in the 2006–2007 rain year. This represents approximately 62 percent of normal. However, San Jose's driest year was in 1877, when 4.83 inches of rain fell. In 1989 San Jose had a rainfall of 8.32 inches. The most rain fell in 1890, when 30.30 inches of rain was recorded. Likewise, 30.25 inches fell in 1983. This gives an idea of how random some rainfall events are. This recent dry spell comes after more than a decade of healthy rainfall. What is clear is that present day mass media exposes the lack or abundance of rain and relate it more recently to global warming, which may or may not be true. But the media's expounding on this subject (and I am not against that) has brought it to the attention of more people, and many people are now scared of the effects that global warming may have on them personally.

Over the past several thousand years the sun has placed a constant amount of energy on the Earth, year by year. At the same time the Earth's ocean levels have remained fairly constant over long periods of time. The result is constant energy, consistently large amounts of water, and a yearly rainfall that has remained constant over the world. To change this requires a huge action of nature to be able to overcome the large enertia provided by the world's large bodies of water and considerable time.

The Cambrian Explosion and the next form of life

Between the time Earth was one billion years old until it was about three and a half billion years old, or about one billion years ago (bya), the Earth evolved toward the world we now experience. However, there were no creatures with bones or shells, based on the fact that no evidence of fossils exists, or any other evidence that anything existed except for multi-celled organisms until about 540 million years ago (mya).Then, came an event that is called the "Cambrian explosion." (12) (The Cambrian is named for Cambria, the classical name for Wales, the areas where rocks from this time period were first studied.)

The Cambrian Explosion occurred about 535 million years ago (mya) as indicated by fossils that showed for the first time that marine invertebrates, such as shell-making ammonites, appeared, followed by fish, amphibians, reptiles, birds, and eventually mammals. The Cambrian is the earliest period in which are found numerous large, distinctly fossillizable multicellular organisms that are more complex than sponges or medusoids in rocks. During this time, roughly fifty separate major groups of organisms, or "phyla" (a phylum defines the basic body plan of some group of modern or extinct animals), emerged suddenly, in most cases without evident precursors.

Though this life explosion began in the Earth's seas, it can be attributed, if only in part, to the increased free oxygen levels in the warm, stable marine and atmospheric environments. As mentioned, once oxygen existed in the atmosphere, the sun's ultraviolet rays split the oxygen into ozone, O_3. The ozone shield was created, and it was at this point that life moved out of the oceans and evolved into land-dwelling organisms capable of respiration. Likewise, land plants reached another level of sophistication with plants like conifers and flowering plants. It is not known why this step-like function of complex living things occurred in what is now called the Cambian Explosion. So, the Cambian Explosion still remains something of a mystery to be solved.

Here's my educated guess at what happened during the Cambrian time period. At some point, the amount of atmospheric oxygen that evolved as a result of photosynthesis had an effect on the oceans and the oxygen in the oceans that made up the water at that time. It allowed the oceans to reach a form of balance between the oxygen in the water and the oxygen in the atmosphere. This may have been enough of a change to make it an easier transition for sea life to move onto land. Perhaps this is where heavy water originated. Heavy water is H_2O where the hydrogen has a nucleus of a proton and neutron instead of just a proton. This makes it heavier. It is called deuterium and is found as one part in five to ten thousand parts of water, varying around the globe. Perhaps this isotope of hydrogen, although a low percentage, increased and was a sufficient change for this transition. Perhaps it affected the amount of water vapor in the atmosphere which may have provided a transitional media for sea life to move from the oceans to land's atmosphere through a media that was similar to their ocean environment. Remember, we are not talking about very sophisticated life forms as we would recognize them today. It was complex compared to what had gone on before this evolutionary process began. As more and more atmospheric oxygen was available, sea life and animals in general grew more complex and became more able to breathe air. Thus began the transfer of many species of sea life to land which is seen in the fossils found today.

On the other hand this transition may relate to the atmospheric pressure obtained in this balance, since atmospheric pressure equals the weight of the atmosphere above the ocean level. As more and more oxygen was generated into the atmosphere, it must have increased the weight of the atmosphere at sea level. The fact is that oxygen existed in the water for some time before the atmosphere began to achieve some level of oxygen and water vapor was released from the oceans and lakes, which resulted in a smooth transition from the ocean to outside air.

There is another probable scenario. As the oxygen level increased in the oceans, it bred a fish-like creature that could almost exist on this level of oxygen and could remain beneath the surface for a length of time, but was required to swim to the surface and stick its nose out and take in some oxygen from the air every so often, sort of like what a whale does. As the atmospheric oxygen increased, this fish-like creature began to spend more time with its nose protruding outside the water, breathing oxygen. Eventually descendents of this amphibian made its life on land rather than in the water, and with this we have an evolutionary phenomenon taking place and more animals living on Earth rather than in the water. It is interesting to consider that Mother Nature was up to some more tricks.

With an oxygen atmosphere having evolved from the output of plant life in the oceans, there was less and less carbon dioxide available for the plants. Plants can't live without at least 50 ppm of CO_2 in the atmosphere, so maybe this was Mother Nature's way of providing animals that would breathe out carbon dioxide to provide a balance. The coming of animals that expelled carbon dioxide while breathing began to provide the carbon dioxide needed for the plants to exist. So here we find a change in the balance of nature. Where before, the Earth was essentially water and land with some single-cell creatures living in the ocean, we now had this transformation to oxygen-breathing animals evolving. These animals were now providing carbon dioxide to the plants that previously had provided them the oxygen. It also became safe for the amphibians to crawl out of the oceans without the fate of being killed by ultraviolet light. This was significant, since fossils found since the Cambrian period show a continuous migration from sea creatures to land creatures during the evolution towards a higher form of animal in the food chain. Life on Earth had begun. Also, our third atmosphere was born, an oxygen-rich one. Here was another of the wonders of life.

The Buildup of Oxygen

The amount of oxygen in the atmosphere increased gradually at first and shot up rapidly around 2.2 to 1.7 billion years ago to about 10 percent of its present level of twenty two percent. This 2.2 percent level at the time was still quite a low oxygen level, but was a beginning of the build up of our third atmosphere and was one of the most important events in the history of life on Earth. The presence of large amounts of dissolved and free oxygen in the oceans and atmosphere may have driven most of the anaerobic organisms then living to extinction during the "oxygen catastrophe" about 2.4 billion years ago. However, the high amount of oxygen creates a large potential energy drop for cellular respiration, thus enabling organisms using aerobic respiration to produce much more ATP (adenosine triphosphate). ATP is thought of as the fuel for human and animal growth. Aerobic respiration makes them so efficient that plants and animals have come to dominate Earth's biosphere. Photosynthetic production of oxygen and cellular respiration of oxygen allowed for the evolution of eukaryotic cells (cells with a nucleus) and ultimately complex multi-cellular organisms such as plants and animals.

If we look at the last 4.5 billion years of Earth's existence we see less than 3 parts per million of oxygen, rising to approximately 9,000 ppm four billion years ago. It continued a rise to approximately 900,000 ppm by 3.0 billions years ago, when oxygenic photosynthesis began to raise the level in the atmosphere. It stayed on that linear growth curve until approximately 1.5 billion years ago. At that time there was a dramatic shift in the rate, which increased to approximately 1.5 percent (one and a half million parts per million) oxygen in the atmosphere, and different types of plants grew. Approximately 540 million years ago during the Cambrian era, the amount rose to close to 10 percent. Shortly after that time there was a slower increase to the 20-plus percent of oxygen present today. During this slow growth period, animals began to appear on Earth. I assume that the slower growth in the atmospheric oxygen was due to the appearance of animals, which breathed oxygen and increased the generation of carbon dioxide.

The atmospheric abundance of free oxygen in later geological epochs and its gradual increase up to the present was largely due to synthesis by photosynthetic organisms. Over the past 500 million years, oxygen levels fluctuated between 15 and 35 percent per volume. (See figure 1 below.) Toward the end of the Carboniferous era (coal age) about 300 million years ago, atmospheric oxygen levels reached a maximum of 35 percent by volume, allowing insects and amphibians with limiting respiratory systems to grow much larger than today's species. Today, oxygen is the second most common component of Earth's atmosphere (about 22 percent by volume) after nitrogen. About 75 percent of the free element is being produced by algae and green microorganisms in the oceans and one quarter from terrestrial plants.

The graph in figure 1 below shows the buildup of oxygen over the past 550 million years and lists the disposition of the oxygen. (14)

Molecular oxygen, O_2, is essential for cellular respiration in all aerobic organisms. It is used as an electron acceptor in the mitochondria (a section within our cells) to generate chemical energy in the form of adenosine triphosphate (ATP), the multifunctional nucleotide that is most important as an intercellular energy transfer. It is produced as an energy source during the process of photosynthesis. Later in the book you will meet again with ATP, one of the energies key to the proliferation of human life, as it was during oxidative phosphorylation.

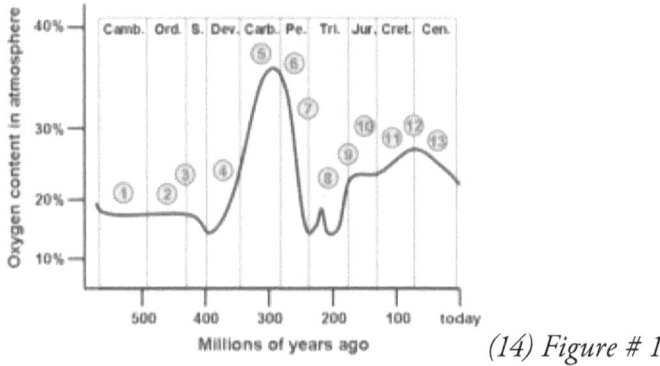

(14) Figure # 1

Fluctuations oxygen levels in the atmosphere over the past 500+ million years, with accompanying events: 1) Radiation of animal phyla Cambrian explosion) - 2) First land plants - 3) Ordovician-Silurian extinction events - 4) Huge forests form on land, first land animals and seed plants - 5) Coal formation, first conifers, insect and amphibian giantism - 6) Low ocean levels, (supercontinant formation) (8) stabilization as land born animals exist that breath oxygen

The present atmospheric composition is made up of the following gases.

Nitrogen	78.1percent
Oxygen	21.0percent
Carbon Dioxide	0.038percent - 380 parts per million
Methane	0.0015percent -15 parts per million
Water Vapor	0.5 to 1.0percent - 5 to 10 thousand parts per million

Various other gases make up the remainder of the atmosphere

AND THEN CAME A METEOR

Evidence shows that there have been several mass extinctions since the Cambrian explosion, the last occurring 65 mya when a meteorite collision probably triggered the extinction of the dinosaurs and other large reptiles, but spared small animals such as mammals, which then resembled shrews. (15)

This meteorite collision may have eliminated the large reptiles, but it had to result in energy gained by Earth in addition to the energy gained from the sun on an everyday basis. This resulted in a huge gain of energy, in agreement with Einstein's theory represented by the equation $E=mc^2$, as the large mass of the meteorite plus the kinetic energy were converted into heat and potential energy. This added energy eventually resulted in several phenomena, one of them being the transformation of the dead carcasses and other material into oil and the energy supplied by the oil. The second effect was to fill the atmosphere with dust, which helped to cover up the carcasses as it fell back to Earth. This dust blocked the sun and oxygen from the Earth and caused the death of the large reptiles. This unused energy, which was a form of entropy at the time it occurred, lay rotting in the subsoil of Earth for over 65 million years. To give one an idea of the amount of energy this meteor strike provided for Earth, it is estimated to be equal to 1.19×10^{20} Calories, which is a little over ten times greater than the estimated energy in the today's fossil fuel reserves of 9.32×10^{18} Calories, as of the year 2003.

This chronology about the major climate events over the last 65 million years provides the reader information about how the Earth has bounced around on climate and temperatures without the influence of man. I wanted the readers to understand the kind of major changes that have occurred on Earth without any influence by man so as to provide information on what nature brings to the present picture of climates around the world. There were other incidents over time where the energy of the Earth, the sun, and the weather brought their powers to bear with dramatic results. For example, weathering of rocks freed up significant amounts of oxygen over time and became one of the major contributors to the salt in the oceans. (64)

Back to evolution on Earth

With these types of phenomena occurring, sea life began its evolutionary process and life evolved into more complex forms. Later fossil findings show that sea life gained the ability to breathe oxygen, and there is an evolutionary metamorphic change whereby amphibians began to leave their water homes and migrate onto land. The creation of the ozone layer, as previously noted, allowed animals leaving the water to be free of the problem of the ultraviolet wave lengths and their dramatic energy. Thus began the major change of life forms on Earth, whereby large, oxygen-breathing animals began to roam the Earth. Most fossil findings show that there were small and large oxygen-breathing life forms that evolved after the Cambrian Explosion, only to be eliminated by a meteor strike on Earth 65 million years ago.

AND THEN CAME MAN

I have discussed the torturous stages that Earth had to go through for human life to reach this level and survive. It is especially significant when you consider what had to exist on Earth for humans and other forms of life to exist. There had to be DNA and RNA (I will discuss these later) brought to Earth for life to have begun. If genetic materials came with the dust that made up the planet, then it had to continue to exist in some form while Earth was going through its phases, as I discussed. Remember, the short ultraviolet sun's rays hit the Earth on a continuous basis before Earth obtained the oxygen atmosphere that eventually leads to the ozone that stopped these rays. It is questionable that DNA and RNA could have existed with these high energy rays beating down on them. The fact that these are needed for life to exist in any form has brought the scientists to form two points of view about how and when they arrived on Earth. One point of view is that they arrived with the planet and were protected from the ultraviolet rays by some form of sheltering; perhaps within the internal structure of Earth as it proceeded through the differentiation process. The other point of view is that they arrived much later from space in a fairly advanced form, perhaps via a comet's dust, or a meteor's impact, or other space material. For these two genetic structures to reach the level of sophistication that is found in present day life would take billions of years, as estimated by most scientists. This arrival to this state of complexity on Earth is a subject of considerable study by scientists. For now, let's say it's sufficient to say that DNA and RNA were not even known to exist by man in the early stages of human evolution. A later part of this book will spend considerable time on this subject. For now, let's look at other levels of obstacles that man has progressed through to reach today's level of existence.

We know that for man to exist he had to have an oxygen atmosphere and the plants that preceded us. We know the oceans and the sun's heat beating on the oceans to separate out the salt-free water that became the fresh water of life were necessary. We know humans had to have the sun's energy spread across the world to provide the climate we could exist in. We know that man had to find the food to support his existence. We were later to find the secrets of life itself. It would take creativity, sophisticated investigation, and many years of searching to find these keys. This is what this book is about.

Fossils have shown that the Cambian Explosion resulted in the evolution of life forms outside of the oceans. Later came more complex and sophisticated life forms. Fossils show that several mya (million years ago), an African ape-like animal, gained the ability to stand upright and is believed to be the forerunner of what is now man. Scientists hypothesize that this ability to stand upright allowed for the use of his limbs to perform tasks that were more complex, which further improved on his learning curve, and his brain became more advanced. Here is one of the wonders I write about. Here was an animal that had no means of the protection that is normally provided to all animals against their predators or as a means of acquiring food. Prehistoric man had no large teeth to attack other animals and to protect himself from other animals. Man had no beak to provide him that protection and method of acquiring food. Man had no claws with which to protect himself or provide him a method of climbing and acquiring food. Man could not run as fast as most of the animals on Earth when he appeared. Man had no capacity for swimming long distances, nor did he have the ability to swim well enough to hunt and capture food in the water. In fact, early man had very little means of communication, even with his own type. Man was smaller (much smaller than present-day man) than many the animals and therefore did not have the strength to overcome his potential prey. Man started out seeking plants for food. It is unknown exactly when man began to eat meat to fulfill his energy requirements. Since man was limited in his ability to move long distances from where he was born, he probably began to eat the meat of animals because he had consumed all of the plant food in his given territory. But he had a brain that provided him with certain abilities that the other animals did not possess. From this step in evolution, there are several theories as to how his brain increased in relation to his small body size. One theory is that because man was borne by the mother in a sack called the placenta, it allowed his head to grow and a larger brain to develop prior to birth, thus giving him the advantage he needed to reach the top of the food chain.

There is evidence that there was a major step in the development of agriculture by early man, and then civilizations began, allowing humans to influence the Earth in a short time span as no other life form had.

Recent man

Several hundred years before Christ, there were approximately one hundred million people on Earth. So you can see that man has been busy propagating his kind on Earth. As busy as he has been, he had no idea where he came from or why there were certain people that were of color and certain people without color. Nor did he know within a given color of man what caused some to have big noses and some not, why some had slanted eyes and others did not, why some had blond hair and blue eyes and others had black or dark hair and brown eyes. He did know there was a difference, and this provided food for thought and generated the drive toward his gaining knowledge about this difference.

And so each of these groups of people seemed to live together and gain habits that were common to the group from which they came. Most of the differences were attributed to the area of Earth where they were born. There also were wars between the various groups, seeming to emanate from leaders that had certain priorities in mind relative to the group he came from. Some were religious in nature, some just ego-related, some ethnically related, some race-related; but they came no matter what. Wars existed since the coming of man. Wars came and ended rapidly, and warriors brought with them their ethnic habits, and there has been a blending over time of the various characteristics of each group. Little by little there was a little more tolerance, or so it would seem, toward a more civilized nature among the people of the known world at that time.

Diseases

Meanwhile there were other enemies about. These were not human, but unseen enemies. Something would cause terrible sicknesses to come and wipe out large numbers of all races; no matter the color of their skin or the color of their hair. These were unseen enemies. These enemies were invisible coming or going. It was a wonder that, no matter how terrible these infiltrators, they would eventually disappear, or so it would appear. Did the enemy disappear or was it the ability of man to overcome their poison, or disease, as it was called? Since they were not visible, it was thought they were demons, or something the "gods" brought on them. Humans had various names for these "gods," some nice, some strong, some bad, some lovely, some not so lovely. But whatever the case, it was noted as man's ignorance of man. Man would continue to search these demons down forever and eventually overcome some of the unknowns.

Man's continual hunt for his beginnings

Man's journey through the early years of his existence was mainly occupied with staying alive. This meant seeking food for his body and protecting his body from predators and his human enemies. This basically describes the Mesolithic period, 10,000 to 7,000 years before Christ. This is sometimes called the Stone Age because the use of ground stone tools was discovered to date back to this time. These tools were used for cutting and smoothing things. Of course tool use advanced to the use of killing animals for their food. This was the time of the hunting and gathering of food stuff. Man would regularly search for food for his mate and their offspring. When the offspring was young, food was provided by nursing by the female, but as time proceeded, the young would eat the same as the parents. This made the finding of food a more dangerous task, so man began to find ways of coping with this problem. There was no development of the land for food or shelter. In fact, the animals they killed for food provided their robes to protect them from the weather. As time passed in this period, there were advancements in the tools and the traps made to catch prey. The beginning of this period was the ending of the Ice Age, and it is considered complete between 8000 BC and 7500 BC.

Around 7000 BC, large animals that could exist in the colder climate, such as mammoths and bison, began to disappear as the Earth warmed. Smaller animals were hunted again, and traps were again more sophisticated. This made hunting for food different and in many ways more difficult. Small animals didn't supply the quantity of food as large prey did, but hunters had found that when they had large kills, the young would get sick when the large kill was only a couple of days old. This led toward developing agricultural communities, where animals were bred and some agriculture occurred. Man made a move toward determining his own fate as far as food was concerned. He also found that it worked best when there was more than one person involved, so tribes developed, and groups found better ways to survive through communal living. But the unseen enemy still came and brought the deaths of many. Now it became obvious that whatever the enemy, it wasn't a one-person phenomenon. Many would be felled by this unseen enemy, and death came in large numbers. They soon began to realize that there were certain times of the year when some of these unseen enemies would appear, and they began to find crude means of warding it off. But as the centuries passed, more people were affected, and what had worked before with some of this unseen enemy required a new approach. Soon some people among them were considered as guides when these illnesses would arrive. Some were called witch doctors, some were called chemists, and eventually some would be called doctors.

The search

As we look back at these crude beginnings, we wonder about how humans lived and how they survived. *The Wonder of Life* is a fantastic story of the history of man's ability to find new ways of recording events as we track down the periods that were considered the worst for the invasion by the unseen enemy. In the search for fossils, evidence was found that Neanderthal man was evidently around approximately thirty-two thousand years ago. This is determined by hieroglyphics on the cave walls where he must have lived. This early life was made up of small groups of humans living together. Nature provided a driving force for early man to expand his existence through some form of communication. At least two things were obvious, even to this early human inhabitant. He knew that each day he craved food, and he had sexual desires that nature provided him. The craving for food was a natural desire each day, because his stomach told him he was hungry, and if he didn't eat he got weak. The desire for sex was also a natural urge brought on by unknown desires as he approached the female of the species. These urges resulted in the propagation of man, and populations continued to grow on Earth, broadening the necessity for mass farming and domestication for food. Man began to realize it was better to have an inventory of many animals around so he could pick from them as the need arose. He also was smart enough to realize that the meat caused sicknesses if it lay around for any length of time. So, he only killed the basic amount needed to cover certain periods of time. Thus began management of time and periods of priorities. All animals have these inbred capabilities to a certain extent, but not to the extent of man.

Precursors of man

Even if the existence of DNA and RNA could be explained as existing at an early time in the life of Earth, there still would not be any life as we know it without oxygen to breath. This may explain why, to this day, no fossils of oxygen-breathing animals have been found that predated the Cambrian Explosion. It is also a fact that human life could not exist prior to photosynthesis. Photosynthesis was needed to establish plants to provide an oxygen atmosphere. All that plants required was to have some form of seeds available in the presence of light, water vapor, and carbon dioxide. Light was provided by the sun following about 50 million years of darkness. Water vapor and carbon dioxide were provided as they spewed out of the volcanoes along with other gases. One of the wonders of life was that plants did not need other plants in order to eat. They were purely a chemical reaction that took place in two phases: one phase was light dependent and began the action, and the second phase was completed when the plant took in carbon and gave off oxygen. During these processes the plant's assimilation of carbon provided the fundamental food for the plant. So, the plants securing of energy was through chemical actions with the sun, water vapor and carbon dioxide. This seems like a simple process, but it is the only method on earth for capturing the energy of the sun, while eventually providing food for man and animals. Man and animals have to consume plants or other animals that eat plants. They have no method for securing energy from the sun. However, for plants to begin an existence there had to be DNA and/or RNA available. As you will learn later in this book, plant cells are made up of DNA. How plants leaped from this beginning of cells containing DNA to plants as we see them today has not been explained. There are several hypotheses, but none that has been accepted. Perhaps seeds were either brought here or were a part of Earth's original makeup. There are those that believe that DNA and RNA in some form existed on the planet and that a combination of chemical events with the early environment resulted in the activation of one, or both of these, leading eventually to the source of DNA that evolved into plants. There is also a possibility that certain non-oxygenic organisms began to be established and somehow synergistic events resulted in a mutation to a plant form that was also non-oxygenic. Whatever the way, plant life was successfully established, which is a required pre-requisite for the eventual arrival of animals.

So, here was life on Earth in its simplest form. Plants didn't need other plants to eat and plant food was abundant, as the sun and chemicals were their only requirement. Plant life has cells and various other structures similar to man and animals, as I will discuss in the later parts of this book. Plants, animals, and humans all have eukaryotic cells, and how they relate will be discussed later. For now, we are at the first level of life on Earth in the form of plants. Once plants were established at a significant level, Earth gained an oxygen atmosphere, which would allow the evolution of plant-eating animals and eventually man. Can you imagine how Earth would have looked prior to this—almost like a bald-headed man who began to grow hair, but without the bald-headed man? Over thousands of years, during which there were periods of ice covering the Earth, the Earth became greener and greener. Eventually, as if by another miracle, the Earth's atmosphere was converted to richer oxygen, and as oxygen became a higher percentage of the atmosphere, the atmosphere started to become perilous for the plants, since the atmosphere became decreasingly composed of carbon dioxide. If the percentage of carbon dioxide in the atmosphere drops below 800 parts per million, some plants can not exist. At about 50 parts per million, no plant can live, or at least plants of any substance.

Man, Communication, and Education

The appearance of animals on Earth, and eventually man, was the next miracle of life; animals breathed out carbon dioxide and the plants took it into their system and then provided the animals with oxygen. Isn't Mother Nature wonderful?

During the early millennia, communication and education were by word of mouth, since there were only crude means of communicating. Writing was limited to what a person could handwrite on some form of material that was primitive at best. To further complicate the issue, there was no standard alphabet or language in the world as it was then. There were no means of copying what someone printed or wrote. So, anything of importance was mainly relayed by word of mouth. And, as indicated, word of mouth was sometimes challenging, since the spoken word was different across the world that was known then.

As time proceeded, so did life, but not as we know it now. Life was to be a long and torturous journey forward from this crude and ignorant beginning. As time proceeded, man would follow a learning curve that continuously reached levels of understanding beyond his individual lifespan as he passed on his learning's to his offspring. In the years that followed came a movement toward a form of education that focused on bright individuals. There were areas of the world that became more organized and intellectually advanced; and these societies recognized that man was better off educating those that lived among them during these times. The organization was in the form of governments established within the areas. Greece and Egypt are two parts of the world that gained the most from this movement toward improving the social and philosophical sharing of ideas. It would be many years before these capabilities would be realized. Yet man continued to thrive and spread his knowledge. Early education was by sight and experience, not steeped in mathematics or science, led by men who were philosophers. Each of them gained some form of advanced education by discussing things among themselves and then extending their knowledge to others. When you consider that philosophers were qualitative in their ways of thinking and teaching, you wonder how so much progress was made in the advanced building of structures. It may be better understood that progress is made by those that philosophize in generalities and that these generalities are sometimes stated as hypotheses. From these beginnings, man progressed by proving these generalities or hypotheses to be correct or incorrect. Those proven correct became postulates or laws, or information for further investigation. Those proven as incorrect always brought some learning that added to man's increasing knowledge. One of man's main strengths came from his failings—learning from when he did something that didn't perform as he expected and making sure he noted this and took another direction the next time it came up.

Man's main strength was his ability to think. With this ability as a strong baseline, he rose above ignorance, and civilization improved fairly rapidly. There were advancements in several directions. As the philosophers expounded on their thoughts, not all that was communicated was accepted since there were questions that were brought forth for which they had no immediate answers. These questions were taken back to the other philosophers and discussed, with some answers coming forth. This back-and-forth approach to communicating new thoughts and new ideas between philosophers resulted in the broadening of man's scope of the world and allowed for great progress. Man became better educated, but it was slow and was not quantitative. As time passed, education became more quantitative, and the first mathematics began to take hold.

Some of the first forms of mathematics related to right triangles. In approximately 1000 BC there is evidence that mathematics relating to right triangles existed in Egypt and China. A Greek named Pythagoras who was born around 500BC went to Egypt and studied their ways. He is given credit for developing the Pythagorean Theorem. He later moved to Italy and taught mathematics, which included significant teaching about what is now known as geometry.

Education through wars

Other mass means of education developed due to wars fought in those times. Wars were a result of one group of people wanting to overcome other groups in society. It's amazing what ingenuity comes from wars. Man thought about how to build ships to carry them to other lands. They then built the ships to fight wars, and those ships were different than the ones they used for fishing. They come up with new weapons and the means of using them to overcome their enemies. The conquerors brought their education to the people they conquered and they absorbed whatever knowledge they could gain from those that they oppressed. As they returned to their homelands, they took back their new learned ideas, which resulted in new questions.

But conquering isn't always a real win. With death all around from the battles came sicknesses that were not understood. Sometimes the conqueror ended up being conquered due to mass diseases that struck him in foreign lands. This was not understood, and some studied the sicknesses and came up with reasons and some solutions, but they were up against an invisible foe. However, some success developed with forms of medications that did help relieve some of these sicknesses. Early in this period, there were discussions of where man came from and why he was different from other animals. This bordered on the discussion of life, but it was more about why man was different from other forms of life rather than about life itself. Some education came from man trying to understand why other species didn't get some of the illnesses that prevailed at the time.

Philosophers enter the picture

Several hundred years before the birth of Christ, education was qualitative and was provided by philosophers who would generalize about the world around them at the time. At this time there were approximately one hundred million people on Earth. One of the first recognized was a philosopher named Aristotle. (17) He was one of the great thinkers of the early world, and it was thought that he knew everything that was known at the time.

Aristotle was born in 384 B.C. and lived to 322 B.C. He was born in a small town in Macedonia. His father was a physician at the time, and much of Aristotle's knowledge about the human body came from his father. He was considered an aristocrat and as such was expected to receive some higher learning. At the age of eighteen he went to study at Plato's academy in Athens, Greece. He was so bright that Plato accepted him as a disciple. Aristotle remained in Athens at this academy for approximately twenty years and left after Plato's death. He went to Asia and researched the botany and zoology of the continent. He was considered the first of the educated to begin to teach biology, and when this subject was taught it always led to inquiries into the beginnings of man.

Aristotle was one of the first philosophers to quantify things he learned, and he began to teach quantitatively; i.e. he didn't generalize as much as the philosophers before him. He would ask for data, and, once found, he wrote it down. The question of where man came from had always been a topic of interest, and he was one of the first to try to organize this subject. Life was important, and Aristotle tried to explain where it originated. He was one of the teachers who thought that man made decisions through his heart rather than his brain. Interestingly enough, at about the same time the Egyptians believed the decision making and the thought process was made by the brain. Maybe they both were right to some extent.

Right or wrong, there were philosophers who had their own spin on what makes the world go around. There were several theories of how babies were conceived and how flowers and their seeds worked. They all knew that children were conceived by the mating of a man and a woman, but they had their own thoughts on what was happening. The Greek philosophers had several thoughts on the matter. Theophrastus felt that male flowers caused female flowers to ripen. Hippocrates got more detailed and felt that seeds were produced by various body parts and transmitted to offspring at the time of conception. Aristotle proposed that male semen mixed with female semen during conception. Aeschylus, in 458 BC, proposed the male as the parent, with the female as a sort of nurse that looked over the child within her and acted as a nurse upon birth. So, there were these philosophies about birth early in the world of philosophers. Each was trying to assess an obvious issue using common sense, which at times wasn't close to the facts. Time and the learning curve would provide answers, as we shall see as time moves on and people become more and more educated.

Alexander the Great

Aristotle was the first teacher of logic, and some of this must have worn off on one of his star pupils, Alexander, who would soon be known as Alexander the great. (18)

Alexander, on the death of his father, became the ruler of Macedonia, and at the early age of about twenty years he began to invade and conquer the countries around Macedonia. Over the course of thirteen years he conquered the countries of the Middle East and went as far as what is now known as India. One of the countries he conquered was Egypt, and he became interested in their way of thinking. Alexandria, the capital of Egypt, was named after this conqueror. During this time period, he spread the culture he had learned from Aristotle as well as the cultures of different countries he subdued. Here was an example of war spreading knowledge. There would soon be several cities named Alexandria in that part of the world, and they still remain. Alexander had intended to turn around and begin to conquer the countries that make up Europe, but he became sick and soon died at the age of thirty-three.

I bring Aristotle and Alexander into the picture to illustrate how knowledge was gained and passed on—much of it passed on during and after the events related to war. Many events of this nature would follow in the chronology of the world, and the world became bigger and better educated in the eyes of man, but there was no good response to where life came from. In those early days each religion that was formed also had its God and creator, and this was spread also as an offshoot of war.

As a companion to war, sickness seemed to follow the conqueror and the conquered, as well as some cures for certain illnesses. In fact the world would start to be better educated about life due to many forms of disease and sickness that would follow. Each brought bad times and an increased knowledge of what was not known about life to the people in the world. A review of the major calamities in the world would show how little was known and how so much was learned as a result of these events.

The Roman Empire

Not long before the exploits of Alexander the Great, there were exploits by what became known as the Empire of Rome. This began as early as 500 BC, which was before Alexander but the Empire didn't reach its peak till around Alexander's time. (19) This Roman Empire eventually stretched from England, Wales, Portugal, Spain, France, and parts of Germany, out to the Black Sea. Italy and Greece were included, and the empire stretched southward to Syria, Lebanon, and all of northern Africa, including Egypt, Libya, Tunisia, Algeria, Morocco, and west of Gibraltar. In essence it controlled what Alexander wanted to control before his death. Probably the most powerful personality to come along with the Roman Empire was Julius Caesar, who was born around 100 BC. He is credited with putting France, England, Spain, and parts of North Africa under Roman control. It is said he was very disturbed when he proceeded to Alexandria, Egypt, and realized that Alexander had conquered Egypt at a much younger age than he was at the time. One of the important things that came out of Caesar's triumphs was the letters he wrote describing all the events. This information was sent back to Rome. His letters included not only his battles, but the various things he learned from the people of these countries. Caesar was assassinated by the senators of Rome when he was 56 years old in approximately 44 BC. Once again, war had spread a form of civilization that carried good things as well as bad. The Roman culture was to spread as far as what is now known as Romania.

During Caesar's time the culture of Rome was spread. As he took command of Egypt, he learned of their ways and what Alexander had brought from Greece. Egyptians were quite advanced in their thinking, especially in what was known of mathematics at the time. The letters that Caesar sent back to Rome contained messages about the new findings he had encountered in Egypt, and so there was another blending of education. Those in search of learning or teachers of what was known, much of it gained from conquests of Egypt, spread out from Greece and from Rome. The conquests of Alexander and Caesar and those before Caesar resulted in the clearing of routes to the various countries that now make up all of Europe and parts of northern Africa, and those teachers traveled along these routes. Roman culture was spread throughout Europe and the countries of Northern Africa.

Rome sent its teachings to the North, the South, and the East. Meanwhile, Greek culture was spread from about where Rome's reach ended all the way to parts of India. Rome's influence lasted until the end of the fifth century, around 476 AD, when the Roman Empire ended.

During Rome's influence in the Mid-East, Jesus was born around 2 BC in the town of Nazareth, and he began his teachings in mid-20s AD. Jesus was crucified in Jerusalem on April 7, around the year 30 AD, on order of the Roman governor Pontius Pilate under the charge of sedition against the Roman Empire.

Jesus' actual birth and death dates are controversial, but were established by Dionysius in the year of 532 AD. His birth date was set at December 25, 1 BC. AD 1 was assigned to the following year. AD represents Anno Domini, which translates to "in the year of the Lord". And thereby was established the system of numbering years from the birth of Jesus. The system was accepted almost two centuries later and became the established calendar in Western civilization.

I bring this information into this book because it represents probably the biggest spreading of culture after the failure of the Roman Empire around 476 AD. Christianity began to be accepted in Rome around 50 AD, and it spread east into the land that Alexander had conquered. (20) It spread using the Latin language of the Church of Rome. However, Christianity was not considered legal in the state of Rome until Galerius issued an edict permitting the practice of the Christian religion under his rule in April of 31 AD.

Constantine would become the first Christian emperor to embrace this religion and the first emperor to openly promote the newly legalized religion. However, there were many pagans during his rule, and he found it necessary to appease these factions. Constantine supported the church financially and granted certain privileges, such as exemption from certain taxes by clergy. Between 324 and 330 AD, Constantine built from scratch a new imperial capital in what is now known as Turkey. The town was named Constantinople, and it was the first city built to represent the Christian faith. This city contained many churches of Christian faith, and there were no pagan temples.

Constantinople became a strong member of the Christian faith. Eventually there were essentially two major players: Rome represented the Western power and Constantinople represented the Eastern power.

Rome continued their teachings using Latin, and Constantinople's teaching were in Greek.

Around the year 476, the political influence of Rome in the Western culture began to fail. This was the demise of Roman control over the countries in what was called the Western World, where Roman teachings prevailed. Although Roman rule would fail, this was not the case with the Christian world. Christianity continued to spread. A split between the West and East (Rome and Constantinople) began in 1054 and was finalized as a result of the sacking of Constantinople by the Fourth Crusade in 1204.

Rome remained as the center of the Christian faith. Christianity faith gained momentum due to the conversion of many countries to the faith, which then interpreted and conveyed doctrine through the native languages rather than in Latin or Greek. People native to the various countries and to the language of their country found it much easier to understand and convey the doctrine to their offspring. Several times representatives of these countries were called back to Rome to have them use the Latin language for their teachings, but finally Rome gave in to the wishes of these countries.

Why I chose to cover this part of history by discussing Christianity

It was not my intent to spend a great deal of time on the discussion of the Christian faith. My intent was to show how the Roman and Greek political situations occurred. As they fell or were rendered less powerful, the Christian faith sustained the teachings of these two powerful political influences beyond their political demise. Reviewing the history of the world as it was known then, between Alexander and his exploits from Greece to what is called the Eastern world and the Roman power that, through people like Caesar, controlled the Western world as it was known then, you see that these two political powers essentially controlled these huge areas of civilization. As the political powers of these two began to fade, the religious power of Christianity quietly spread, but largely within those political borders. What is called the Great Schism began in around 1054 and extended until 1204, when these two great religious powers of the Christian faith began to split due to differences in interpretations within their religions. The Eastern sector continued to spread eastward from Greece into Bulgaria, Czechoslovakia, Yugoslavia, Romania, Russia, and Moravia; spreading the Orthodox interpretation of Christianity.

During all this expansion of political and then religious power, extraordinary teaching and learning occurred. Although a great amount of the teaching and learning was through the momentum of these all consuming powers, there was also a special sector that was a part of the religion but practiced it in a different way. This was the way of the monasteries and the monks. The monks were essentially hermits who lived within the monasteries that began appearing in the fourth century and expanded through all of the years mentioned (300 AD to the present). There were two factions of monks, ones who lived like hermits in solitude, and the other monks who lived in communities, normally in a monastery. In both cases their lives were more devoted to working on problems separate from the religious and more focused on secular efforts. Each would spend years working on one difficult problem that eventually provided those outside the religion with facts that would require a lifetime of solitude to solve. Within the monasteries, monks also became teachers of the Christian faith to young people. They were strict in their ways, and those that learned under them were taught with very little in the relaxed way of modern public schools. Later in the book you will read of some of the monk's findings.

The Silent Deaths

As wars, conquests, and religion brought more and more people together, there were also silent deaths that showed no clues as to their cause. There were no instruments to allow the chemists of those days to observe the infiltrators that seemed to relate to these deaths. These killers came silently and left silently in most cases. They were worse than war, where the enemy could be seen. There were no battles to win, or so it seemed. The wealthy were stricken as well as the poor. Peaceful people who fought no wars and had no mortal enemies were taken down with the rest by these silent invaders of the human body. Names were given to these scourges based on the results rather than the culprits. The several that I will cover would be called pandemics by today's definition. A pandemic is a disease that is spread from human to human and is manifested all over the world, from country to country. The present-day definition of a pandemic involves three phenomena; it is new, causes serious illness, and is infectious, so it spreads easily and can sustain itself within humans. There are many traumatic illnesses that cannot be called pandemic even though they are widespread. Cancer is widespread, but it is not contagious and therefore does not fall under the description of a pandemic.

The Black Death

The Black Death, or the Black Plague, was one of the most deadly pandemics in human history. (21) Although there were outbreaks of the Black Plague, or Bubonic Plague, in the sixth and eighth centuries, these were rather mild compared to the massive attack by this disease in the mid-fourteenth century. It began somewhere in the south or middle of Asia. It was carried to Europe by the late 1340s. However, it spread over all of what was known of the world at the time. The pandemic (prevalent over a wide geographic area) is estimated to have killed 75 to 100 million people worldwide. When one considers that there were approximately 300 million in the world at the time, this is an enormous percentage of the whole population. The deaths in Europe alone were estimated at 20 million deaths. The plague was estimated to have killed approximately half of the people in Europe, where there was a population of approximately 40 to 45 million in the middle of the fourteenth century.

The plague disease, believed to be caused by *Yersinia pestis*, is prevalent in populations of ground rodents in central Asia, but it is not entirely clear where the fourteenth-century pandemic started. The most popular theory places the first cases in the steppes of Central Asia, though some speculate that it originated around northern India. There are others that point to a probability that the Black Death originated in Africa and spread to central Asia, where it then became entrenched among the rodent population. Nevertheless, from central Asia it was carried east and west along the Silk Road by Mongol armies and traders making use of the opportunities of free passage within the Mongol Empire offered by the Pax Mongolica (peace in Mongolia). It was reportedly first introduced to Europe in the trading city of Caffa in the Crimea in 1347. After a protracted siege, during which the Mongol army under Janibeg was suffering the disease, they catapulted infected corpses over the city walls to infect the inhabitants. The Genoese trader fled, bringing the plague by ship into Sicily and the south of Europe, whence it spread.

Whether or not this hypothesis is accurate, it is clear that several pre-existing conditions, such as war, famine, and weather, contributed to the severity of the Black Death. Medieval people called this catastrophe the "Great Pestilence," the "Great Death," or the "Great Plague." Later the "Black Death" predominated. It has been thought that the name came from a striking late-stage sign of the disease in which the sufferers' skin would blacken due to subepidermal hemorrhages (purpura) and the extremities darkened with gangrene.

Because the Black Death was, according to historical accounts, characterized by buboes (swellings in lymph nodes) like the late nineteenth-century Asian Bubonic Plague, scientists and historians at the beginning of the twentieth century assumed that the Black Death was an outbreak of the same disease, caused by the bacterium *Yersinia pestis* and spread by fleas with the help of animals like the black rat. However, this view has recently been questioned by scientists and historians.

The plague would disappear for a time, followed by a resurgence of the disease. It spread across many countries in Europe but spared Poland, Belgium, and the Netherlands. This cycle continued in England for years, disappearing at times for a hundred years and then returning.

The latest occurrence was in 1665–66. The Great Fire of London in 1666 may have killed off any remaining plague-bearing rats and fleas, which led to a decline in the plague.

An interesting hypothesis about the appearance, spread, and especially disappearance of plague from Europe is that the flea-bearing rodent reservoir of disease was eventually succeeded by another species. The black rat was originally introduced from Asia to Europe by trade, but was subsequently displaced and succeeded throughout Europe by the bigger brown rat. The brown rat was not as prone to transmit the germ-bearing fleas to humans. This is just a theory by some but not proven. (85)

It is believed the Europeans were susceptible to disease because they lived in crowded surroundings with very poor sanitary conditions. They often ate stale or diseased meat because refrigeration had not yet been invented. Also, medicine was primitive and unable to remedy an illness that modern technology might have cured. Bad medical advice also advanced the plague. People were often advised not to bathe because open skin pores might let in the disease. Good hygiene was not a practice until the beginning of the twentieth century.

As bad as this disease was, it probably would not be called a pandemic under the present definition because it is not contagious from human to human. For a person to contact this disease they would have to be bitten by a flea from a specific species of rat.

Famine

Famine cannot be considered a disease since it is not a sickness and is not contagious. However, famine leads to sickness. Societies suffering from famine end up debilitated by unrelated diseases, due to their weakened condition. Malnutrition drags the body and all its defenses down. Most of today's world is not in this condition. However, there are countries in Africa that suffer from malnutrition and the resultant illnesses that can be expected from this weakened condition. In the years 1315 to 1322, a catastrophic famine known as the Great Famine struck all of Northern

Europe. The famine was one result of a large population growth in the centuries leading up to the Black Death. Europe became overpopulated in the early fourteenth century, and, as a result, the number of Europeans began to exceed the productive capacity of the land and farmers. (2) In northern Europe, new technological innovations such as the heavy plow and the three-field system were not as effective in preparing new fields for harvest as they were in the Mediterranean because the north had poor, clay-like soil. Food shortages and skyrocketing prices were a fact of life for as much as a century before the Plague. Wheat, oats, and hay, and consequently livestock, were all in short supply, and their scarcity resulted in hunger and malnutrition. The result was a mounting human vulnerability to disease, due to weakened immune systems.

Standards of living then fell drastically as diets grew more limited, and Europeans as a whole experienced more health problems. In autumn of 1314, heavy rains began to fall, which led to several years of cold and wet winters. The already weak harvests of the north suffered, and the seven-year famine ensued. The Great Famine was the worst in European history and carried away at least ten percent of the population. This Great Famine probably weakened and made the population more vulnerable to the Black Plague.

In 1318 a pestilence of unknown origin, sometimes identified as anthrax, targeted the animals of Europe. The disease decimated sheep and cattle, further reducing the food supply and income of the peasantry. This added to the strain on both the economy and health of the European countries.

Typhus

Typhus, sometimes call "camp fever" because of its pattern of flaring up in times of strife (also known as "ship fever" for its tendency to spread wildly in cramped quarters such as ships), emerged during the Crusades. It had it first impact in Europe in 1489 in Spain. While fighting the Christian Spaniards and the Muslims in Granada, the Spanish lost 3,000 to war casualties and 20,000 to typhus. In 1528, the

French lost 18,000 troops in Italy and lost supremacy to the Spanish. In 1542, 30,000 people died of typhus while fighting the Ottomans in the Balkans. (86)

Cholera

Cholera is a severe diarrheal disease cased by the bacterium *Vibrio cholerae*. It is transmitted to humans by ingesting contaminated water or food. (22) The major reservoir for cholera was long assumed to be humans, but some evidence suggests that it is the aquatic environment.

Cholera was originally endemic to the Indian subcontinent, with the Ganges River likely serving as a contamination reservoir. It spread by trade routes (land and sea) to Russia, then to Western Europe, and from Europe to North America. It is no longer considered an issue in Europe and North America, due to filtering and chlorination of the water supply.

1816–1826: The first cholera pandemic began in Bengal and by 1820 had spread across India. It extended as far as China and the Caspian Sea before receding. (84)

1829–1851: The second cholera pandemic reached Europe, London, and Paris in 1832. In London, it claimed 6,536 victims; whereas in Paris, 20,000 succumbed (out of a population of 650,000), with about 100,000 deaths in all of France. It reached Russia, Quebec, Ontario, and New York in the same year and the Pacific coast of North America by 1834.

1849: The second major outbreak in Paris occurred in 1849. In London, it was the worst outbreak in the city's history, claiming 14,137 lives, many more than the number in the 1832 outbreak. In 1849 cholera claimed 5,308 lives in the port city of Liverpool, England, and 1,834 in Hull, England. An outbreak in North America took the life of former U.S. President James K. Polk. Cholera spread throughout the Mississippi River system, killing over 4,500 in St. Louis and over 3,000 in New Orleans, as well as thousands in New York. In 1849 cholera was spread along the California and Oregon Trail, and hundreds died on their way to the California Gold Rush, Utah, and Oregon.

1852–1860: The third cholera pandemic mainly affected Russia; with over a million deaths. Between 1853 and 1854, a London epidemic claimed 10,738 lives.

1854: An outbreak of cholera in Chicago took the lives of 5.5 per cent of the population

Outbreaks continued to pop up in 1863, 1866, 1881, 1899, 1961, and 1991. As recently as 2007, the U.N. reported outbreaks in Iraq; probably as a result of the war and living conditions.

Anthrax

Anthrax is an acute infectious disease in humans and animals that is caused by the bacterium *Bacillus anthracis*. It is highly lethal in some forms. Anthrax is one of only a few bacteria that can form long-lived spores. When the bacteria's life cycle is threatened by factors like lack of food caused by their host dying or by a change of temperature, the bacteria turn themselves into more or less dormant spores and wait for another host to continue their life cycle. (23)

When breathed in, ingested, or entering a cut in the skin, these spores reactivate themselves and multiply very rapidly in their new host. Anthrax spores in the soil are very resilient and can live many decades, perhaps centuries. The bacteria are known to occur on all continents except Antarctica. Anthrax most commonly occurs in wild and domestic grass-eating mammals (ruminants) that ingest or breathe in the spores while eating grass. Anthrax can also be caught by humans who are exposed to dead, infected animals or who eat tissue from infected animals or are exposed to a high density of anthrax spores from an animals' fur, hide, or wool. Anthrax spores can be grown outside the body and used as a biological weapon. Anthrax cannot spread directly from human to human; but anthrax spores can be transported by human clothing, shoes, etc. If a person dies of anthrax, their body can be a very dangerous source of anthrax spores. The word *anthrax* is the Greek word for coal; the germ's name is derived from *anthrakitis*, the

Greek word for anthracite (coal), in reference to the black skin lesions victims develop in a cutaneous skin infection.

Anthrax is one of the oldest recorded diseases of grazing animals such as sheep and cattle and is believed to be the Sixth Plague mentioned in the Book of Exodus in the Bible. Anthrax is also mentioned by Greek and Roman authors such as Homer (in the *Iliad*) Virgil (*Georgics*), and Hippocrates. It was prevalent in the nineteenth century in Europe and was previously mentioned in the section discussing the famine that occurred in the fourteenth century..

Robert Koch, a German physician and scientist, first identified the bacteria which caused the anthrax disease in 1877. His pioneering work in the late nineteenth century was one of the first demonstrations that diseases could be caused by microbes. His groundbreaking experiments not only helped create an understanding of anthrax, but also helped elucidate the role of microbes in causing illness at a time when debates were still held over spontaneous generation versus cell theory. Koch went on to study the mechanisms of other diseases and was awarded the 1905 Nobel Prize in Physiology for Medicine for his discovery of the bacteria causing tuberculosis. Koch is today recognized as one of history's most important biologists and a founder of modern bacteriology. You will hear more about Koch as I discuss the ventures of people important in the advance of medicine and life-seeking secrets. (65)

Smallpox

The history of the rise and fall of smallpox is a success story for modern medicine and public health. Even though the disease has been eradicated, the threat of its return has once again brought it to the forefront of public controversy.

The origin of smallpox is uncertain, but it is believed to have originated in Africa and then spread to India and China thousand of years ago. (24) The first recorded smallpox epidemic was in 1350 BC during the Egyptian-Hittite war. Smallpox reached Europe between the 5th and 7th centuries and was present in major European cities by the eighteenth century. Epidemics occurred in the North American colonies in the seventeenth and eighteenth centuries. At one time smallpox was a significant disease in every country throughout the world except Australia and a few isolated islands. Millions of people died in Europe and Mexico as a result of widespread smallpox epidemics.

The demise of smallpox began with the realization that survivors of the disease were immune for the rest of their lives. This led to the practice of variolation— a process of exposing a healthy person to infected material from a person with smallpox in the hopes of producing a mild disease that provided immunity from further infection. The first written account of variolation describes a Buddhist nun practicing around 1022 to 1063 AD. She would grind up scabs taken from a person infected with smallpox into a powder and then blow it into the nostrils of non-immune person. By the 1700s, this method of variolation was common practice in China, India, and Turkey. In the late 1700s, European physicians used this and other methods of variolation, but reported "devastating" results in some cases. Overall, 2 to 3 percent of the people who were variolated died of smallpox, but this practice decreased the total number of smallpox fatalities by ten-fold.

The next step toward the eradication of smallpox occurred with the observation by English physician Edward Jenner that milkmaids who developed cowpox, a less serious disease, did not develop the deadly smallpox. In 1796, Jenner took the fluid from a cowpox pustule on a dairymaid's hand and inoculated an 8-year-old boy. Six weeks later, he exposed the boy to smallpox, and the boy did not develop any symptoms. Jenner coined the term "vaccine" from the word "vaca," which means "cow" in Latin. His work was initially criticized, but soon was rapidly accepted and adopted. By 1800 about 100,000 people had been vaccinated worldwide.

The "modern" vaccine that was licensed by the FDA was taken from a weak strain of virus called the New York City Board of Health strain. It was produced by Wyeth Laboratories and licensed under the name Dryvax. The last outbreak of smallpox in the United States occurred in Texas in 1949, with eight cases and one death. Even though most of North America, Western Europe, Australia, and New Zealand were free of smallpox by this time, other countries such as Africa and India continued to suffer from epidemics.

IN 1967 the World Health Organization (WHO) started a worldwide campaign to eradicate smallpox. This goal was accomplished in ten years, due in a large part to massive vaccination efforts. The last endemic case of smallpox occurred in Somalia in 1977. On May 8, 1980 the World Health Assembly declared the world free of smallpox.

Spanish Flu: The worst of the worst

The 1918 flu pandemic, commonly referred to as the Spanish Flu, was a category 5 influenza pandemic caused by an unusually severe and deadly influenza; a virus strain of subtype H1N1. (25) Many of its victims were healthy young adults, in contrast to most influenza outbreaks, which predominantly affect juvenile, elderly, or otherwise weakened patients.

The Spanish flu pandemic lasted from 1918 to 1919, spreading even to the Arctic and remote Pacific islands. While older estimates put the number of killed at between 40 and 50 million people, current estimates are that 50 million to 100 million people worldwide died; possibly more than those taken by the Black Death. This extraordinary toll resulted from the extremely high infection rate of up to 50 percent and the extreme severity of the symptoms, suspected to be caused by cytokine storms. Between 2 and 20 percent of those infected by Spanish flu died, as opposed to the normal flue epidemic mortality rate of 0.1percent. Unusually, the epidemic mostly killed young adults, with 99 percent of pandemic influenza deaths occurring in people under 65 and more than half in young adults 20 to 40 years old.

The disease was first observed at Fort Riley, Kansas, on March 11, 1918. The Allies of World War 1 came to call it the Spanish flu, primarily because the pandemic received greater press attention in Spain than in the rest of the world, as Spain was not involved in the war and had not imposed wartime censorship. The word flu came from an Italian derivation of the word influenza, which means "from the cold," meaning that this illness came during the cold time of the year. Each of us knows this is still true today, since the flu starts around November and lasts through March here in the United States.

Scientists have used tissue samples from frozen victims to reproduce the virus for study. Given the strain's extreme virulence, there has been controversy regarding the wisdom of such research. Among the conclusions of this research is that the virus kills via a cytokine storm, which explains its unusually severe nature and the unusual age profile of its victims. A cytokine storm is not a scientific term and is simply used to describe the result of a massive immune response that releases huge amounts of cytokins, normally meant to fight infection in the person's system. The over-reaction leads to excessive inflammation and damage to the lungs, which causes the death of victims. Here's a case where the human response system over-reacts. This explains why the distribution of deaths of the 1918-1919 Spanish flu resulted in the deaths of young adults who have the best response system, compared to children or elderly people. *Nature Medicine* published an article in September 2006, authored by Menno de Jong, that supports the hypothesis that the cytokine storm is caused by the rapid replication of the H5N1 bird flu virus. (67)

Studies of the 1918 pandemic flu, the H1N1 virus that also originated in birds, show that patients also died as the result of an exaggerated immune response. Doctors who did autopsies on some victims of the 1918 pandemic flu were shocked to discover that the lungs of the victims were completely saturated with fluids. Normal, healthy lungs are light and flexible, ready to expand and contract as we breathe, but diseased lungs full of fluids are heavy with liquids and unable to absorb oxygen.

To give the reader a feel for the impact of this flu, it is estimated that it killed as many as 25 million in its first 25 weeks; in contrast, AIDS killed 25 million in its first 25 years. This pandemic has been described as "the greatest medical holocaust in history" and may have killed as many people as the Black Death. Keep in mind that the Black Death occurred over many years, whereas this flu was over in approximately eighteen months. My wife's grandparents and their sons and daughters (uncles, aunts and mother of my wife that totaled eight persons) all were hit with this flu and were near death, but miraculously none died.

Ebola Virus and other lethal diseases

Ebola virus and Bolivian hemorrhagic fever are highly contagious and deadly diseases with the theoretical potential to become pandemics. (68) Their ability to spread efficiently enough to cause a pandemic is limited, however, as transmission of these viruses requires close contact with the infected vector. Furthermore, the short time between a vector becoming infectious and the onset of symptoms allows medical professionals to quickly quarantine vectors and prevent them from carrying the pathogen elsewhere.

HIV, the virus that causes AIDS, is now considered a global pandemic, with the infection rates as high as 25 percent in southern and eastern Africa.(69) Effective education about safer sexual practices and blood-borne infection precautions training have helped to slow down infection rates in several African countries sponsoring national education programs. Infection rates are rising again in Asia and the Americas. I will cover HIV virus and the resultant AIDS in detail in a separate section later in the book.

SARS. There was an outbreak of SARS in 2003 that began in parts of China. This is a highly contagious form of atypical pneumonia, caused by a coronavirus dubbed SARS, which had the potential to become a pandemic; however, rapid action by the World Health Organization (WHO) helped to slow transmission. (66) The spread was isolated by quarantine. Canada got hit but took swift action to control the spread, and SARS was eliminated. However, this disease is not completely eradicated, and the world organizations for heath keep an eye out for any reoccurrence.

Summary of Disease

This book is about the wonder of life, so why should I spend considerable energy discussing the things that kill life? I feel that one of the wonders of life relates to how many challenges man has met and dealt with. In some cases man did not deal with the listed diseases as much as he survived them. This is a wonder. The strength of man, and in many cases the strength of his immune system, to be able to endure such periods while in close contact with those that suffered and died from the diseases is a wonder. In some cases individuals would have a mild case of the disease or be tolerant for some reason, but once the disease was contracted and recovered from, the body built immunity to that particular disease. Man had learned that for some diseases, the best cure was to avoid them. This was done by quarantine in many cases. Man had learned that if you keep the sick or dead away from the living, the living had a better chance of escaping its spread. Man recognized that many of the diseases arrived via boats on the trading routes, and ships were stopped from entering harbors if they came from countries that had a pandemic-type disorder. Later, there were wondrous actions taken, like the one Dr. Edward Jenner started on small pox. This was the first vaccination that prevented a person from acquiring a disease such as small pox. Others would come, and I am going to describe some of the other conquests of man against these unseen foes. As time progressed the learning curve of man would progress right along with it to take on the foe of disease.

One must keep in mind the lack of communication that existed during these terrible periods. There was only word of mouth until the fifteenth century (I will discuss what happened then to overcome this lack of communication). Imagine living now with only that capability. There were no books, newspapers, or other type of mass communication of any substance. This lack caused everything to take longer, and many new findings never got transmitted until years passed. Around the year 1000 AD, a form of printing existed called hand printing and was done by a person one book at a time. The world as it existed at the time looked for better means.

The Printing Press

As the world population grew, in the world as it was known at the time, it became harder and harder to communicate to the masses. It was almost as if time was moving too fast for the communication that was needed to thrive within this growth. When a disease occurred in Asia, it was unknown in other parts of the world until a boat from Asia arrived in those countries and passed the word. This could take many years. There was no form of communication to pass around this news rapidly. There also was no means of communicating the cures if they were found. Word of mouth was the sole provider and this could be very slow. In Europe, Africa, the Middle East, Russian, China, and India were trade routes to and from these continents as things happened the world over. Still, man was restricted in keeping up with what was happening because of the lack of a communications medium. A book or letter was hand-written, which was slow and laborious at best. Then came the block printing, which was an improvement. However, block printing was very time consuming and was not very precise. In addition, writing and printing were done in Latin in Europe and the countries that had been more or less colonized by Rome or by Alexander during his conquests. If not in Latin, it was in Greek. During the thirteenth and fourteenth centuries, the various countries began to write things in their own native tongues. Still, this was crude and slow and made it hard to keep up with the events in the world.

Then one of the most significant inventions in man's time arrived: the printing press. The printing press is a mechanical device for applying pressure on an inked surface that rests upon a media (such as paper or cloth), thereby transferring an image. The systems involved were first assembled in Germany by goldsmith Johann Gutenberg (4) in the 1430s.

The invention of Gutenberg's printing press depended primarily upon a diffusion of technologies from Asia, with their paper and the demand for books. Here's an idea of the quantity of books available in that day and age: by 1424, Cambridge University Library owned only 122 books – each of which had a value equal to a farm or vineyard. In Europe, the scarcity of books resulted in the decline of Latin and the ascent of the various vernaculars and the development of scientific journals and their specialist vocabulary, or jargon. The level of importance of the printing press is rivaled by few other inventions, so much so that it is often used as a reference to the social, political, and scientific change experienced by Europe after the press's introduction.

The demand for books was driven by rising literacy among the middle class and students in Europe. At this time, the Renaissance was still in its early stages, and the populace was gradually removing the monopoly the clergy had held on literacy. This alone diluted the influence of the church on people's lives. Scientists could now submit letters that were printed and disseminated. The world of knowledge experienced a major jump forward.

Having previously worked as a professional goldsmith, Gutenberg made skillful use of the knowledge of metal he had learned as a craftsman. He was the first to make type from an alloy of lead, tin, and antimony, which was critical for producing durable type that produced high-quality printed books. It also proved to be more suitable for printing than the clay, wooden, or bronze types invented in East Asia. To create these lead types, Gutenberg used what some considered his most ingenious invention, a special matrix enabling the quick and precise molding of new type blocks from a uniform template. He is also credited with the introduction of an oil-based ink, which was more durable than the previous water-based ink. For printing material, he used both vellum and paper, the latter having been introduced in Europe a few centuries earlier from China by way of the Arabs.

Printing in Europe also was a factor in the establishment of a community of scientists who could easily communicate their discoveries through the establishment of widely disseminated scholarly journals, helping to bring on the scientific revolution. Because of the printing press, authorship became more meaningful and profitable. It was suddenly important who had said or written what and what the precise formulation and time of composition were. (87) This allowed the exact citing of references, producing the rule, "One Author, one work, one piece of information." Before, the author was less important, since a copy of Aristotle made in Paris would not be exactly identical to one made in Bologna. For many works prior to the printing press, the name of the author was entirely lost.

The development of the alphabet

Of great importance relative to the invention of the printing press was the acceptance of the alphabet as we know it now. With a fairly common alphabet in use, books could be printed in various languages and translated into whichever language was appropriate. It is interesting to review the development of the alphabet. You will note as I proceed through this development of the alphabet how the alphabet gained its letters through some of the wars I had previously mentioned as the means by which knowledge was passed. You will see that many letters came from the countries the Romans and the Greeks invaded, and the culture of each country (the conqueror and the conquered) spread in both directions.

I will begin when the alphabet almost looked like the one we use today. (27) An early alphabet was initiated in Egypt in about 1000 BC. It was modified several times and added to. The alphabet used to go from right to left until the Etruscans in early Roman times. They transformed the alphabet so that it read from left to right. The main reason was that the farmers used to plow their fields in this direction. They considered the alphabet like the line in the dirt that the plow makes, so the letters were shaped like these plow lines, without curvature. The *A* was scratched out going from the bottom of the left side of the *A*. Where *A* stopped, the *B* would begin. It wasn't shaped like the *B* is today, since they wanted it to follow as if going from the plowed *A* to the plowed *B*. So the Etruscans made a contribution to our present alphabet. Now we enter the time of the Romans and the Church of Rome. See History of the Alphabet. (70) en.wikipedia.org/wiki/History_of_the_**alphabet** - 115k

The early Roman alphabet

Romans adopted writing from both the Etruscans and the Western Greeks in about the fifth century. They had no use for the Z or other characters of the Western Greek alphabet, so they dropped them from their alphabet. (3)

Romans needed a letter to represent the *f* sound in their language. The Etruscan language didn't have an *f* sound, and neither did Western Greek. The Greek was at that time pronounced *ph*, that is, a *p* with an *h* sound after it. They adapted the Etruscan letter F, which was pronounced "w," and gave it the sound *f*. They adopted an Etruscan three-lined zig-zag S and then curved it to make the modern curvy S. They used the gamma < to represent both the Etruscan *k* sound and the Greek *g* sound. The Romans and Greeks were provided a good base by the Etruscans who were probably instrumental, because of this, in providing the religious teachings of the time. The early Roman alphabet looked like this:

A B C D E F H I K L M N O P Q R S T V X

There are a few differences from the modern alphabet.

C represented both the hard *k* sound in cat and the *g* sound in garden. It represented both the vowel we call i and the *y* sound that starts the word yellow. V represented both the *u* sound in "put" and a consonantal sound that was somewhere between our *v* and *w*.

The letter G

The Romans had three letters in their alphabet for the *k* sound, C, K, and Q. In addition, the C did double time as a *g* sound. The sensible thing to do would be to drop the Q completely and use C only for the *g* sound. Instead, the Romans continued to use Q in certain circumstances before U, and invented the new letter G by adding a bar across the C.

It's a mystery why, when they added G to the alphabet, they put it after F, rather than after C. Perhaps because Z had been removed from its position between F and H and discarded, they felt that there was a gap. Whatever the reason, G has been firmly ensconced after F ever since.

With this cleared up, they had no real need for K, but they held on to it in case it became useful later, while using mainly C and Q for the writing of Latin.

Eastern Greek

In the third century BC, the Greeks led by Alexander the Great conquered the eastern Mediterranean and as far east as India. Over the next few centuries, knowledge also spread out from Greece in all directions, and the Romans absorbed a lot of ideas from Greek culture. Greek words started to be used in Latin. There was a need to be able to write down these words.

The Romans translated most of the letters, making do with such combinations as PH instead of f and TH instead of t. But they had no way of writing two particular Greek sounds, so in about 100 AD, the Romans borrowed two letters from the Eastern Greek alphabet. One was Y, which was very much the same as the V they had already got from Western Greek. In Eastern Greek it had retained a long stem, while in Western Greek it had lost it. The Eastern Greek pronunciation was by now slightly different as well, using the slender *u* sound we get in the German word *fünf* or the French *tu*. The other letter the Romans borrowed was the Zeta Z, for the *z* sound. Both the Y and the Z were only used for writing Greek words, so the letters were placed at the end of the alphabet, although Z had centuries before been positioned after F.

So, by the time the Roman Empire reached its peak in the fourth and fifth centuries, the alphabet looked like this:

A B C D E F G H I K L M N O P Q R S T V X Y Z

Due to the Roman dominance of Europe, the Roman alphabet became the standard alphabet throughout Western Europe, and eventually it spread throughout the Western World.

More new letters

After the Norman invasion of Britain in the eleventh century, the Anglo-Saxon language was written down using Roman letters. There was no letter for the *w* sound in Anglo-Saxon, which didn't exist in Latin. At first, they used the Runic wen, which looks like a narrow triangular P, but it was too easy to mix up with an actual P, so they started to write it using a double U, hence the name "double u." At that time, there was only one letter for both the vowel sound *u* and consonant sound *v*, and it looked like a V, so W looks like two Vs. The W was placed in the alphabet beside the V to which it was related.

Another letter was introduced into English at that time, from the runic alphabet: Thorn Þ. This was used to represent the *th* sound in English. Thorn died out later on, although it is still used in Iceland. The only place you'll see it now in English is in a corrupted form as a Y at the start of Ye Olde Tea Shoppe.

The letter U started off as a written variation of the letter V. The V symbol represented mainly the *u* sound, but could also be used for the *v* sound. In some forms of handwriting, V was written with a rounded bottom, but it still represented both the vowel U and the consonant V. Some time later, people started using the pointed V when they meant the consonant and the rounded U when they meant the vowel. Because these were considered to be variations of the same letter, they were put side by side in the alphabet.

The last letter to be added to the English alphabet was the letter J. Similarly to the evolution of U and V, I and J started out as variations of a single letter. Scribes might put a long tail on a final I if there were a few in a row. For example, Henry the Eighth could be written "Henry viii." It was up to the scribe to decide which version of the letter he wanted to use.

In Rome, I represented both the vowel I and the consonantal *y* sound at the start of the English word yellow. Gradually over the centuries, the consonant was changed: in Spain it became an H, in Germany it remained a Y, and in France it became a *j* sound. When the Normans invaded England in 1066, they brought the *j* sound with them, but continued to spell it with the letter I, which could be written I or J depending on which looked good.

In about the fifteenth century (around the time of the printing press), people started to fix on the I for the vowel and the J for the consonant, but this was not fully accepted until the mid-seventeenth century.

So from the seventeenth century onward, our alphabet contained the same 26 letters as we now use. But even then, many scholars still treated it as having only 24: they still considered U and V as one letter, and I and J as one letter. For example, Samuel Johnson's dictionary, published in the mid-eighteenth century, had all the I and J words mixed together. It was only in the mid-nineteenth century that scholars fully accepted that these were separate letters and that there are 26 letters in the alphabet. (70)

Conclusion of the modern alphabet

With the invention of J (thank goodness for the J—my name is John and my oldest son's name is Jay), the English alphabet contained the 26 letters that we know so well. Other languages in Europe added accents to many letters to cue extra sounds, for example á, Å, and Ä, but English has avoided this. There have also been attempts to revise the alphabet and introduce new letters to represent the ng sound, the ee sound, and so on. All such attempts have so far been doomed to failure. The vowels of A-E-I-O-U were accepted for pronunciation.

Fortunately the alphabet reached a level of maturity just before the invention of the printing press or readers of much of what was printed would have needed an interpreter. Likewise, the combination of printing books in a common alphabet and each country's' own language allowed each country to maintain records in their common language, not exclusively in either Greek or Roman. In this manner, education within a country could be accelerated and, with the common alphabet, could be translated into the language of other countries to further enhance the transfer of knowledge from one country to another.

The common alphabet and the printing press accelerated the spread of knowledge. The spread of knowledge beyond the sixteenth century was gigantic. To make an even bigger expansion of the world's knowledge, the New World was colonized by the leaders of the world at that time, and they brought their languages and books and teachings to the New World early in the seventeenth century.

You can appreciate the impact of the alphabet and the printing press as they allowed solutions to problems to be documented and shared, avoiding the need to resolve the same issues time after time. I might comment that progress through the centuries has been lead by the invention of some better means of communication. Examples are the phonograph, telephone, the telegraph, the radio, the television, the computer, the cellular phone, the FAX machine, the home printer, the internet, the specialty items like the ipod and iphone and the list goes on and will continue in the near future.

But other types of invention were needed to carry man further. He needed new tools to allow him to continue his progress toward learning more about the enemies he could not see. Man was rewarded by the skills of a janitor in the country of Holland (the Netherlands) when he polished the round glasses that were to make the next giant step toward solving many of man's problems.

He polished his lens to make a better microscope.

THE MICROSCOPE

In the next sections of this book I will discuss various additional illnesses and diseases and how they affected the world. I consider this a part of the evolution of man on Earth. I previously covered some of the wars and religion and how they spread the learning of man. In a sort of back-handed way, the diseases I will be discussing also spread the learning of man. Each disease that affected humans the world over resulted in communication the world over. Cures for diseases began to spread to countries other than the ones where the cures originated through books and articles. Advancements in the instruments that helped to find and cure diseases reached the peoples of the world. It seems that nothing is communicated faster than a disease that strikes or a cure that is found.

When I was in the Navy I spent the last three years off-ship stationed at the Patuxent Naval Air station. While there, in 1954 I read a very interesting book called *Microbe Hunters* by Paul De Kruif. (27) This book had been originally published in 1926 and was republished in 1954. This thoroughly interesting book is about the invention of the microscope and how doctors and scientists used this piece of equipment from the middle of the seventeenth century through early in the twentieth century. I will cover several of the scientists that were included in the book.

The invention of the microscope

The next significant achievement, one that generated a big surge in the scientific world, was the invention of the microscope. It began with the crazy love for the grinding of lenses by a Dutch janitor. Antony Leeuwenhoek was born in 1632 in Delft, Holland. (27) He left school at the age of sixteen and became an apprentice in a dry goods store in Amsterdam. At the age of twenty, he left this job and went back to his hometown, married, and set up a dry goods store of his own. He had several children. Antony became very interested in the use of a microscope while reviewing cloth in his store. He used a 10x microscope, which is all the world had at the time, to count the threads. He began to grind and polish his own lenses (named after the lentil because of the shape) and looked at things under his superior microscope. He did this for years while serving as a janitor for the town's city hall. By the age of forty he had about one hundred microscopes When he found a way to improve one, he would return to the early versions and make changes. His interest in the various aspects of the device, such as the metals used to hold the lenses and other parts of the microscope, were evident in his lenses and scopes.

He would study a frog's leg try to understand how every little thing worked. He observed the eyes of flies and would tell people about them. Many thought he was not of sound mind. He heated glass tubes and shaped them into needle-sized tips that allowed him to pick up very small objects.

When he was around forty years old, he went out into his yard and took a drop of water from one of his plants. He brought it into his work shop and looked at the water under his microscope. What Leeuwenhoek saw would result in the war on bacteria (Although he didn't know it at the time. It would be many years before what he saw were called bacteria). He couldn't believe his eyes. There were little animals running around in the water. He wondered where they came from. He took a saucer from the cabinet and washed it and cleaned it with some chemical and looked to see if anything was on the saucer. It was clean. He then set it out in the rain and brought it in and looked and saw nothing. He took a pepper seed and placed it in the water and saw nothing. He left it to sit for a couple of days, and when he looked he saw the normal ones that he previously had seen and one very big one that seemed to be eating the smaller ones. He decided to try to find out where they came from. He would look at his saliva and be very excited to see that these little creatures were there also. One day after drinking a very hot cup of coffee, he looked at a drop of saliva and found none. He picked around in his mouth and finally found a place in a back tooth that had many. He then did experiments with hot coffee and found that it could kill the creatures; when the coffee cooled down, they remained motionless.

At about this time in history, a group of men founded a little group called The Invisible College, which would secretly meet in England to discuss things they had done or seen. These meetings had to be secret because if the men of Cromwell heard about anything like this they would think that it was a conspiracy against the government. This group of men included Isaac Newton and Robert Boyle, who was the founder of the science of chemistry, so they were scientists of note. They began to get word that a Dutch janitor had made microscopes that allowed one to see very small creatures. They found it hard to believe and determined that this janitor had microscopes that magnified by a factor of 200, when normal ones magnified by ten. (I would like to make a note here for the reader's benefit. A microscope can only resolve things that are bigger than one-half a wavelength of light. The average wavelength of light is 0.55 micrometers. So the best microscopes that worked off of light could resolve things as small as 0.275 micrometers. If you were to look through one of Leeuwenhoek's best microscopes, which magnified by approximately 270, it would look like 75 micrometers—or three-thousandths of an inch (human hair is between three- thousandths and seven-thousandths of an inch), which is about the smallest thing that the human eye can detect. What this says to me is that his microscope in the middle of the seventeenth century was almost as good as today's microscopes.)

Newton decided to visit Leeuwenhoek. During his visit he was allowed to look through the microscopes, but was not allowed to touch one. Newton was very astounded at what he saw and convinced Leeuwenhoek that he should take notes of what he found and send them to The Invisible College. Thus began cooperation between this janitor and the highest of high scientists of England. Leeuwenhoek would investigate many things in his life and continue until he was ninety. He died when he was ninety-one. On his death bed, he asked his best friend to forward the last two reports that he had written. They had to be converted into Latin and sent to the Royal Society in England. The microscope of this janitor was as big an invention as the printing press, since now science could use it to visit another world of living things.

Robert Hooke, the English father of the microscope, made a copy of Leeuwenhoek's light microscope and then improved upon his design. (28) Although his microscope was easier to use than Leeuwenhoek's, he commented that his microscope didn't resolve small dimensions as well as Leeuwenhoek's. In 1678, after Leeuwenhoek had written to the Royal Society with a report of discovering "little animals"—bacteria and protozoa—Hooke was asked by the Society to confirm these findings. He successfully did so, thus paving the way for wide acceptance of Leeuwenhoek's discoveries. Hooke was the author of the book *Micrographia*, which detailed the various things he had observed with very accurate drawings. His observation of the details of cork contained information that was the first description of cells. He described the cells of the cork as being like a honey-comb. Until that time there was no understanding of living things being composed of cells. Of course, without the microscope it was impossible to be aware of this. The same is true of the discovery by Leeuwenhoek of bacteria and protozoa. Hooke is credited with discovering the basic unit of life, the cell. Hooke is also credited with being the first to use the basic three-lens configuration that is still used in microscopes today. There has not been a major change in the basic light microscope in these past 330 years.

Hooke examined fossils with his microscope, the first person to do so. He noted close similarities between the structures of petrified wood and fossil shells on the one hand, and living wood and living mollusk shells on the other. Most people at the time didn't believe that fossils represented forms of life that had lived previously on Earth. He described how fossils really represented previous living creatures and how they would become like these fossils. This work was done 250 years before Darwin. He described how these fossils found on high ground had previously been under water and how these remains could be used to determine the history of life.

Improvements in the microscope

I have been writing this book more or less in chronological order. However, I am going to cover the improvements in the microscope regardless of time so as to bring a clearer picture to the reader.

Improvements in the resolution of microscopes required that three basic problems be resolved: The first related to chromatic aberration, which is the unequal bending of different colors of light that occurs in a lens. (29) This was solved by Chester Hall in the 1730s by using a second lens with a different shape and light-bending properties. He found that he could realign the colors without losing the magnification of the first lens. The second related to spherical aberration, which was solved by Joseph Jackson Lister; it relates to the unequal bending of light that hits different parts of a lens. He resolved this problem by placing the lenses at precise distances from each other, which eliminated the aberration from the first lens. Also, if a low-power, low-curvature lenses could be made with minimal aberration and placed as the first lens in the series; this virtually eliminated spherical aberration. The third problem was that for a microscope to be as good as physically possible, it must collect a cone of light that was as wide as possible. This problem was solved by Ernst Abbe with the use of water and oil immersion lenses. The maximum resolution that Abbe was able to achieve is about ten times better than the resolution that Leeuwenhoek had achieved a hundred years earlier. This resolution of 200 nanometers (0.2 micrometers) is a physical limit placed by the wavelength of light. Remember I previously mentioned that a light microscope could resolve one half of a wavelength of light and used the average wavelength of light, which is 0.550 micrometers. The actual lower limit of light that man can see is 0.400 micrometers, so Ernst Abbe was able to take the microscope down to the lower limit, which is lower than the average wavelength I previously mentioned.

The first electron microscope

Instead of glass being used to bend and focus light, electron microscopes use magnetic coils to do the same thing with electrons. (29) H. Busch was the first to use a magnetic coil like a lens, in 1926. E. Ruska made the first image-producing electron microscope in 1933, which passed the 200-nanometer optical limit. Ruska and his company, Siemens of Germany, produced the first commercial electron microscope in 1939, and structures never seen before in science and engineering became visible. Much of what we know about the nano-universe, we owe to the scanning electron microscope. There were many improvements in the electron microscope over the years. I remember in 1964 seeing Westinghouse display their improved version at the integrated circuit plant where I ran the Custom Products Group and I could practically see inside of silicon. I was to purchase several electron microscopes over the years during the development of integrated circuits. They were much smaller in physical size, yet resolved as well as the large older ones. They also became affordable for use in industry, and their use spread rapidly.

The first scanning probe microscope

This system did not used electron beams to image a sample. Instead, it used a tiny, needle-like probe that scanned back and forth across a sample's surface. The interactions were recorded into a computer to form an image. This was invented by IBM in Switzerland by Gerd Binnig and Heinrich Rohrer. They were awarded the Nobel Prize in physics in 1986 for their work. The major advantage is that this can be used without a vacuum and even in a liquid. This made three-dimensional images available with very high resolution. I had one of my groups purchase one in 1993 for use in resolving very small dimensions in the development of advanced integrated circuits.

Microscopes and the men who used them to conquer diseases

I covered the main advances in microscopes to the present, since they have brought medicine, biology, physics, and other sciences to the forefront over the last 365 years. With these revolutionary pieces of equipment, much could be learned about the makeup of man and how to resolve many of the diseases that could have shortened man's life on Earth. I will now continue my discussion of the various advances made with the standard microscope that brought advances in life for man and discuss how the various microbe hunters battled the ailments of man.

Spallanzani

Lazzaro Spallanzani was born in 1729 in a small Italian village, just six years after Leeuwenhoek died. (27) He had been educated as a scientist at the University of Reggio. He had heard of the Dutchman and began to observe the "beasties," as many called them by this time. In the mid-1700s, many scientists and others felt that the beasties came about by spontaneous generation. In other words, they felt that they were not born; they just appeared out of nowhere, spontaneously. Lazzaro didn't believe this. He did many experiments to prove this wrong. Science had advanced by this time, and there were ways to make up a soup, or culture, that would result in many beasties in a day or so. As he did his experiments, others were doing experiments to show that they could cork a flask that had the soup in it and heat it. After opening it up there were just as many beasties as before, if not more. As Spallanzani did experiments, he would take flasks and heat them and taper down the ends and then seal them off and then heat them in boiling water for different times, demonstrating that after a certain length of time, there were no beasties to be found. This would be refuted by other scientists with experiments that they conducted.

Then Spallanzani devised another experiment that he thought would prove his point. He took a tube and put beastie soup in the tube and hooked one end to a vacuum pump. Then he sealed the other end off by heating the tip again. He let it pump and pump, and no matter how much he did this, the beasties lived. He couldn't believe it. All animals had to have oxygen to live. Why were they not dead? He was befuddled.

One day Spallanzani had an idea. He went to his lab and put a cleaned glass dish under his microscope. On one side he placed a drop of the soup with the beasties and on the other side of the microscope nozzle he put a drop of clean water that had no beasties. Then he took a needle he had cleaned and stuck it in the water forming a line from the water to the clean soup. It was like making a river for the beasties to swim toward his clean water, which was under the microscope. Spallanzani then watched while the beasties moved down this line of water. When the lead beastie was under his microscope, using a very clean, fine paint brush, he swished it through the channel of water and cut the "river" so no other beasties could swim into position under the microscope. With this deft movement he had captured one beastie under his microscope lens. He watched the beastie for hours. Then something remarkable happened. The beastie got longer and skinnier and then there were two beasties. He continued watching; two became four and then those four became eight. He got up and danced around his laboratory. The beasties did not appear spontaneously. Instead, each multiplied by dividing up into two beasties, and those two divided into two more, all at a rapid rate. Spallanzani had proven that the beasties were not spontaneously generated. Thus, the next advance for the microbe hunters was completed.

Pasteur

Pasteur was born in France in 1822. He attended a Paris university and received degrees in chemistry. (27) Pasteur first found the little animals in his microscope when he was trying to understand why some of France's grape crops were not producing the wine they were famous for. He viewed the good and bad wines under the microscope and found that the bad wine had no yeast in it and the good wine had yeast in it. Many experiments later, he proved to himself that the yeasts were what turned the sugar in the mix to alcohol and that the wines that did not have these rich yeasts were devoid of these little animals he normally could see under the microscope. He proved that these little creatures were responsible for the generation of yeasts. So, the little beasties could do good things as well as bad. At the time scientists didn't know the good from the bad bacteria. Eventually, his experiments and results saved the wine industry in France.

The belief that the little beasts were formed by spontaneous generation remained. People had forgotten about Spallanzani's experiments a hundred years before and believed that the beasties appeared by spontaneous generation. Pasteur established several experiments to prove that the beasties were actually air-borne and entered his mixture of broth that he grew bacteria) or other things in by falling into the broth. It was known that if you had a clean bowl of broth and left it out for a day or two and viewed the broth, it would be full of bacteria—they now had a proper name for the beasties. Pasteur demonstrated that the bacteria were due to the growth of microorganisms, not spontaneous generation. He exposed a bowl of boiling broth to air via a filter that prevented air particles from passing into the broth and allowed the broth to sit around for days. No bacteria could be found in the broth. He proved that the bacteria therefore came from the air as dust or spores, or were carried by other means. As soon as he removed the air filters, bacteria appeared in a short time. Through these experiments, he proved the existence of germs and developed germ theory.

Pasteur proved there were good germs and bad germs. Observing the bacteria in milk, he determined that sour milk had bad bacteria and good milk did not. He found that in milk heated to a certain temperature, the bacteria were killed while the integrity of the milk was maintained. Below that temperature, bacteria would not only remain but would multiply. If the milk were heated too high above that optimal temperature, the milk would be ruined. This was a great step toward ridding the world of problems related to milk. This process became known as pasteurization, in honor of his work. Milk pasteurization is the process of heating to eliminate harmful bacteria in the milk. This is used in every qualified supplier of milk and milk products. Heat milk at 72 degrees C (162 Fahrenheit) for 16 seconds and the bad bacteria are gone, whereas at 63° C (145 Fahrenheit), the milk must be heated for not less than thirty minutes. Milk is deemed pasteurized if it tests negative for alkaline phosphatase.

Pasteur's work also provided the clues necessary for providing sterile operations that were developed by other great men at that time.

Pasteur also developed methods, through the use of good bacteria, for improving wines and the yeasts that were required for other foods

Pasteur worked on the diseases that resulted in cholera in chickens. Part of this was through good fortune. The culture that had been set aside for inducing cholera in chickens mistakenly sat around for an extended period. He then injected the cholera culture into some chickens, and they didn't develop cholera. He took some new culture and tried to induce cholera in these chickens, and it failed to make the chickens sick. He went back over his work and realized that the initial culture had probably been weakened while sitting around and therefore was not strong enough to cause cholera to appear in the chickens. However, it was strong enough for the chickens to build up immunity to the disease. He repeated the experiment and proved to his satisfaction that this was indeed true. Thus through good fortune and good observation of critical details, he found a source of immunity for chicken cholera.

Later, Pasteur was to apply this same method in developing an immunization for anthrax; which affected sheep and cattle and resulted in their death. He demonstrated his anthrax cure by taking a number of cattle and giving half of them his anthrax serum, without injecting the other half. He waited a certain number of days, and then he returned. In front of a crowd of observers, he gave each of the cattle a shot of anthrax. He left the field and told the observers to return in a given period. Upon their return, the sheep, cattle, and pigs that received no serum were dead, and those that did receive the shots were walking around like nothing had happened. This proved that a vaccine could be made as he had demonstrated on chickens and cattle.

Pasteur later developed a vaccine for rabies. At the time, there was an almost 100-percent death rate in people bitten by rabid dogs. He studied how rabies developed in a dog's body and how it finally got to its brain and killed the animal. It took fourteen days for the rabies to reach the brain and kill the dog. He then took a weakened culture and injected it into a rabbit. He waited a number of days and took some blood from the rabbit and injected it into another rabbit. He kept doing this, and each rabbit eventually died. However, after a number of rabbits died, the next rabbit did not die. Microscopic study showed that the rabies carried in the blood of the animals weakened as it was passed down. He allowed dogs with rabies to bite healthy dogs and then he gave them these shots for fourteen days, and the dogs did not become rabid.

A youngster in the neighborhood was bitten by a rabid dog, and the father appealed to Pasteur to give the boy the treatment. Although he had never tried his cure on a human, Pasteur knew the boy would die without the vaccine, so he went through with the treatment. It was a success, and the news traveled fast and far, and Pasteur was hailed as a hero.

Not long after this, a pack of wild dogs bit nineteen children in a town in Russia. The czar of Russia, hearing about Pasteur's work, sent the children to France to be treated. Pasteur was given advanced warning and realized he would not have enough time to develop the serum. He needed fourteen days with his present approach. He hurriedly changed his routine with the rabbits, giving them more rapid treatment, and provided the serum within seven days. The nineteen children were treated, and sixteen of them survived. The Czar of Russia was so pleased that he provided money to build the Pasteur Research Lab in Paris, the biggest research laboratory in the world at the time.

Pasteur was considered the captain of the microbe hunters.

Koch

Robert Koch began his medical practice in small towns while traveling as a young married man; then his wife brought him a microscope for his twenty-eighth birthday. He focused on studying microbes and less attention to his patients. (27) His first major interest was to try to find out what Antrax looked like and discover how it killed cattle and sheep. He was rather poor, and when he needed to inoculate an animal to see the results, he couldn't afford any big animals. They didn't have much room in the house where they lived, and therefore, he picked mice for his experiments. He was probably the first person to use mice to study a disease. His practice was out in the countryside, and he couldn't obtain needles to inoculate the mice. He removed the spleens from cattle that had died of Antrax, and he studied what he saw in his microscope. The bacilli he studied were motionless and looked like sticks. He wasn't sure this is what caused Antrax, but he believed it was. He made sharp sticks out of slivers of wood and collected some of these stick-like curiosities on them and injected them into the mice. The mice would die, and he would see a large number of these stick-like curiosities in their spleens. He wanted to discover if they were the actual cause of death. So he figured a way of isolating the microbes he thought were Antrax. He placed one of his sticks in a drop of the fluid from an ox's eye and placed it on a glass slide. Then he immediately put a thicker glass slide in which he had etched a depression over the culture, so that the glass wouldn't touch the culture. The thicker glass slide also had a coating of Vaseline-like material around the outside edge as a sealant. Then he very delicately turned the slide structure upside down so the culture hung in the depression. He believed that no other bacteria could then fall on the culture, even though the two glass slides should have sealed the culture from the outside world. He placed this in a homemade incubator heated by an oil lamp (remember this was a time before electricity) to body temperature and left it there for a couple of days. Then he checked it for these "sticks" that didn't move.

After several observations, he saw them move Then he saw them stretch and thin out and become two, and before long there were thousands of them under his microscope. He placed some in a drop of oxen eye fluid and repeated the experiment. He did this eight times, each time the moving sticks grew and multiplied. He injected this culture he had developed into a mouse, and the next day the mouse was dead. When he viewed its spleen, it was full of the long, non- moving sticks. He now knew that what he had taken from the original dead animals was causing death in a mouse. He was the first person to develop deadly bacteria outside of the body of an ox. He became famous for isolating the bacteria that caused tuberculosis in 1882. He repeated his performance on isolating cholera vibrio in 1883. Koch was awarded Nobel Prize in Physiology and Medicine for his tuberculosis findings in 1905. He is considered the father of bacteriology

Koch also researched why Antrax would reappear after long periods had passed without problems, sometimes many years. His studies showed that when the Antrax lay in the dead body of a victim for some length of time, it then transformed into endospores that could last a long time. These spores might wait on the ground for a hundred years until cattle or sheep would breathe them in and become ravaged by this deadly disease. He announced that every animal that died needed to be burnt or buried deep in the ground where the temperature is too cold for the bacteria to be active. These became the accepted procedures.

These endospores, embedded in soil, were the cause of unexplained "spontaneous" outbreaks of anthrax. Koch published his findings in 1876 and was rewarded with a job at the Imperial Health Office in Berlin in 1880. In 1881, he urged the sterilization of surgical instruments using heat.

In Berlin, he improved the methods he used in Wollstein, including staining and purification techniques and bacterial growth media, including Petri dish, named after its inventor, his assistant Julius Richard Petri. These devices are still used today. In 1883, Koch worked with a French research team in Alexandria, Egypt, on cholera. Koch identified the vibrio bacterium that caused cholera, though he never managed to prove it in experiments. The bacterium had been previously isolated by Italian anatomist Filippo Pacini in 1854, but his work had been ignored due to the predominance of the miasma theory of disease. Koch was unaware of Pacini's work and made an independent discovery. His greater status meant that the discovery would be widely spread for the benefit of others. In 1965, however, the bacterium was formally renamed *Vibrio cholera Pacini 1854*.

In 1885, he became professor of hygiene at the University of Berlin and later, in 1891, director of the newly formed Institute of Infectious Diseases, a position which he resigned from in 1904. He started traveling around the world, studying diseases in South Africa, India, and Java.

Probably as important as his work on tuberculosis, for which he was awarded the Nobel Prize, are Koch's postulates, which say that to establish that an organism is the cause of disease, it must be:

* Found in all examined cases of the disease
* Prepared and maintained in a pure culture
* Capable of producing the original infection
* Even after several generations in culture, be retrievable from an inoculated animal and cultured again

After Koch's success, his pupils found the organisms responsible for diphtheria, typhoid, pneumonia, gonorrhea, cerebrospinal meningitis, leprosy, bubonic plague, tetanus, and syphilis, among others, using his methods.

He died on May 27, 1910, at age sixty-six. The Koch Crater on the moon was named after him. The Robert Koch Prize and Medal were created to honor microbiologists who make groundbreaking discoveries or who contribute to global health in a unique way. The first non-German to be awarded the medal was Professor Bill Hutchison of Glasgow.

Metchnikoff and the phagocytes

Metchnifoff was born in Russia in 1845 and died in July 1916. He was accepted at Kharkov University in 1863 to study natural sciences and completed the four-year course in two years. (30)

After reading about Pasteur, he became interested in studying microbes. He began to look at starfish that he kept in his laboratory. Starfish larvae have crystal-clear bodies, and you can see what goes on inside them. Metchnikoff was watching one under a microscope when he saw something swarming through the fish's body and consuming various things. He thought that maybe the body of the fish had a built-in immune system that included these cells that gobbled up any invading microbes. He thought about the fact that after a thorn pierced a finger, the finger would soon swell with pus. He immediately made the conclusion that the pus was caused by these cells in one's body trying to rid the body of the invaders. He wondered how that would affect the starfish. He went into his garden and got a stem from a rose bush. He stuck one of the thorns in the starfish and then watched the actions of these moving creatures inside the fish. Sure enough, they swam toward the thorn and began to swallow up the intruders. He and a friend decided they had to give a name to these cells that did this work. He wanted to give it a Greek name, since Greek names are prevalent throughout science. After a time they decided on *phagocytes*, from the Greek work for "devouring cell."

Next Metchnikoff studied water fleas, since they also have a crystal-clear body. Study showed that they also had a built-in mechanism that worked like the larva of the starfish.

Eventually, Metchnikoff went to the Pasteur Institute to work under the man himself. Pasteur gave him a laboratory of his own. Pasteur believed he was on the right trail toward understanding why humans didn't always die from an infection. Metchnikoff preached about phagocytes for twenty years at the research laboratory and converted many to this way of thinking. The only argument that his opposition ever gave him was that the phagocytes devoured everything, including food. But Metchnikoff always had a good argument.

Metchnikoff was awarded the Nobel Prize for Medicine in 1908 for his theory on phagocytes, which are white blood cells. It was found that they do elevate immunity levels in the human body and fight infection. Some form of them is still called phagocytes.

Oxygen and the breathing of air

Before I go much further into the details of the brilliant advances made by the people of science and medicine, I would like to bring to the reader's attention something that really shocked me as I reviewed these accomplishments; and this relates to oxygen.

Oxygen was discovered by Joseph Priestley and Carl Wilheolm Scheele in 1774. On August 1, 1774, Priestly focused sunlight on mercuric oxide inside a glass tube, which liberated a gas he named dephlogisticated air. (31) He noted that candles burned brighter in the gas and that a mouse was more active and lived longer while breathing it. Unknown to Priestley, Swedish pharmacist Carl Wilheolm Scheele had already produced oxygen by heating mercuric oxide and various nitrates some time in 1772. Noted French chemist Antoine Lavoisier later claimed to have independently discovered the new substance.

My point is this: oxygen was not discovered until late in the eighteenth century. The bigger shock is that it was not known that the important part of the air that humans breathe is oxygen. This was discovered just before the Civil War in the U.S. around 1865. My shock related to my ignorance that this was discovered so late in the life of man. I assumed we knew this. It wasn't till after the Civil War that the percentage of oxygen we breathed in and how much we breathed out was realized. Isn't that a shock when you consider all the progress made by scientists and medical doctors up to this time, who didn't know what kept us alive? This goes to show you that one cannot take anything for granted. At times you may think you are ignorant, or dumb, or behind times, or whatever; but don't take it that way. There is much to learn as we go through this wonder of life.

No light bulbs or lights

I always have to keep reminding myself that certain things were not available to man as he proceeded on his advancements. Remember there were no light bulbs during these early times. There were candles and oil lamps. Microscopes had no lighting. Electricity was just making a big impact on the world early in the 1800s. Electric lights really started in 1900 and were not yet widespread across the country or the world. There was no central heating or air conditioning in the world, and these developments didn't make any inroads in the United States until after World War II. As you read about these accomplishments on diseases and other facets of life's improvements, keep these things in mind. Amazing accomplishments were achieved under very difficult conditions.

Other microbe hunters.

There were several other microbe hunters during the last part of the nineteenth century and early twentieth century that paved the way for understanding and curing diseases. These pioneers paved the way for improving human life through their findings.

Emile Roux (under Pasteur) and Emil Behring (under Koch) studied the cause and cure of diphtheria (which killed 50 percent of the children struck by this disease), typhoid, pneumonia, and meningitis. They followed the procedures established by Louis Pasteur and Robert Koch (here is knowledge being passed along to ensure continuity without needing to learn lessons over again) with the high degree of patience required to follow every clue and every detail. Sometimes serendipity helped them identify the microbe causing the issues and develop an antitoxin that would cure disease. Their accomplishments helped to reduce the fear and destruction that prevailed where these diseases had previously run rampant.

Theobald Smith became the first American microbe hunter. (32) He was a pioneering epidemiologist and pathologist and is widely considered to be America's first internationally significant medical research scientist. He became famous for finding the cause of tick fever, or Texas fever, a debilitating cattle disease. This was an unusual disease. Cattle could be shipped to Texas from the north without problems; however, cattle that were shipped from Texas to the north came down with this disease. Smith, in 1889, discovered the tick-borne protozoan parasite responsible for Texas fever. It turned out that the cattle that were born and raised in the north were immune to tick fever, but the cattle that were transferred to the north were not immune. The adult tick would take blood from infected cattle and then drop to the ground and lay eggs. The small ticks would crawl up the legs of the cattle and transfer this disease to the cattle when feeding on blood. This was the first time that an arthropod had been definitively linked with the transmission of an infectious disease, which presaged the eventual discovery of insects as important vectors in a number of diseases.

David Bruce was a British bacteriologist born in Melbourne Australia in 1855. In 1894 he went to South Africa. (27) (33) For many years he searched for a cause for sleeping sickness; in 1894 he discovered the micro-organism not only for that disease but also of the tsetse fly disease, as well as the method of transmission. In 1903, he went to Uganda to investigate sleeping sickness. In 1904, he proceeded to Malta to conduct additional investigations into Malta fever. In every case a great advance in the study of tropical medicine was the result. Once you find the culprit, you then can find a way to reduce its effect.

Ronald Ross, of Scottish descent, was born in India and completed his study of medicine at St. Bartholomew's Hospital in London in 1875. (27) (34) He studied malaria between 1881 and 1899. He worked on malaria in Calcutta at the Presidency General Hospital. In 1897 Ross was posted in Ootacamund and fell ill with malaria. After this he was transferred to Secunderabad, where he discovered the presence of the malarial parasite within a specific species of mosquito, the Anopheles. He initially called them dapple-wings, and he was able to find the malaria parasite in a mosquito that he allowed to feed on a malaria patient named Hussain Khan. Later, using birds that were sick with malaria, he was able to ascertain the entire life cycle of the malarial parasite, including its presence in the mosquito's salivary glands. He demonstrated that malaria is transmitted from infected birds to healthy ones by the bite of the mosquito, a finding that suggested the disease's mode of transmission to humans. In 1902, Ross was awarded the Nobel Prize in Physiology or Medicine for his remarkable work on malaria.

Dr. Walter Reed

Although many researchers had been trying to solve the mystery of the yellow fever epidemic throughout the nineteenth century, it was the brief Spanish-American War of 1898 that provided the pressure that resulted in a solution. (27) (35) The United States had gone to war with Spain to support rebels in Cuba and Puerto Rico who wanted to be free from violent and repressive Spanish control. The American public was particularly supportive of the rebels because of the "yellow journalism" of William Randolph Hearst, who published a series of exaggerated stories on Spanish atrocities. When the U.S.S. Maine was sunk in a Havana port, battle cries of "Remember the Maine" sent the U.S. into war against Spain. The U.S. defeated Spain n less than one year, because of its naval superiority. Early in the war, a severe yellow fever epidemic broke out among Cuban peasants and American soldiers stationed in Havana

For many years, scientists had struggled with solving the problem of the puzzling epidemic, but it wasn't until the outbreak of yellow fever in Havana that the problem was solved by an American-led team of scientists. The U.S. Army was incredibly motivated by the war to halt this deadly epidemic, which could be fatal to soldiers. In an effort to find ways to control yellow fever epidemics, the U.S. Surgeon General commissioned a team of researchers, led by army medical scientist Dr. Walter Reed, to go to Cuba and accelerate all efforts to figure out how the disease spread. Dr. Reed had considered many ideas and began testing them, including looking into insects. Epidemics seemed to follow the course of wind currents, and they would stop when cold stopped mosquitoes from breeding. Dr. Reed's bold experiments proved that yellow fever was indeed spread by the bite of the mosquito *Aedes aegypti*. He had one set of volunteers sleep on the soiled clothes and beds of yellow fever patients in a room screened so that no mosquitoes could get in. None of these people contracted the disease. He had another control group of volunteers stay completely away from sick patients; except he let mosquitoes that had been allowed to feast first on people sick with the disease to bite the volunteers. These volunteers did get sick. There was no doubt; although yellow fever was not directly contagious from one person to another, it was spread by insect bites.

Dr. Reed's discovery had an immediate and powerful effect and has since rid much of the world of this horrible disease. As a result of his discovery, yellow fever patients were kept in a room with mosquito screens, and any nearby breeding grounds of the insect were destroyed. Within three months yellow fever was eliminated from Havana, for the first time in over 150 years. The same techniques were used a few years later in Panama, which had suffered epidemics. Panama has not seen even a single case since. It is widely held that it was only then possible to build the Panama Canal. This is another example of how the pressures of war can lead to a powerful and useful medical innovation.

Paul Ehrlich 1854–1915

Although he lacked formal training in experimental chemistry and applied bacteriology, Paul Ehrlich was introduced by his mother's cousin, the pathologist Carl Weigert, to the technique of staining cells with chemical dyes, a procedure used to view cells under the microscope. (27) (36) While working on his medical degree, he continued to experiment with cellular staining. The selective action of these dyes on different types of cells suggested to Ehrlich that chemical reactions formed the basis of cellular processes. From this idea he reasoned that chemical agents could be used to heat diseased cells or to destroy infectious agents, a theory that revolutionized medical diagnostics and therapeutics.

After receiving his medical degree from the University of Leipzig in 1878, Ehrlich was offered a position as head physician at the prestigious Charite Hospital in Berlin. There he developed a new staining technique to identify the tuberculosis bacillus (a bacterium) that had been discovered by Robert Koch. Ehrlich also differentiated the numerous types of blood cells of the body and thereby laid the foundation for the field of hematology.

Ehrlich was a brilliant man. He read that there were only two compounds of arsenic that could be given to a rabbit without killing the rabbit. He didn't believe this and within days had already proven ten compounds of arsenic that wouldn't kill a rabbit. Between 1892 to 1910, he continued this work. He developed the best book on arsenic and arsenic compounds, which is considered the bible of arsenic. In about 1896 he claimed that one day he would find one of these compounds that wouldn't kill a rabbit but would cure syphilis. This drove him to continue his search for the "magic bullet." In 1910, he gave a rabbit that had a cancerous cell compound 606, and the rabbit not only survived but it got better within days. Ehrlich had his magic bullet: number 606 of the compounds of arsenic.

Here was a disease that was not only a killer, but men or women got syphilis, they were outcast and thought of as dirty. This disease was worldwide and was spread by the love of man rather than the hate of man. A person that had this disease would only require one shot of the arsenic compound to be better by the next day. No medicine had ever had an immediate impact as this. It was called Salvarsan. Ehrlich's biggest problem was having enough of the medicine produced. He had to teach the pharmaceutical companies that began supplying the medicine to doctors the world over. This medicine proved effective for many years.

Joseph Lister 1827–1912

Lister attended the University of London. In 1854, Lister became first assistant surgeon to James Syme at the University of Edinburgh in Scotland. After six years he got a professorship of surgery at the University of Glasgow. (37)

Hospital wards were occasionally aired out at midday, but Florence Nightingale's doctrine of fresh air was seen as science fiction. Facilities for washing hands or the patient's wounds did not exist, and it was even considered unnecessary for the surgeon to wash his hands before he saw a patient.

Lister became aware of a paper published by Louis Pasteur that demonstrated that rotting and fermentation could occur without any oxygen if micro-organisms were present. Lister confirmed this with his own experiments. If micro-organisms were causing gangrene, the problem was how to get rid of them. Pasteur suggested three methods: to filter them out, to heat them up, or expose them to chemical solutions. The first two were inappropriate in a human wound, so Lister experimented with the third.

Carbolic acid (Phenol) had been in use as a means of deodorizing sewage, so Lister tested the results from spraying instruments, surgical incisions, and dressings with a solution of it. Lister found that carbolic acid solution swabbed on wounds markedly reduced the incidence of gangrene, and he subsequently published a series of articles. "Antiseptic Principle of the Practice of Surgery" described this procedure in the journal *The Lancet* on March 16, 1867.

He also made surgeons wear clean gloves and wash their hands with 5 percent carbolic acid solutions before and after operations. Also, he first persuaded Charles Goodyear to manufacture rubber gloves for his nurse, since the carbolic acid caused her to suffer from contact dermatitis. Instruments were also washed in the same solution, and assistants sprayed the solution in the operating theater. One of his recommendations was to stop using porous natural materials in the manufacture of the handles of medical instruments.

As the germ theory of disease became more widely accepted, it was realized that infection could be better avoided by preventing bacteria from getting into wounds in the first place. This led to the rise of sterile surgery. Some consider Lister "the father of modern antisepsis." Listerine mouthwash is named after him for his work in antisepsis.

Lister moved from Scotland to King's College Hospital in London and became the second man in England to operate on a brain tumor. He also developed a method of repairing kneecaps with metal wire and improved the technique of mastectomy. His discoveries were greatly praised, and he was made Baron Lister of Lyme Regis and became one of the twelve original members of the Order of Merit

OTHER MAJOR IMPACTS OF THE NINETEENTH CENTURY

I can not leave the nineteenth century without covering three major contributions made by three men during that century. These three contributed significantly to the progress of man and did so without specifically working on diseases or illness, though their work did indirectly affect these areas. The three that made contributions with their work were Gregor Mendel, on the basics of genetics, Charles Darwin, on the theory of evolution, and Wendell Holmes on hygiene.

Gregor Mendel and Genetics

The scientist known as the father of genetics is Gregor Mendel. (38) Born in July of 1822 in what is known today as the Czechoslovakia Republic. Mendel pursued various studies of science from 1851 to 1853; however, he converted and became a monk at the age of 21. Remember when I was discussing religion and mentioned that there were those who spent their lives dedicated to working on other things besides religion. These were the monks in the monasteries. Here was one of the most famous, although it wasn't recognized for years after he was dead.

Gregor Mendel played a very important role in the discovery of genes and heredity. He is considered to be the father of genetics, known for his famous experiments on peas that explained the patterns of inheritance.

He began his famous hybrid cultivation of pea plants in the year 1856. Mendel originally hypothesized that in every generation, a plant inherits two "units of information" (they were not called genes at the time) for a trait, one from each parent. He carried out his experimental work in the monastery garden. At first the cultivation resulted in unpredictable results, but after careful work, Mendel noticed certain similarities when breeding the plants, such as patterns among plant generations involving dependent factors such as stem length, stalk height, round or wrinkled seeds, and other characteristics. He crossed-fertilized two true-breeding pea plants, one with purple flowers and one with white flowers, and observed the offspring's characteristics; both had purple flowers. Then he let the offspring self-fertilize, and he saw that some flowers were white, but purple predominated. He continued to let the pea plant self-fertilize. Eventually he saw that his hypothesis was correct. Both "units of information" from each parent flower existed, and one trait was dominant, in this case the purple one. After spending eight years working on various plants, including upwards of twenty-eight thousand different experiments of this nature, he wrote a set of rules, or primary tenets, relating to the transmission of hereditary characteristics from parent organisms to their children. It underlies much of what is known as genetics today.

Mendel's experiments resulted in his making rules for the field of study based on his work. Mendel reasoned an organism for genetic experiments should have:

* A number of different traits that can be studied
* A plant should be self-fertilizing and have a flower structure that limits accidental contact
* Offspring of self fertilized plants would be fully fertile

Mendel's experimental organism was a common pea, which has a flower that lends itself to self-pollination. The male parts of the flower are called the anthers. They produce pollen, which contains the male gametes (sperm). The female parts of the flower are the stigma, style, and ovary. The egg (female gamete) is produced in the ovary. The process of pollination (the transfer of pollen from anther to stigma) occurs prior to the opening of the pea flower. The pollen grain grows a pollen tube, which allows the sperm to travel through the stigma and style, eventually reaching the ovary. The ripened ovary wall becomes the fruit (the pea pod). Since pea plants are self-pollinators, the genetics of the parent can be more easily understood. Mendel tested all thirty-four varieties of peas available to him through seed dealers. These studies took eight years.

In February 1865, he presented his findings to the Natural History Society of Brunn, calling them "Experiments in Plant Hybidization." No one seemed interested in Mendel's findings. He tried again, sending his work to Professor Karl von Nageli at the University of Munich, but success did not come. Mendel's results were largely neglected: though they were not completely unknown to biologists of the time, they were not seen as important. Even Mendel himself did not see their ultimate applicability and thought they only applied to certain categories of species. Despite his accomplishments, his labor would not be appreciated and recognized until thirty-four years later, when his work was rediscovered by several scientists in Europe. It was recognized that he did not merely study hybridization, but also worked with the heredity of the plants. He had developed the "rule of three," whereby the third-generation offspring would result in the dominant characteristic re-appearing. I would like to interject here that I am a perfect example of this phenomenon. I am a twin and my parents had two sets of twin boys. Three generations later, my son and his wife had a set of twin boys. This is three generations from my parents.

When Mendelian inheritance tenets were integrated with the chromosome theory of inheritance by Thomas Hunt Morgan in 1915, they became the core of classical genetics. Mendel's experiments brought forth two generalizations, which later became known as Mendel's Laws of Heredity, or Mendelian inheritance. These are described in his essay "Experiments on Plant Hybridization," which was read to the Society of Brno on February 8 and March 8, 1865, and was published in 1866. (71)

The "re-discovery" made Mendelism an important but controversial theory. It's most important promoter in Europe was William Bateson, who coined the terms "genetics," "gene" (containing information), and "allele" (gene types) to describe many of it tenets. The model of heredity was highly contested by other biologists because it implied that heredity was discontinuous, in opposition to the apparently continuous variation observable. Many biologists also dismissed the theory because they were not sure it would apply to all species, and there seemed to be very few true Mendelian characters in nature. However, later work by biologist and statisticians such as R. A. Fisher showed that if multiple Mendelian factors were involved for individual traits, they could produce diverse amount of results observed in nature. Thomas Hunt Morgan and his assistants would later integrate the theoretical model of Mendel with the chromosome theory of inheritance, in which the chromosomes of cells were thought to hold the actual hereditary particles, and create what is now known as classical genetics, which was extremely successful and cemented Mendel's place in history.

Mendel's findings allowed other scientists to simplify the emergence of traits to mathematical probability. A large portion of Mendel's findings can be traced to his choice to start his experiments only with true breeding plants. He also only measured absolute characteristics such as color, shape, and position of the offspring.

His data was expressed numerically and subjected to foresight to examine several successive generations of his pea plants and record their variations. Without his careful attention to procedure and detail, Mendel's work could not have had the impact it made on the world of genetics.

The Law of Segregation, also known as Mendel's First Law, essentially has four parts. (72)

Alternative versions of genes account for variations in inherited characteristics. This is the concept of alleles. Alleles are different versions of genes that impart the same characteristic. For example, each human has a gene that controls eye color, but there are variations among these genes in accordance with the specific color for which the gene "codes."

For each characteristic, an organism inherits two alleles, one from each parent. This means that when somatic cells are produced from two alleles, one allele comes from the mother and one from the father.

These alleles may be the same (true-breeding organisms), or different (hybrids). (73)

If the two alleles differ, then one, the allele that encodes the dominant trait, is fully expressed in the organism's appearance; the other, the allele encoding the recessive trait, has no noticeable effect on the organism's appearance. In other words, only the dominant trait is seen in the phenotype of the organism. This allows recessive traits to be passed on to offspring even if they are not expressed. Not all traits have a dominant-recessive relationship, however. There is also codominance; for example, human blood types where A and B are codominant and O is recessive.

The two alleles for each characteristic segregate during gamete production. This means each gamete will contain only one allele for each gene. This allows the maternal and paternal alleles to be combined in the offspring, ensuring variation.

The Law of Independent Assortment, also known as "Inheritance Law" or Mendel's Second Law, states that the inheritance pattern of one trait will not affect the inheritance pattern of another. (72) While his experiments with mixing one trait always resulted in a 3:1 ratio between dominate and recessive phenotypes, Mendel's experiments with mixing two traits (dihybrid cross) showed 9:3:3:1: ratios. His 9:3:3:1 table shows that each of the two genes are independently inherited with a 3:1 ratio. Mendel concluded that different traits are inherited independently of each other, so that there is no relation, for example, between a cat's color and tail length. This is actually only true for genes that are not linked to each other.

Rationale for these laws

The reason for these laws is found in the nature of the cell nucleus in our chromosomes. (I will cover human cells and chromosomes later in the book when I cover DNA and it will include discussions concerning the nucleus where the DNA is located and how it affects human traits.)

The cell nucleus is made up of several chromosomes carrying genetic traits. In a normal cell each chromosome has two parts, the chromatids. However, during reproduction, a reproductive cell, which is created in a process called *meiosis*, usually contains only one chromatid (half the total chromosomes of the human cell; twenty three instead of the forty six chromosomes in each of a human cell) from the chromosomes from one party and one set of chromatids from the other party. By merging two of these cell chromatids (usually one male and one female), the full set is restored and the genes are mixed. The resulting cell becomes a new embryo. The fact that this new life has half the genes of each parent is one reason for the Mendelian laws. The second, most important, reason is the varying dominance of different genes, causing some traits to appear unevenly instead of averaging out (whereby dominant doesn't mean more likely to reproduce—recessive genes can become the most common also).

There are several advantages of this method (sexual reproduction) over reproduction without genetic exchange. Instead of nearly identical copies of an organism, a broad range of offspring develops, allowing more varied abilities and evolutionary strategies.

There are usually errors in every cell nucleus. Copying the genes usually adds more of them. By distributing them randomly over different chromosomes and mixing the genes, such error will be distributed unevenly over the various offspring. Some will therefore have very few such problems. This helps reduce problems with copying error somewhat. This effect is supported by the chromatids of half of the one sex partner mixing with the chromatids of the other partner. This rather random distribution is what helps prevent the carrying forward of errors.

Genes can spread faster from one part of a population to another. This is useful for instance if there's a temporary isolation of two groups. New genes developing in each of the populations don't get reduced to half when one side replaces the other; they mix and form a population with the advantages of both sides.

Sometimes a mutation (for example sickle-cell anemia) can carry positive side effects (in this case malaria resistance). The mechanism behind the Mendelian laws can make it possible for some offspring to carry the advantages without the disadvantages, until further mutations solve the problems.

Mendelian Trait

A Mendelian trait is one that is controlled by a single locus and shows a simple Mendelian inheritance pattern. (73) In such cases, a mutation in a single gene can cause a disease that is inherited according to Mendel's laws. Examples include sickle-cell anemia, Tay-Sachs disease, cystic fibrosis, and xeoderma pigmentosa. A disease controlled by a single gene contrasts with a multi-factorial disease, like arthritis, which is affected by several loci (and the environment), as well as those diseases inherited in a non-Mendelian fashion. The Mendelian Inheritance in Man database is a catalog of, among other things, genes in which Mendelian mutations cause disease.

Charles Darwin: The Theory of Evolution

The theory of evolution, formalized by Charles Darwin, is as much a theory as is the theory of gravity, or the theory of relativity. Unlike theories of physics, biological theories, and especially evolution, have been argued long and hard in socio-political arenas. (39) Even today, evolution is not often taught in primary schools. However, evolution is the binding force of all biological research. It is the unifying theme. In paleontology, evolution gives scientists a powerful way to organize the remains of past life and better understand the one history of life. The history of thought about evolution in general and paleontological contributions specifically is often useful to the scientists of today. Science, like any iterative process, draws heavily from its history.

Charles Robert Darwin (180 –1882) was an English naturalist . After becoming eminent among scientists for his field work and inquires into geology, he proposed and provided scientific evidence that all species of life have evolved over time from one of a few common ancestors, through the process of natural selection.

The fact that evolution occurs became accepted by the scientific community and the general public in his lifetime, while his theory of natural selection came to be widely seen as the primary explanation of the process of evolution in the 1930s. It now forms the basis of modern evolutionary theory. In modified form, Darwin's scientific discovery remains the foundation of biology, as it provides a unifying logical explanation for the diversity of life.

Darwin's five-year voyage on the ship the Beagle established him as a geologist whose observations and theories supported Charles Lyell's uniformitarian ideas, and publication of his journal of the voyage made him famous as a popular author. (74) Puzzled by the geographical distribution of wildlife and fossils he collected on the voyage; Darwin investigated the transmutation of species and conceived his theory of natural selection in 1838. Having seen others attacked as heretics for such ideas, he confided only in his closest friends and continued his extensive research to meet anticipated objections. In 1858, Alfred Russel Wallace sent him an essay describing a similar theory, causing the two to publish their theories early in a joint publication.

His 1859 book *On the Origin of Species* established evolution by common descent as the dominant scientific explanation of diversification in nature. He examined human evolution and sexual selection in *The Descent of Man* and *Selection in Relation to Sex*, followed by *The Expression of the Emotions in Man and Animals*. His research on plants was published in a series of books, and in his final book; he examined earthworms and their affect on soil.

Darwin's journey on the Beagle took him to South America and the islands around South America. During this expedition, he spent most of his time as a geologist, but from his findings he began his work on the evolution of species. (75)

The Beagle survey took five years, two-thirds of which was spent on land. He carefully noted a rich variety of geological features, fossils, and living organisms, and he methodically collected an enormous number of specimens, many of them new to science. At intervals during the voyage he sent specimens to Cambridge, together with letters about his findings, and these established his reputation as a naturalist. Before they set out, FitzRoy, a geologist at Cambridge, gave Darwin the first volume of Charles Lyell's *Principles of Geology*, which explained landforms as the outcome of gradual processes over huge periods of time. On their first stop ashore at St Jago, Darwin found that a white band high in the volcanic rock cliffs consisted of baked coral fragments and shells. This matched Lyell's concept of land slowly rising or falling and gave Darwin a new insight into the geological history of the island that inspired him to think of writing a book on geology. [74] He went on to make many more discoveries, some of them particularly dramatic. He saw stepped plains of shingle and seashells Patagonia as raised beaches, and after experiencing an earthquake in Chile saw mussel-beds stranded above high tide, showing that the land had just been raised. High in the Andes, he saw several fossil trees that had grown on a sand beach, with seashells nearby. He theorized that coral atolls form on sinking volcanic mountains, and he confirmed this when the Beagle surveyed the Cocos (Keeling) Islands.

In South America, Darwin found and excavated rare fossils of gigantic extinct mammals in strata with modern seashells, indicating recent extinction without change in climate or signs of catastrophe. Though he correctly identified one as a Megatherium, and fragments of armor reminded him of the local armadillo, he assumed his finds were related to African or European species. It was a revelation to him after the voyage when Richard Owen showed that they were closely related to living creatures exclusively found in the jungles. Owen's second volume, which argued evolutionism and explained species distribution by "centres of creation," was sent out to Darwin. He puzzled over all he saw, and his ideas went beyond Lyell. In Argentina, he found that two types of rhea had separate but overlapping territories. On the Galápagos Islands, he collected mockingbirds and noted that they were different depending on which island they came from. He also heard that local Spaniards could tell from their appearance on which island tortoises originated, (Which gave him some support of what he had found that the birds of the same species were slightly different on each of the islands. This provided him thought for the fact that the birds each had a change in their genetic structure to accommodate the weather differences on the various islands.) but he thought the creatures had been imported by buccaneers. In Australia, the marsupial rat-kangaroo and the platypus seemed so unusual that Darwin thought it was almost as though two distinct Creators had been at work. In Capetown, FitzRoy met John Herschel, who had recently written to Lyell about that "mystery of mysteries," the origin of species. When organizing his notes on the return journey, Darwin wrote that if his growing suspicions about the mockingbirds and tortoises were correct, "such facts undermine the stability of Species", then cautiously added "would" before "undermine." He later wrote that such facts "seemed to me to throw some light on the origin of species." (74)

Three natives who had been taken from Tierra del Fuego on the Beagle's previous voyage returned there to become missionaries. They had become "civilized" in England over the previous two years, yet their relatives appeared to Darwin to be "miserable, degraded savages." A year on, the mission had been abandoned, and only Jemmy Button spoke with them to say he preferred his harsh previous way of life and did not want to return to England. Because of this experience, Darwin came to think that humans were not as far removed from animals as his friends then believed, and he saw differences as relating to cultural advances towards civilization rather than being racial. He detested the slavery he saw elsewhere in South America, and was saddened by the effects of European settlement on Aborigines in Australia and Maoris in New Zealand.

Captain FitzRoy was committed to writing the official narrative of the Beagle voyages, and near the end of the voyage, he read Darwin's diary and asked him to rewrite this journal to provide the third volume, on natural history.

JOHN DURBIN HUSHER

Inception of Darwin's evolutionary theory

While still a young man, Charles Darwin joined the scientific elite. After visiting his home in Shrewsbury, England, and seeing relatives, Darwin hurried to Cambridge to see Henslow, a fellow geologist at Cambridge, who advised him on finding naturalists available to describe and catalogue the collections and agreed to take on the botanical specimens. Charles Lyell met Darwin for the first time on October 29 and soon introduced him to the up-and-coming Richard Owen, who had the facilities of the Royal College of Surgeons at his disposal to work on the fossil bones collected by Darwin. Owen's surprising results included sloths, a hippopotamus-like skull from the extinct Toxodon, and armor fragments from a huge extinct armadillo (as Darwin had initially surmised). The fossil creatures were unrelated African animals, but closely related to living species in South America.

In mid-December, Darwin moved to Cambridge to organize work on his collections and rewrite his journal. He wrote his first paper, showing that the South American landmass was slowly rising, and with Lyell's enthusiastic backing read it to the Geological Society of London on January 4, 1837. On the same day, he presented his mammal and bird specimens to the Zoological Society. The ornithologist John Gould soon revealed that the Galapagos birds that Darwin had thought a mixture of blackbirds and finches were, in fact, separate species of finches. On February, Darwin was elected to the Council of the Geographical Society, and in his presidential address, Lyell presented Owen's findings on Darwin's fossils, stressing geographical continuity of species as supporting uniformitarian ideas. Gould now revealed that the Galapagos mockingbirds from different islands were separate species, not just varieties, and the wrens were yet another species of finches. Darwin had not kept track of which islands the finch specimens were from, but found information from the notes of others on the Beagle, including FitzRoy, who had more carefully recorded their own collections. The zoologist Thomas Bell showed that the Galápagos tortoises were native to the islands. By mid-March, Darwin was convinced that creatures arriving in the islands had become altered in some way to form new species on the different islands, and he investigated transmutation, while noting his speculations in his "Red Notebook," which he had begun on the Beagle.

The question of human evolution had been taken up by his supporters (and detractors) shortly after the publication of *The Origin of Species,* (75) but Darwin's own contribution came more than ten years later with the two-volume *The Descent of Man*, and *Selection in Relation to Sex*, published in 1871. In the second volume, Darwin introduced in full his concept of sexual selection to explain the evolution of human culture; the differences between the human sexes, and the differentiation of human, as well as the beautiful (and seemingly non-adaptive) plumage of birds. A year later Darwin published his last major work, *The Expression of the Emotions in Man and Animals*, which focused on the evolution of human psychology and its continuity with behavior of animals. He developed his ideas that the human mind and cultures were developed by natural and sexual selection, an approach which has been revived in the last three decades with the emergence of evolutionary psychology. As he concluded in *Descent of Man*, Darwin felt that, despite all of humankind's "noble qualities" and "exalted powers:" "Man still bears in his bodily frame the indelible stamp of his lowly origin."

His evolution-related experiments and investigations culminated in books on the movement of climbing plants, insectivorous plants, cross-self-fertilization of plants, different forms of flowers on plants of the same species, and *The Power of Movement in Plants*. In his last book, he returned to the effects earthworms have on soil formation.

He died in Downe, Kent, England, April 19, 1882. He had expected to be buried in St Mary's churchyard at Downe, but at the request of Darwin's colleagues, William Spottiswoode (President of Royal Society) arranged for Darwin to be given a state funeral and buried in Westminster Abbey, close to John Herschel and Isaac Newton. (74) Darwin's works and books provided scientists with a baseline to work from, both for and against his theories. Without his work, the general subject was fairly mixed up and confusing. However, Darwin's works brought many into the subject and gave them much argumentative material to work from. However, as time went on many in the scientific community came to agree with Darwin's work. The combination of his work and the work of Mendel on genetics gave many scientists baseline work in the twentieth century to do mathematical studies of these issues. Mendel's work on peas had preceded the work of Darwin, and when scientists began to put two and two together they could see where Mendel's work provided reasons why animals and humans could evolve with slight differences and eventually into evolution.

Many still argue against Darwin's theories, but as time passes, the evidence points toward his theory.

Later in this book I will cover more genetics, and the reader will obtain a feel for how much our understanding of genetics and evolution comes from Mendel and Darwin.

The Importance of Human Hygiene

The greatest American medical genius was Dr. Oliver Wendell Holmes (1809–1894) from Harvard University. (76) He was also father of the greatest American justice, Oliver Wendell Holmes. Dr. Holmes stated before he died: "Hygiene will always remain the most important discovery in medical history."

No one listened, and disease continued to rage across the USA, where the average lifespan was thirty-nine years. Dr. Holmes enforced hand washing and hygiene in his son Oliver. When Oliver Jr. was on the Supreme Court at 92 years, aging in splendid intellectual condition, all the other justices marveled. Justice Holmes replied, "My father taught me the vital importance of hygiene, despite my many objections at the time."

Today 99 percent of Americans have poor personal hygiene and fail to understand the consequences.

One section of the health history of the world shines above all others: hygiene. Consider: the cave man had wonderful exercise, fresh air, no pollution, plenty of nutrients, wide diet, calorie restriction; plenty of sleep, no modern-day stress, yet the typical lifespan was 19 years. One hundred and fifty years ago, the average life span in the

USA and Europe was only 38 years. The average life span curve was fairly flat from 1800 to 1900, and then a big change occurred. This change in the curve is believed to be the result of several things, one of which was better hygiene. The move to better hygiene came as a result of overcoming the idea that people shouldn't wash their hands or take a bath because doing so opened the pores and allowed germs to enter the body. In England, where the idea that bathing just opened pores to let germs in prevailed, the work by various microbe hunters showed that cleaning areas of the body eliminated many of the surface germs. It is hard to imagine that the queen had a bath at birth, and bathed only two other times in her life before 1900. "Three baths in a lifetime" reflected the general public's notions that germs entered opened pores.

Results of Lister's focus on the cleanliness of surgical equipment helped to convince people, since it was proven that using Lister's approach, including cleaning all instruments and having everyone clean their hands before operating, showed a definite trend towards reduced death after operations. Hygiene began to be taught in the schools in developed countries. This included washing hands each morning, after any work, before and after a meal, and before going to bed at night. Brushing of the teeth and using mouth rinses are known to have helped not only teeth, but health in general. Practices of extra cleaning when there was a sickness in the general area helped. Another related thing that helped was the installation of drains in homes and work places, as well as improved sewers. These improved drains and sewers moved contamination from around the home to areas of cleanup. Proper sewage plants treated the water being carried from the homes and sent it on its way to rivers, lakes, or oceans in a proper condition.

The average life span increased as a result to around forty-nine in 1920. In the late 70s, it reached seventy. Today the average life span in the world is seventy-seven years. Much of the improvement is the result of good hygiene. Today, in Japan the average person can expect to reach ninety in sound health, with a good mind. The magic is hygiene, and super hygiene will help you achieve maximum lifespan that may eventually exceed 125 years. It is also believed that proper diets and nutrients help achieve longer life.

Advances in sanitation, nutrition, and medical knowledge made possible improved life expectancy in the United States and throughout the world. In the United States, only 50 percent of children born in 1900 could reasonably hope to reach the age of 50. Life expectancy improved immensely during the twentieth century, and this will be covered in the later parts of this book.

Many common sicknesses like the common cold and ear, nose, and throat infections would be greatly reduced if everyone washed their hands more often. It's a fact that "germs do not fly, they hitchhike," as some wise man once said. Germs pass from one person to another when a dirty hand touches a door knob and someone then touches that knob. The second person then carries it to the next rendezvous. Washing would have caught that germ. It's interesting that bacteria can lie around for ages in a dormant stage, but then be picked up and activated many years later. Bacteria don't need to be on a live host to live. They can wait. Remember the section on anthrax? It can wait in the ground for centuries until a cow happens to eat some when feeding in the fields—and bingo, it can start right up. A virus is a different issue; it needs a host to live. It is a parasite and needs to be carried around to the next host. A virus can be stopped from spreading by practice of segregating the sick from all others for a length of time (quarantine) while the sick are being treated.

It is important to keep in mind that life expectancy averages include infant mortality in the numbers. The life expectancy figures also include women who lose their lives during child birth. There has been considerable improvement in both of these areas. Infant mortality has been improved due to better sanitation in the hospitals and because more children are born in the hospitals instead of at home. The life expectancy for women has improved considerably, since many women use to die during child birth. If the child and mother survived past the newborn's infancy, then the life expectancy for both increased dramatically. The reasons for the reduction of mothers dying during and after childbirth are covered in a latter section of this book.

A good example of how things spread via the hitchhiker method is evident when a family has a couple of children in school; almost instantly the child starts having illnesses and bringing them home, and then the parents get the illness. When the kids are all through school and away at college, the health of their parents improves immensely. Young people who have no children are in better health because they don't have a child in school hitchhiking germs into their home. Much of this could be improved if the family instills good hygiene practices in their children, as well if the children and parents wash their hands upon the child's return home. Good hygiene goes on for life. You don't grow out of needing to follow good hygiene habits. Unfortunately, underdeveloped countries don't have the facilities to meet these hygiene goals. They have no clean bathrooms, good drainage systems, chlorinated water supplies, soap, or water. The rest of the world could help the undeveloped countries by supplying them the facilities and materials to help them immediately.

THE TWENTIETH CENTURY AND INFECTION

Early in the twentieth century improvements in life expectancy came from the contributions of doctors and scientists made during the nineteenth century. Illnesses such as tuberculosis, diphtheria, pneumonia, cholera, and meningitis were caused by bacteria, and with the aid of the microscope cures were developed. Cures for sicknesses caused by parasites such as the mosquito and yellow fever were also discovered. However, during the first thirty-one years of the twentieth century, not much additional progress was made against bacterial infections. Most of the early part of the twentieth century showed improvement due to the installation of sanitary methods in hospitals, improved hygiene in the homes, and improvements in the treatment of sewage and the installation of sewage drains in the home..

However, significant progress was about to be made. As I previously mentioned, wars bring bad and good to the world. The bad is obvious, and the good can only come from the fact that much is seen by medical people during war, leading to a concentrated effort to overcome these new-found problems. This is the learning curve that it seems we must follow, i.e. to make the best out of the worse. Man was now to have another chance at following this learning curve, as a war broke out in Europe. This soon became a world war, and many countries and many people were involved. As is the case with war, the medical people tried to cure and save the many wounded, which involved a concentrated effort on many levels.

During World War I, the German army advanced to just outside of Paris, France, in 1914, and the battle was fought between the two countries, with the English also helping on the side of France. Eventually the United States would enter the war. This war was a war of attrition, as the battles were fought between the trenches just north of Paris. This part of the war lasted an eternity for some, and those were the ones that were not wounded or hurt in any way. Others were not so lucky. Eleven million soldiers were killed in the few years that the battle stalled above Paris. It was a frustration of sorts, this loss of life. Most of the soldiers died not due to a direct kill by a bullet, but from the infections that followed any kind of wound. It might be nothing more than a scratch: a bullet that skimmed off of a person, the nick of a bayonet on the arm or leg. In some cases, there was no visible wound to take care of, as the war in the trenches resulted in sloppy, muddy, filthy, and contaminated conditions. When a soldier was wounded in the early phases of these battles and his flesh was opened in some manner, the treatment was to pour some alcohol on the wound and sew it up. Later it was found that this was almost surely a death sentence. It was found that it was better to leave the wound alone, open and almost unattended. It seemed the body took care of itself better in such cases. Why? That was the question.

The answer was there. The doctors and medical people on both sides of the trenches knew what was killing the soldiers; it was infection. (41) Staphylococcus and streptococcus were the enemies, more so than the soldiers on each side of the trenches. The weather didn't help. It was damp and ideal for disease, especially these two bacteria, which seemed to be able to proliferate infections in the sloppy, muddy trenches. By the end of the war there were eleven million deaths, and nine million were due to infection.

One of the medical people on the German side of the trenches was Gerhard Domagk, who was witness to this terrible loss of life. He had only about a year of medical training before he was sent to the front to take care of the wounded. After what appeared to be dramatic operations on the wounded that he felt would survive, in a couple of days the wounded man awakened to pain; the carefully closed incisions were now swollen, red, and painful. They gave off a foul odor, and dark liquid oozed out of the incision of the wound that he thought was healing the day before. The skin around the wound would take on a half-gelled look and puff up. This is what the physicians feared, since this was the first sign of gangrene. In this state it was called Gasbrand, for gas gangrene caused by a bacterial infection. If one of the doctors passed his gloved hand across this area, it would crackle from the rotting tissue that was releasing gas, causing the crackling. (47) This meant amputation of the limb or death. Sometimes one amputation was followed by another amputation. If nothing could stop the infection, the wounded would become silent and die of green-black gangrene.

Gas gangrene was furiously contagious, especially as it progressed. It would cause such things as leg swelling and then came hard sores that cracked and released a gas. The gas was able to spread the bacteria to others. Once set loose in a medical ward, the patients were now isolated in wards filled with others suffering from the same fate. Going into a Gasbrand ward was like walking among the walking or lying dead. Gerhard Domagk was witness to this dreadful scene. After spending his time on the line, Gerhard was transferred to Belgium as a medical aide, joining the German troops that were readying for their offensive. Now Domagk met another silent death. Remember the flu epidemic I described in an earlier part of this book. It reached throughout the world in 1918 and lasted about eighteen months. This flue was not a part of the war, but the war spread it. Soldiers were crowded into different modes of transportation and eventually into the trenches. Soldiers were dying from the flu or from staff infections or strep infections. All of this was depressing for a medical technician. For the Germans, if the medical problems were not enough, they now were being pounded backward to whence they came, and soon the war ended.

The war ended for the soldiers, but not for Gerhard. He enrolled at Kiel University in the north of Germany to work on his medical degree. He wanted to learn how to fight the diseases he saw in the war. In 1921, Domagk, age twenty-six, graduated from medical school.

He received a sehr gut, the highest possible mark for his doctoral dissertation on the biochemistry of muscle cells. Gerhard worked in the laboratory of the University of Munster until 1927. He began to become discouraged because his work wasn't being recognized, even though he wrote several papers about the interactions of the body and bacteria. However, Heinrich Horlein from Bayer Chemical had read his papers. Bayer was now expanding their pharmaceutical research programs and he contacted Gerhard. Horlein had been given the go-ahead to construct a new research building including a state-of- the-art laboratory for pathology. Bayer had sold Bayer Aspirin brand to a United States company, Sterling Products, but eventually became part of IG Farben, which was the biggest corporation in Germany. With this muscle, Bayer was in a better position to grow after the war. Gerhard Domagk was offered the position as Director of Experimental Pathology. In 1927 he joined this company with research muscle.

Bayer was big and profitable, largely because of their dye business. They manufactured dye for almost every enterprise that required dye. Most importantly, it was the biggest supplier of dye used to stain microbes, bacteria, and other minute things. This gave Gerhard a great starting point. He figured if the dye could stain bacteria, then he should be able to use the dye to carry various selected compounds into the cells of the body where the bacteria was doing its worse. He began the long and tedious task of finding what could attack staphylococcus and streptococcus.

This war that Gerhard Domagk fought was his war in the small confines of a laboratory, staining various compounds to identify and hopefully attack these bacteria. He was especially interested in the fact that different dyes stained different kinds of tissues. He benefited because Paul Ehrlich (the scientist previously introduced who invented the "magic bullet") was with the company, and he worked with the other scientists to develop dyes that were magic for people like Paul Ehrlich. The microscope was every bacteriologist's central instrument, but it had a terrible drawback; much of the microscopic world could not be seen. Under a microscope, water was transparent, serum was transparent, white blood cells looked like clear blobs, and bacteria were ghosts. The solution was dye. Properly stained with some of the new synthetic dyes chemists were making from coal tar, human cells and bacteria popped out of the background showing cell wall, nuclei, and granules preferentially. They were somehow matched. You could stain bacteria one color and the human tissue around it another. Domagk had a brilliant assistant in his war on infection.

Domagk was fortunate in that he had a great chemist working with him over the years as he tried different compounds with the various dyes. If one compound didn't work, he would feed that information back to Josef Klarer. Klarer and Domagk turned out to be a good team, with Klarer working out the chemical compounds on paper and then in actual fact. Klarer was reputed to be something of a genius; tall and a few years younger than Domagk; he was hired as part of the same 1927 expansion as was Domagk. Klarer had received his doctorate summa cum laude in Munich under the tutelage of Hans Fischer, himself a Nobel laureate. Observers had called Klarer's thesis on dye structures "sensational." He seemed destined for a stellar career in academia, but had, it was said, turned down a professorship to come to Bayer. He was brilliant, but also, as brilliant people often tend to be, slightly unstable. {47}

Some chemists were theoretical, carefully thinking through structures but clumsy in the lab. Klarer, by contrast, was a natural hands-on scientist with an inborn genius for lab work—a Mozart at the bench. Many chemists worked slowly and deliberately; Klarer was spontaneous and fast. He worked without any apparent plan, and he made it look easy. Yet there was something manic about him. At Bayer he could be found toiling fiercely at all hours. He ate irregularly and disappeared for days at a time. He avoided talking with people and seemed gruff and touchy when forced into conversation. In the absence of communication, his co-workers gossiped. Klarer never slept; he had been severely wounded in the war and had undergone a long convalescence. Most of his colleagues left him alone. The tradition at Bayer in any case was for chemists to work on their own, reporting up the ladder, not across the aisle to other chemists. It was a style suited to industrial secrecy, and it suited Klarer. The company appreciated his talents, so they allowed him to set his own work schedule, looked the other way when he took off, and let him work all night when he needed to. Klarer made new molecules at a fantastic rate and sent them to Domagk for testing. He was the most productive chemist the company had. No one else could come close to his output. Domagk worked just as hard and just as diligently as Klarer, taking the compounds mixed with certain dyes and applying them to the streptococcus bacteria and summing up the results. Then, the two of them together would determine the next move.

Klarer worked well with another chemist named Mietzsch. They worked in Workroom 4, tracing the patterns of atoms, unlocking the structures of chemicals, finding ways to take them apart and re-form them, altering them slightly, creating new compounds, hoping that one would become Bayer's next miracle medicine. Meanwhile Domagk would apply their wares to the task of conquering the strep bacteria.

At first the team of Domagk and Klarer worked on finding a compound of dye and molecules that would kill streptococcus. One would wonder today why they spent their time on that particular germ, since all it causes today is a sore throat, but in the 1920s and into the 1930s, it was one of the most feared killers on Earth. No one was safe from strep or staff infection.

In the summer of 1924, the son of the President Calvin Coolidge got a blister on his toe while playing tennis. In a couple of days he got a fever and an analysis of his blood showed he had an infection from Streptococcus. Everything that could be done was done in the days that followed but on the seventh day from when he got the blister he died. This is an example of how staff or strep infection could cause the least of harms to end in tragedy. It is an example of how little we knew back then about how to take effective action against the bacteria would knew was doing the damage. I felt that this description of a person with a fatal blister on his foot would demonstrate the power of this streptococcus germ and why Domagk and Klarer spent so much time working on a medical cure for this deadly infection. This was the same problem that Domagk had seen in the trenches of France in

1914, twenty-four years before, and it still persisted in causing bodily harm to man—with no end in sight. Strep along with staff infection were every doctor's nightmare. These germs could be found anywhere. Remember that bacteria could lie around for years, just waiting for a chance to give man an infection. Most strains of strep were harmless, but a few were deadly, and if they got beneath the skin or in a cut they could cause a significant number of human diseases. The worst strains of strep could secrete three poisons, wipe out red blood cells, raise fevers, eat through tissue, fight their way through the body's natural defenses, and create havoc in strong human beings. They didn't affect only the weak; they had no supranational thoughts. They just waited or hitchhiked to wherever they could find an opening. For the readers who are interested in reading about these diseases, they should read the referenced book.

So, day after day, week after week, Domagk and Klarer fought this battle. Klarer was fantastic in finding new molecules by changing a carbon atom on the end of a string of atoms, or adding a hydroxyl to the string of atoms. Sometimes they would stay with the same dye and try combinations of different molecules; no combination affected the strep germ. Then they tried a combination of dyes while holding a molecule constant to see if the different dyes would penetrate the evil germ and carry a molecule with it, perhaps to end in a kill. But none would come. Each failure would make Domagk stay in the lab and think about what had been tried to date. He kept meticulous files on the various combinations of chemicals and dyes.

The year 1928 passed. At times they thought they had found a combination that worked, but when they tried it a second time they didn't get the same results. It gave them hope, as Domagk tried to determine what had changed. It had worked the previous time; why not this time? He repeated the experiments over again and again. Finally he would send a message to Klarer to work on another combination.

The year 1929 passed, and Domagk began to think that there was no combination that would work. It was frustrating, because they believed at times that they were on the right trail and then the results they were looking for eluded them. He was fortunate that Klarer didn't lose any of his energy or run out of combinations. They say that "misery loves company;" here was misery, and he was glad that Klarer was his company. The year 1930 passed. . .

1931, their fifth year in this battle, found Klarer and his partner Mietzsch trying compound after compound. Each compound was identified with letters preceding the number, so "Kl" meant it came from Klarer and "M" meant it came from Mietzsch. They had produced hundreds of compounds, which Domagk had injected into the strep germ with little success. Every so often there would be a hint of success, only to find that something had given them the wrong answer. Each of these compounds found their way into the tropical-disease group to be tested there against other diseases besides the strep. Klarer slowed the use of the Azo dyes with some of his compounds. Some of the Azo dyes began showing activity against tropical diseases, fighting bird malaria, rat leprosy, and sleeping sickness. Finally encouraging strep results emerged with some mice on one of the compound, Kl-517. Like his Kl-487 it included a chlorine atom. It had a great effect on mice that had been injected with a super strep; some mice recovered completely after receiving Kl-517.

Meanwhile, the Bayer Company remained very patient. Domagk was working on other tropical medicines on another project with some success. They were having very prosperous years as their market grew, and their profits allowed the research lab to continue their research. At times Domagk wondered how the company could be so patient when he was losing his patience, but the funds kept coming and his experiments continued.

One day Klarer's boss happened to be talking to him about how well sulfur had worked for dying wool some years before. This got Klarer thinking about adding sulfur as a side chain. In the first week of October 1932, Klarer delivered a compound that included a sulfur molecule. The compound was noted as Kl-695. While Domagk was away, the technicians kept his program going. They noticed that the mice who received compound Kl-695 didn't die and, in fact, were running around in their cages with a great deal of energy. When he returned, Domagk reviewed the notebook that he kept that the technicians had maintained while he was gone. As he looked down the list, there were Ws with double and triple plus signs, meaning they had worked well; it was nothing like Domagk had ever seen

Domagk relayed this information to Klarer and told him to try some sulfonamide with a certain dye. The next afternoon he had this mixture. Domagk couldn't believe what he was seeing in the microscope. The germ was curling up and dieing. He told Klarer about the effects he was seeing, and they tried to duplicate it. Sure enough, it killed the strep. They waited a day and tried it again; the results were rapid and thorough.

Domagk decided to keep this success quiet until he tested whether this mix worked on the staff infection as well. The next day he had his mix and went to work on the staff germ. He had a hard time believing it but he had the same results. At this time Domagk knew he had produced the secret formula. He could have patented the medicine, but he thought about the French. He feared the French and their ability to make improvements on a patent of the German's. Every time one of the pharmaceutical companies came up with a new medicine and took it to the market, the French would copy it, improve it, and gain a bigger market share. They were better at marketing their products. So, he decided to hold off. He got with Klarer and told him to try every combination of sulfur compounds with the dye. He wanted to find the very best version, so that when it was patented and introduced to the market, maximum market share and profits would result. In early 1932 a cure was found, but they decided to delay and see which of the sulfur compounds gave the best results.

I am going to jump from this point in the story and cover another dilemma that was occurring during this time frame that eventually relates to this work with bacterial infections. I will bring you back to this point so as to review the progress..

Bedside fever and deaths

Meanwhile, the British doctor who had been on the French side of the trenches was back in England working on problems that were unbelievable. Leonard Colebrook was second in command at the St. Mary's Inoculation Department in London. He was a baby doctor, not one who delivers the babies, but the one who was responsible for developing possible cures for the problems associated with the birth of children and the safe recovery of the mother throughout this ordeal. In the 1920s and early 30s, the field of obstetrics was formed; a field made up of male doctors that were highly trained and skilled had taken the place of midwives, only to find themselves surrounded by much illness and death of the mothers and babies. Postpartum death often came in double doses, taking both the baby and the mother. Birth was looked upon as a major operation; and, worse of all, the biggest killer was the strep germ. The obstetricians could see the problem but had no defense against it.

There was a shift in the early 1900s toward mothers giving birth in hospitals instead of at home. Hospitals took over, thinking that this was the best place to have a child and thus avoid the sanitary obstacles in the homes. It was much like today where we consider the hospitals much cleaner than our homes and the major number of births in the U.S. is in the hospitals. The problems faced by the obstetrician in the 1920s and early 30s related to infections that were overwhelming. Colebrook had tried Ehrlich's Salvarsan that had been developed for syphilis to fight the disease, with no success. Doctors were convinced by the success of Salvarsan with syphilis that there would be other diseases to be fought with chemicals. Chemicals could work against a bad disease as traumatic as syphilis, so why not work against infection. They worked day in and day out to try and find something that would relieve the world of infant deaths at birth and the deaths of many of the mothers as well. Coleman, like many doctors was frustrated that the death rate for mothers had increased instead of going down. He tried everything. He had the female ward cleared of patients and the rooms scrubbed and disinfected. Bedding was burned. He took every step that should resolve any issues of death being caused by poor hygiene or other problems that might prevail in hospitals more than in homes. He stayed awake at night looking up at the ceiling and going over the various phenomena that go on in the hospital that could escalate this problem. The next day he would begin again.

Hospitals themselves had become the centers for infection by strep, rather than providing relief. Coleman had seen this sort of thing in France during the war. Some of the routines used in the war were tried without success. Coleman tried other arsenic compounds, remembering Ehrlich's successes with an arsenic compound, but he had the same failure. The problem was so bad and so prevalent that it had a name: "childbed fever." One out of every five new mothers died. History has shown this type of disease as far back as records was kept, even in the time of Hippocrates in ancient Greece. A terrible bout with this problem occurred in the seventeenth century several times.

Childbed fever led to the psychological breakdown of the doctors, who were stressed to the point of illness themselves. (77) It was frustrating to take the many precautions that they knew were not taken by the midwives who had previously attended births at the homes of many mothers under much worse conditions than at the clean hospitals. Yet nothing worked.

By the time that Leonard Colebrook became involved in this predicament in the 1920s, childbed fever had been responsible for the deaths of tens of thousands of new mothers every year. He believed the only way to resolve the issue was through the use of chemicals. He went to Germany and spent the summer learning their language and learning about the use of chemicals for fighting diseases. By 1929 he was considered an expert in the use of chemicals to fight diseases, only to find frustration when it came to childbed fever. In 1930 he stopped giving transfusions and trying new chemicals and gave up trying to find a cure, returning to the old-fashioned approach of providing new mothers and their infants with the best nursing care and otherwise leaving them alone. He endured unbearable frustration. (47)

In 1931 Colebrook took a new position at Queen Charlotte's brand-new maternity hospital, which included a hospital-within-a hospital devoted to the isolation, care, and study of childbed fever victims. At the age of 48 he began this new venture and his fight against streptococcus. He was committed; but so was streptococcus.

I provided this background so that you will be able to relate to this terrible situation and how the progress made by Domagk and Klarer might eventually help relieve this situation. It's hard to conceive of such problems with childbirth these days. Especially at the level they were experiencing in the 1920s and early 30s.

Success at Last

Now refinement became the battle, as the team at Bayer tried to determine the right amount of sulfanilamide for injections, among other refinements. Some were stronger than Kl-695; one in particular, Kl-730, was the most effective and most consistent anti-strep medicine anyone had ever seen. They focused on Kl-730 and looked for side effects. Many drugs work, but some have side effects that were worse than the disease it cured. This labor of patience became the mode of the day. Domagk would take the mice and put a slit in their stomachs and check for problems in this area—no problems. Animals without Kl-730 died by the next day, and animals given the Kl-730 had healthy organs, healthy tissues, and no sign of streptococcus. Now at the height of their exhilaration, they had to make a decision. They now knew they had a medicine that cured strep—should they patent it and allow others to see their work and copy it?

In 1935 Bayer released the new drug called Prontosil, marketed as a cure for streptococcus that had also been successful with several other diseases, including limiting the effects of Staphylococcus. They claimed "remarkable effects," and the world began beating down the doors to obtain some of this miracle medicine. There was a limited supply of the medicine, mainly due to the fact that it had to be mixed properly with Bayer's Azo dye. The company was purposely vague about some details because they wanted to control the market, and they were especially concerned with France.

Enter Colebrook

Sir Henry Hallet Dale, first director of England's National Institute for Medical Research, contacted Bayer and asked for samples to give to Colebrook for studies related to childbed fever. Eventually he got a message from Dr. Horlein of Bayer telling him he could have as much as he needed. Months passed before the Prontosil arrived. In January of 1936, Colebrook reported the results of almost six month of mouse testing, indicating the results were not as good as expected. He felt that he might have to do more tests before trying it on a woman. On January 6, his colleague Ronnie Hare accidentally pricked himself with a glass shard, and within two days an infection had spread throughout his bloodstream. It was doubtful he would live. Colebrook had no choice but to try the Prontosil. He gave it to him intravenously and orally. Hare turned red almost immediately and within two days was completely recovered. The first childbed fever patient that Colebrook decided to use it on was suffering from peritonitis; the strep had entered her abdominal cavity. Her pulse was racing and her temperature was rising, and it appeared she would meet the fate of so many before her. Colebrook didn't know how much to give her, so he gave her a massive dose. Within hours her fever was gone and the infection subsided.

Colebrook felt this may have been just good fortune, but as he tried it on various new mothers he began to realize the miraculous nature of this medicine. As conservative as he was, it became obvious that the new drug worked and it worked fast with every one of the patients he gave the new drug to. (47) Colebrook and another associate, Kenny involved in these tests, submitted a short paper to the *Lancet* on the success they were realizing. This was the beginning of the end of childbed fever—a miracle for mothers giving birth and for the children it helped with other medical issues.

Then came France

In France Ernest Fourneau, a leading French chemist, tried the same path as Colebrook, and he contacted the right people in Germany to try to obtain some Prontosil.

Eventually Fourneau received a small sample of the Prontosil and decided to do some experiments of his own. He injected forty mice with a strong dose of streptococcus and then put twelve without Prontosil in a cage. He intended to inject the remaining twenty-eight with the Prontosil to determine the impact of this magic fluid. Soon after starting his experiment, he realized he might not have enough to dose the remaining twenty-eight mice. As careful as he was in parceling out the injections, after injecting twenty-four of the remaining twenty-eight; he ran out of Prontosil. He still had four mice, so he sat down and thought about what he should do. He looked around his lab; he had some sulfonamide; knowing (from people he had talked to) that the Prontosil had some amount of sulfa drug in it, he decided to give the remaining four mice an injection of the sulfonamide. This he did, and he put them in a box and went on his way.

The next day he could hardly wait to see the results with the forty mice. He rushed to his lab and looked in the cage with the twelve mice that had received no Prontosil—there were twelve dead mice in the cage. He hurried to the second cage, and there were twenty-four mice running around with no apparent effects from the huge dose of strep they had received the day before. He was elated. Then he looked in the box to see how the four that received the Sulfonamide were. To his delight, they were running around as peppy as the twenty-four that had received the Prontosil. He couldn't believe it. He decided to wait another day and visit the two cages of live mice. When he returned the next day, he was met by twenty-eight live mice, including the four that had only received sulfonamide, looking frisky and ready for some food.

Fourneau couldn't believe that the Germans had missed this simple approach. Here was serendipity; if he hadn't run out of the Prontosil, he wouldn't have tried the sulfonamide. He calmed himself and decided to do some additional tests on other mice and with the sulfonamide.

This would take some time; he wanted to make sure he wasn't fooling himself. As the days went by, he became more and more impressed with the sulfonamide. There was not one failure in over a hundred tries. He kept coming back to this question: how could sulfonamide be this effective against this deadly germ?. Fourneau contacted the Pasteur Institute and arranged for them to do some tests on the sulfonamide also, and their results confirmed his results. Within three months of Domagk's publication in the *Lancet,* the Pasteur Institute began distributing their version. It was almost impossible to believe that a simple, common, unpatentable chemical that was used throughout the dye industry and on farms could be so potent a medicine, and no one knew how it worked. It was a miracle; an inexpensive miracle; the first chemical cure for a disease— Prontosil— and now simple sulfonamide. Many lives would be saved by a lot of work from the German group and a case of serendipity for the French group. And many people will benefit through the availability and low cost of sulfonamide.

The announcement by the Pasteur Institute of the results with plain sulfonamide hit the German group like a ton of bricks, and doctors around the world couldn't believe that this devil of a disease could be tamed by a common chemical. (42)

Of course Colebrook in England was elated. He began tests on his childbed fever candidates, and they were released from the hospital within days of giving birth. The average reader today may not be able to appreciate this major conquest. It was like winning a war over this deadly germ. It was like freeing women the world over from fearing death when having a child. This is one of the wonders of life.

United States actions

One of the world's most renowned medical institutions then was (and still is today) Johns Hopkins, located in Baltimore, Maryland. They tried to get some of the Prontosil; two physicians, Perrin Long and Eleanor Bliss, intended to address various illnesses with this drug. However, they were not able to obtain any. Finally a laboratory at

DuPont was able to deliver ten grams of pure sulfa to get them started, and start they did. Bliss got wonderful results with mice, and Long, based on the experience of Colebrook and his doses for childbed fever, began to work directly with patients. A seven-year-old girl with severe erysipelas, skin flaming and a fever of 105, was treated after everything else had failed, and she was cured in days. They used it on scarlet fever, tonsillitis, a botched abortion, with uniform success. The news from Johns Hopkins set off exhilaration around the planet. Here was another world-renowned institution, along with the Pasteur Institute and the reports from Colebrook in England, reporting nothing but great news. It was used on Franklin Delano Roosevelt, Jr. in December of 1935 and January 1936. He was close to death and was saved by this medicine and became a high profile case that helped to solidify its use in the United States.

The first official communication about the breakthrough discovery was not published until 1935, more than two years after the drug was patented by Klarer and his research partner Fritz Mietzsch. Prontosil was the first medicine ever discovered that could effectively treat a range of bacterial infections inside the body. It had a strong protective action against infections caused by streptococci, including blood infections, childbed fever, and erysipelas, and a lesser effect on infections caused by the other cocci. (77)

Later it was discovered by a French research team at the Pasteur Institute that the drug was metabolized into two components inside the body; a smaller, colorless, active compound called sulfanilamide was released from the inactive dye portion. The discovery helped establish the concept of "bioactivation" and dashed the German corporation's dreams of enormous profit, since the active molecule sulfanilamide had been first synthesized in 1906 and was widely used in the dye-making industry; its patent had since expired and the drug was available to anyone.

Of course, with every good there is always the bad. The use of sulfonamide was not to escape this bad portion of this story. Soon little labs around the United States were making their version of sulfonamide; some worked very well, but there were deaths occurring around the

States. Research on the reason soon brought answers. All the deaths occurred when using one supplier's medicine. It was determined that the problem related to the supplier using diethylene glycol (anti-freeze used in cars to prevent radiator water from freezing) in his drug mixture.

As a result of this catastrophe, a federal law was passed in 1938: the Federal Food, Drug, and Cosmetic Act, which controlled how drugs would be tested and approved before their distribution for use and sale.

World War II

As the most effective antibiotic drug to fight many of the diseases that a soldier can receive in a war as gigantic as World War II, the sulfa drug was untouchable. In the battles of the Pacific against the Japanese, it is believed that it played an immense part in the defeat of the Japanese. While Japanese troops were dying from infection, tropical diseases, dysentery, sexual diseases, and others, the American troops were being saved by sulfa drugs of various new combinations and released for duty in rapid order. Each soldier was ordered to carry a pouch that contained sulfa powder, (It's worth mentioning that the term Sulfa Drug was used instead of the bigger name. I was the recipient of Sulfa for sickness in 1947 and 49) to be sprinkled on wounds received on the battlefield or in accidents that occur in large numbers during war.

The war in Europe, although less dramatic in its impact, benefited from the sulfa drugs carried by the Allied soldiers on D-Day and throughout the campaign to defeat Hitler and his army. It must have been ironic to many that its use in Germany, where the research began, helped to defeat the Germans. The pouch the Allied soldier carried with him into battle in Germany contained the antibiotic invented here.

As I mentioned war brings bad and good things. The medical profession wanted to try some new variations on sulfa drugs, but in order to determine the results there had to be a large number of people, to provide both a control group and the medicated group. This is hard to come by, but the military provided just that. During World War I, there were many cases of meningitis, bringing a 70 percent death rate to the soldiers that fell victim to this disease. Early data from the field of war showed that new sulfa drugs, believed to be an improvement over the original sulfonamide drugs, did show definite improvement over the original. As the war proceeded, this death rate eventually dropped to 4 percent, which was an amazing statistic. (77)

During the course of the war, based on the meningitis cure rate, Army doctors wanted to determine if the drug could be used to prevent the disease. Here again, large numbers of people were needed to provide a statistically meaningful sample size. It was decided to study military personnel who were going through basic training. In several cases upwards of fifteen thousand military personnel were split into groups, those who received nothing and those that took one of the pills each day, which were provided to the group that ate in one mess hall and not to the ones in the other mess hall. Over the course of several months the personnel not receiving the pill experienced forty cases of meningitis. The ones receiving the pill experienced none. Other experiments of this nature showed the same rate of response or better. It was then obvious that the drug could be given to children to prevent meningitis. By 1950, meningitis practically disappeared from American children. Sulfa drugs were one of the wonders of life.

A reward for Gerhard Domagk

In 1939 Gerhard Domagk was awarded the Nobel Prize in Medicine and Physiology, an honor that Adolf Hitler forbade him to accept. (78) Hitler was incensed when a Nobel Peace Prize was awarded a few years earlier to an anti-Nazi activist, and he refused to acknowledge its existence. Domagk would accept the award in 1947 when the war was over. It is ironic that when he was receiving his Nobel Prize that the use of sulfa drugs had declined because diseases were able to mutate and began to remain unaffected by sulfa drugs. One of the main uses for sulfa drugs had been to treat gonorrhea during the war, and now it was ineffective against gonorrhea. Gerhard Domagk passed away in 1964 from a disease.

And how did it work?

As good as the development of Prontosil was and as fortunate as the French were to accidentally find the simple sulfonamide solution, none of them knew how it worked. Perplexingly, it had no effect at all in the test tube, exerting its antibacterial action only in live animals. This was unique in itself and still poses a problem with some of today's developments on antibiotics.

It took a couple of years for two English bacteriologists to find out how it worked and why it didn't work in the test tube. When streptococcus enters the body it attacks and consumes an enzyme, dihydropteroate synthetase (DHPS), for its nutritional needs; it swallows them up in great quantities. DHPS catalyzes the conversion of para-aminobenzoate (PAVBA) to dihydropteroate, a key step in folate synthesis. Folate is necessary for the cell to synthesize nucleic acids. (You will find that nucleic acids are essential building blocks of DNA and RNA later in your reading), and in its absence cells will be unable to divide. Ironically, the sulfa drugs acted like the Trojan horse that we all read about, in that it "looked" like the enzyme mentioned above. So the strep consumed the sulfonamide instead of the enzyme and died of malnutrition, so to speak. Isn't Mother Nature wonderful and isn't life a wonder?

Sulfa conclusion

You are probably wondering why I gave so much information on the development of sulfa drugs. There are several reasons. For one, I wanted the reader to develop a feel for the amounts of time and patience required to develop a drug such as this. I also wanted to show how fortunate one has to be to have something this difficult and compelling drop into one's lap when least expected. I also wanted the reader to see the serendipity that can be involved. It took years to get to Prontosil, and there was a French bacteriologist lucky enough to run out of Prontosil and picking up sulfonamide instead, only to find that this readily available chemical could perform like Prontosil. I also wanted the reader to have a feel for the frustration of a person like Klarer and his associate Mietzsch, who got no credit for the discovery of Prontosil. I wanted the reader to read about the first antibiotic and have a feel for the advancements in medicine and how far the world has come since then. I wanted the reader to see the ironic nature of this drug and how it helped the Allied troops in the Second World War, while being of no value to the Germans and the Japanese troops. I wanted the reader to see how tough childbirth was for both baby and mother not too long ago. This is a terrific story. Many of the facts came from the book, *The Demon Under the Microscope* by Thomas Hager and from Wikipedia on medicine and sulfonamide. I considered this a marvelous example of the wonder of life. No fiction approaches the excitement of the wonder of life.

Serendipity with a Fungus: Penicillin

I will now cover some additional serendipity (the gift of finding valuable or agreeable things not sought for; in other words, "luck") that would contribute a step to the education of many and become a wonderful aid to mankind.

In 1928, before the discovery of the sulfa drugs, a doctor from Scotland, Dr. Alexander Fleming, while practicing his art in his London laboratory, made a discovery that can be called a "super serendipity" for the world.(43) Fleming was called "Mr. Petri Dish" because of his practice of keeping many of his bacterial experiments in shallow, saucer-like dishes. In some would be streptococcus and in others there might be staphylococcus, each of which he worked on to try and find a chemical that would make them ineffective. On one weekend, he left for an extended holiday and didn't clean out all the saucers that were left on the window sill of his laboratory. When he returned, he hurriedly looked over the dishes on the sills that he had forgotten to clean prior to leaving. He observed that a stray mold had grown on the outer edge of one of the saucers. the dish. He noticed that the mold had a sort of halo. When he looked at this under the microscope, there was serendipity. The mold on the edge of the saucer had killed all the staphylococcus on the outer edge of the dish. Fleming viewed this mold under the microscope and noted that it was made up of very small stick-like creatures. His observations matched some prior knowledge, and he realized this was called by the name penicillin. Penicillin had been recognized many years before. Although Fleming wasn't the first to identify penicillin, he was the first to recognize the effect it had on powerful bacteria.

I have written about streptococcus and its terrible effect before the introduction of the sulfa drugs, but I didn't go deeply into staph, as it is called. Staph is part of the harmful bacteria family of cocci, and, like strep, the disease they brought on did great damage to people. Remember, I mentioned that the sulfa drugs counteracted certain illnesses, but sulfa drugs were not as effective against staph infections. Staph and strep are harmful germs and under the microscope are easily distinguished one from the other, by the way they line up. Those that line up in a line like a bunch of soldiers are the strep family. These are the ones the sulfa drugs were able to overcome early in the life cycle of the sulfa drugs. Those that do not line up regularly but form groups are part of the staph family. Staph causes blood poisoning, and those with this problem were usually short time in the world in 1928. There was not much to choose from between these two deadly microbes.

Of interest is the difference between mold and bacteria. They both destroy the material they live from. Bacteria in the body and throughout the air thrive in the climate of the human body. It's nice and warm and moist. Molds like moisture also, but they require the temperature of the air they live and grow in. They live in different environments, so to speak. Mold and bacteria are quite different when viewed individually under a microscope. Bacteria come from a biological group named prokaryotes. This group has no nucleus within its cells. Humans, animals, and plants come from a biological group called eukaryotes, whose cells do have a nucleus. Mold is in the latter family.

The biological families of prokaryotes and eukaryotes will be discussed in detail later in the book. I bring them to the reader's attention at this point so as raise the differences and at the same time point out some similarities between these two. It is also interesting that one affects the other, as Fleming noted during his work with mold and the deadly bacteria. Later in the book I will discuss how scientists are able to learn how mold kills the deadly bacteria in a war in the human body. (79)

Fleming discovered one problem with this serendipitous finding—the unexpected gift was not easily reproduced. In fact, as much as Fleming wanted this unexpected gift, it tauntingly went away like a shadow at night. Try as he might, he discovered the mold was not easily found or easily reproduced. Whenever he did produce it in his broths, it would vanish while he tried to separate it. In the same building as Fleming's laboratory was another laboratory that studied such things as molds. Fleming wanted to determine the type of mold and took his mold down to their laboratory, which was under the direction of C. J. La Touche. He noted that the mold studied there was the same as one of the molds in this laboratory, and they described it as a penicillin-type mold. He felt that this may have been where the mold had originated..

Fleming worked on trying to replicate the mold and the action of the mold. His finding was that it indeed annihilated the germs he worked with, but for only a short time. He could not find a way to extend its effectiveness past thirty or so minutes. He was not a chemist and was weak on what chemical he could introduce to make it endure for a longer period. He did give a paper on the actions of this mold, but the presentation was received by a fairly uninterested crowd. He downplayed the fact that its lifespan was limited. It was frustrating, and eventually Fleming dropped his studies on the mold.

However, every so often, Fleming would return to penicillin, when he had an idea on how to increase its durability. After trying and failing, he went about his other business of finding solutions with other approaches. However, his interest would reach a peak every so often. He revisited his work on a solution in 1934 and then again in 1936, but with the same lack of results.

Florey, the Australian

In 1939, Australian scientist Howard Walter Florey and a team of researchers that included Ernst Boris Chain, A. D. Gardner, Norman Heatley, M. Jennings, J. Orr-Ewing and G. Sanders began work on trying to solve the problem of developing a method to create large viable batches of penicillin at the Sir William Dunn School of Pathology, University of Oxford in England. (44)

It is said that Florey was an abrasive Australian who made heavy demands on his peers and the people that worked under him. This abrasiveness rarely came out, but when it did he was like a person possessed, shouting louder than those whom he confronted. It is said that he wouldn't call a spade a spade; he would call it a bloody shovel. As outspoken as he was, the people that worked with him knew it wasn't anything personal against them, and it is said he never said anything good about himself. He was very confident as well as very competent. Florey was promoted to Professor of Pathology at the Dunn School of Pathology. At the age of thirty-seven, Florey interviewed and accepted Ernst Boris Chain, a German Jew, eight years younger than Florey, as his chemist in the School of Pathology. He felt that in order to advance the study of pathology and biochemistry he would need a qualified man, and he got one. His next addition in 1937 was Norman George Heatley. In 1936 Florey had assigned Chain to work on the investigation of carbohydrate metabolism of cancerous tumors. Chain felt he needed someone proficient in micro-dissection to effectively carve the tumors to study them. He recommended twenty-five year old Heatley, and after a long conversation with Florey, Heatley was brought into this technically competent group. Dr. Margaret Jennings also joined the Dunn School's staff and eventually became Florey's general assistant. She had what Florey lacked: a command of written English that was more than acceptable. For the next thirty years she would partner with Florey and present thirty technical papers.

Florey's longest and hardest search was for money. There was very little money for research of the nature he was pursuing. This continued during all the years he worked on solution to penicillin, as well as other programs in the School of Pathology. He needed this support to keep his staff together. He finally was able to convince people in the Rockefeller Foundation to provide funds to support the people he had just added. In due time those who provided funds to Florey would be well rewarded by his accomplishments.

The work on the penicillin mold was done in a very crude manner early in the program. All initial work was done in individual Petri dishes. After a period, it was recognized that the beneficial mold they were seeking could grow to about 1.5 centimeters (about 0.6 inches) in depth, so they had dishes made with little cups in the bottom; this increased production. Afterwards Heatley had dishes made with test tubes in place of the little cups, and this worked even better. Still, this resulted in a very limited amount of the serum they were developing, and, like Fleming, they found that the penicillin gave results for a limited time period. Finally they found a chemical they could inject with penicillin that provided longer endurance. This was late in 1940 and the Germans were bombing England as they had for around two years. Florey and his co-workers tried to ignore the bombing, which at times caused damage to the school.

It was felt that the Germans were bombing England to soften it up for an invasion. (44) As it became more apparent that the Germans were going to invade England, Florey brought his staff together and discussed what action they should take. They had now been having some success with the drug in vitro, but could not make it stay in the body long enough to bring a cure. Their only limitations were being able to make enough to provide complete results and to be able to produce enough to make it a viable drug in plentiful enough quantities to introduce to the country. They didn't want to start something they couldn't finish. The reason for the meeting was to determine how to hide what they had done. They were concerned that the Germans would invade the country, and they didn't want them to have access to this drug that looked as if it could kill almost any germ they tested it against. The decision was made to take some of the mold and put it on each of the staff's wide smocks they wore in the laboratory. In that manner, if the Germans did invade and ended up in their lab, they could destroy what was obviously being worked on and the Germans wouldn't think the mold on their smocks represented anything but dirty smocks. They accepted the idea and they went about dutifully keeping enough mold available in case there was an invasion. Fortunately, the British Air Force won the battle of the air over Britain; Hitler decided he couldn't invade England without having airspace superiority. For those readers who want to read the details of the development of this drug and how they finally were able to have it manufactured in volume, you should read the book *The Mold in Dr. Florey's Coat*. (44) I have provided the reader with the areas of that book that stuck out in my memory as significant while doing my research on how penicillin made its way to the public. I wanted to bring to the reader the significant contributions made in medicine during the 20th century; which included the Sulfa Drugs, Penicillin and, as you will read, the Polio shots that practically eliminated this dreadful disease. They are all exciting, patient, forays by committed research people to solve the mysteries of terrible diseases.

At the point where they were certain of their results and had learned a method for producing it in quantity (but still by Petri type dishes), the only thing that remained was to find a company that would take on the drug production and produce the drug in large enough quantities for distribution. Florey found no pharmaceutical company in England willing to take it on due to constraints of the war effort. At this point Florey decided to take the drug to the United States and see if the large pharmaceutical companies there would take on the job. By this time the United States was heavily involved in the war with Germany, Italy, and Japan, and he felt it was to their benefit to find a way to develop the drug in quantity. At this point he sought the funds to pay for a flight to the States. He made contact with people who had leverage with the pharmaceutical companies in the United States, packed his valuable molds, and flew to the States. There he provided the information for producing the mold and brought to their attention the fact that the mold passed rapidly through the body, and the biggest problem was staying long enough to make a dramatic impact.

Six U. S. firms took on the responsibility for developing the drug to support the war effort. Their first shot at producing the drug was to find some chemical additive to allow it to have a longer reaction in the body. An interesting point is that these firms searched the world over to find a good source of the mold that provides the penicillin. They found a moldy cantaloupe in Peoria, Illinois, that proved to be the best and highest quality source.

Soon volume production was available but was still severely limited domestically in order to meet the war's demand. It is estimated that penicillin made a major difference in the number of deaths and amputations caused by infected wounds amongst Allied forces; saving an estimated 12 to 15 percent of lives. Availability was severely limited. Because of rapid renal elimination of the drug from the body, demand increased due to the need for frequent doses. Since penicillin is actively secreted in urine, with 80 percent leaving the body in almost its initial form within 3 to 4 hours; it became a common procedure to collect the urine from patients being treated so that the penicillin could be isolated and reused.

The American pharmaceutical companies worked on a method to slow down penicillin elimination. They hoped to find a molecule that could compete with penicillin for the organic acid transporter responsible for elimination, such that the transporter would preferentially secrete the competitive inhibitor. The uricosuric agent probenecid proved to be suitable. When probenecid and penicillin were concomitantly administered, probenecid competitively inhibited the elimination of penicillin, increasing its concentration and prolonging its activity. This had a major impact on the drug's ability to eliminate the germs being fought.

The advent of mass production techniques and semi-synthetic penicillin solved supply issues, and this use of probenecid declined. Probenecid is still clinically useful, however, for certain infections requiring particularly high concentrations of penicillin.

Florey and Chain shared the 1945 Nobel Prize in medicine with Fleming for this work.

The American pharmaceutical companies soon corrected the issues of volume and longevity in the body, and forms of different penicillin were produced in volume before long. Considering that it arrived in the U.S. only in 1942, it soon was making a favorable impact with the troops in the later parts of the war. By 1961, pharmaceutical companies could produce upwards of six billion shots a month. The biggest problem became the same one that reduced the effectiveness of the sulfa drugs: overuse. Various bacterial mutations made penicillin ineffective for many illnesses by the late 1980s, and new medicines had to be found for fighting various infections. Bacteria mutate quickly and build defenses against the medicines that kill them. In one sense it is like Darwin's theory, when he theorizes that man and animals evolve to try to overcome weaknesses. Penicillin has since become the most widely used antibiotic to date and is still used for many gram-positive bacterial infections.

Gram-positive and gram-negative bacterial infections

It is interesting to know the difference between the gram-positive bacterial infections and the gram-negative infections. (46) A staining method shows whether a bacterium is gram-positive or gram-negative. This is usually the first test to determine some general information about the bacteria one is viewing. Gram-positive bacteria are those that retain a crystal violet dye during the stain process. Gram-positive bacteria appear blue or violet under a microscope, while gram-negative bacteria appear red or pink. This gram classification is empirical and provides an immediate differential identification. The bacteria that show as gram-positive have one membrane layer and include bacillus, Listeria, staphylococcus, streptococcus, Enterococcus, and clostridium. These bacteria lead to various forms of infection. Penicillin drugs were more effective than sulfa drugs in handling these diseases; although the sulfa drugs are still used for specific diseases.

The gram-negative bacteria are evident in salmonella (a food poisoning), Legionella (sometimes called Legionnaires disease. It is contacted by inhalation of misty droplets that contain the bacteria) (80), Escherichia coli a food poisoning that occurs in the lower intestine (82), acetic acid bacteria, an aerobic that enters the system through breathing (81) and is related to bad wine or vinegar and others that **do not include infection**.

Developments from penicillin

The narrow spectrum of activity among the penicillins, along with the poor activity of the orally active phenoxymethylpenicillin, led to the search for derivatives of penicillin that could treat a wider range of infections. (83) The first major development was ampicillin, which offered a broader spectrum of activity than either of the original penicillins. Further development yielded beta-lactamase-resistant penicillins, including flucloxacillin, dicloxacillin, and methicillin. These were significant for their activity against beta-lactamase-producing bacteria species, but were ineffective against the methicillin-resistant *Staphylococcus aureus* strains that subsequently emerged.

The line of true penicillins (related to the location of the beta-lactam ring) was the antiseudomonal penicillins, such as ticarcillin and piperacillin, useful for their activity against gram-negative bacteria. However, the usefulness of the beta-lactam ring was such that related antibiotics, including the mecillinams, the carbapenems, and, most importantly, the cephalosporins have it at the center of their structures.

Mechanism of penicillin action

You can watch a short online movie of penicillin killing a bacterium. A bacterium is shown, and beside it is the penicillin. The bacterium lengthens just as a cell would before dividing to make two cells where one previously existed. In this demonstration, the cell lengthens and can not divide because the penicillin interferes with the ability to synthesize its cell wall. The bacterium lengthens until the cell wall is stretched so far that the thin cellular wall cannot withstand the osmotic pressure, and it bursts. If you remember, the sulfa drugs worked quite differently. The bacteria normally consume a certain enzyme; the sulfa drug chemically resembles the enzyme and it is consumed instead. The bacteria essentially starve to death. It's a case of misidentification. For those who want to see how penicillin kills bacteria, visit http://www.cellsalive.com/pen.htm. (45)

Polio and Jonas Salk

Doctor Jonas Salk did his development work on a cure for polio at the University of Pittsburgh as part of a group working on a possible vaccine for this dreaded disease. While enrolled in the school of engineering at the University of Pittsburgh,. I heard of Dr. Jonas Salk and his work on a vaccine to provide immunity against polio. Later I heard they were going to provide the Salk vaccine to members of the university, and I volunteered for the shot. I remember standing in a long line that extended outside the Cathedral of Learning, the University of Pittsburgh's main building. The line progressed, and soon I was inside the main corridor of the building and advancing forward to receive the shot. I remembered that my mother had not allowed my twin brother and me to go swimming in any public swimming pools while we were growing up, because of the danger of acquiring polio. This was a true worry for all parents at the time. It had been proven that one could be infected with the polio virus while swimming in water where carriers of the virus swam. I remember these thoughts going through my mind as the line moved forward, and before I knew it, I was having a shot of Salk's vaccine injected into my arm.

President Roosevelt had been crippled by this disease as a young man and began a campaign called the March of Dimes. People would donate money to the March of Dimes to provide funds needed to fight polio. Some of that money went to the university and its virus laboratory. It was here at the university of Pittsburgh medical school in Pennsylvania that Salk developed this vaccine. Several years later, I read about his battle to provide this vaccine.

Salk had arrived at the University of Pittsburgh after working with another doctor at the University of Michigan, where they together developed the flu vaccine. Their flu vaccine proved effective, and they worked on improving its effect. Salk was receiving an annual salary at the University of Michigan of around three thousand dollars per annum. He was then offered the position of heading the virus research lab at the University of Pittsburgh, with an annual salary of approximately seven thousand and one hundred dollars per annum—not much when you consider the amount being paid to people of his level today. A person at his level today would be making several million dollars a year including his bonus and any stock that came with the offer to join a company or university. Some universities provide a stock program based on any new development that was discovered while at the university.

He felt that a vaccine for polio could be developed using a dead virus. There were many people working on a vaccine against polio at the time, and none of them believed in the use of a dead virus (46).

Salk began by injecting the live polio virus into a Rhesus monkey. After the death of the monkey, he ground up the monkey's kidney, where the virus could be found in quantity, and proceeded to kill the virus with the use of chemicals. He then injected the dead virus into another Rhesus monkey and waited for the monkey to develop antibodies against polio. The antibodies appeared when viewed through a microscope and gave him hope that this was the way to proceed (Kluger 2004) (47). This may sound simple to the reader, but I am not doing justice to what Salk had to go through to get to this point. I am skimming over details for the sake of providing the reader the general idea of his approach. For the details, read the book *A Splendid Solution*, by Kluger shown in reference (47).

Salk tried several methods of delivering the dead virus to see which would create the most antibodies against the polio. This involved various chemicals to kill the virus and different fluids for carrying the dead virus so as to make it easier to provide a clean and easy-to-use vaccine. One must appreciate the fact that if one live virus was still in the serum, if it were used, it would result in a case of polio. So the method had to be very clean, very exact, and had to provide 100-percent dead polio virus in the serum to avoid causing instead of eliminating polio .

Salk tried several methods and eventually settled on one.

Once Salk had created what he believed was a viable vaccine, he inoculated himself and his wife and two children. They all developed antibodies against polio. This encouraged him to seek some other test subjects for the vaccine. He eventually found a school for the developmentally disabled in Pennsylvania that agreed to allow him to test his vaccine on the children of that school. This research proved to be successful, and he began to campaign for this vaccine to be accepted for tests on larger numbers of children. He couldn't convince anyone to move on this approach because most of the doctors were against a vaccine based on dead virus. Other doctors felt that this would result in some secondary effects in the long-term, even if it did work. His success while at Michigan didn't seem to pave the way for him. In addition to developing the vaccine, Salk had also determined through experiments that there were three separate forms of the polio virus. These were identified as Type I, Type II, and Type III, with the results progressively worsening from Type I, a crippling disease; to Type II, a disease that forced the victim into an iron lung for the rest of his life to allow him to breath; to death with Type III.

Finally Salk's pleas were answered. Basil O'Connor, head of the National Foundation for Infantile Paralysis, made a decision to support a major effort that would involve 1.8 million children across the States receiving the Salk vaccine on a given day. Nine drug companies were selected to discuss the possibility of supplying the drug. Salk met with them, along with O'Connor, and they proceed to review the steps and thoroughly went over the detailed method devised by Salk. They discussed what was required to be accepted as a supplier. Of these companies, six showed an interest. This was a huge step in ensuring there would be enough of a supply of the vaccine to handle a mass inoculation across the States. In order to prove the viability of the drug each produced, they were each required to inoculate a Rhesus monkey with a shot from each lot they produced. To prove viability, each company was required to inoculate nine monkeys with vaccines from nine lots produced; all the monkeys had to show antibodies for polio and be free of polio.

As the drug companies began production and inoculating the monkeys, plans were made to determine the effectiveness of the Salk vaccine. O'Connor felt that a responsible person had to be selected to collect and analyze the data from this field trial. It had to be a person not related to the program and one who had the capability of analyzing the large amount of data from this large field trial and providing an unbiased report on the results. Professor Tommy Francis of the University of Michigan was selected, and he eventually accepted this responsibility. Professor Francis had worked with Salk while he was at Michigan. The two of them had developed the flu vaccine.

During the mass production by the six companies selected to produce the vaccine and the testing by inoculation of nine monkeys representing nine batches produced at each company, a problem occurred. Several monkeys became sick and died from polio in various parts of the country. A rapid review of the situation and the data showed that all the monkeys had been inoculated by a single drug company. A review of the site and data at this drug company revealed that a poor filter in one of the steps in processing the vaccine was at fault.

After this was cleared up, the program was back on track to begin in full force in February of 1954. However, some supply problems occurred, and the field tests were pushed back to April 1954, just as the polio season was to begin. This delay was a disadvantage, as the team experts had wanted the vaccine to be in place a few months before the peak polio season began. But, since this massive program had begun and had so much momentum, they decided to move on with the program.

A startling event occurred when the program was about to begin. Walter Winchell, a noted news broadcaster's voice came across a radio station that broadcast in all the States with an urgent announcement. I will paraphrase the comments of this well-recognized and popular broadcaster, who started all his programs with "Good morning, Mr. and Mrs. America" in a loud and chipper voice.

> Good morning, Mr. and Mrs. America. Tomorrow they will be delivering one million small white caskets to all the train stations and bus stations all over the country. These caskets are for the bodies of the one million

children who will die after receiving the Salk vaccine that will be injected into their little bodies.

This was shocking to Salk and to the people involved in the program. However, the huge vaccination program began anyway. Of the 1.8 million children chosen, 400,000 would receive the Salk vaccine, more than two hundred thousand would receive a placebo, and 1.2 million would receive nothing. All 1.8-million-plus would be tracked to provide data on a controlled basis. Information from The Smithsonian that 650,000 received the vaccine, 750,000 received placebos, and 430,000 received nothing, which adds up to a little over 1.8 million.

A form showing the name, date, address, location including address of lab, city, state, and other data would then be forwarded to Professor Francis at the University of Michigan. At a later date, each of these children would be checked for antibodies for the three forms of polio. As well, statistics would be maintained on how many came down with polio in each of the controlled groups. The reader must keep in mind the immensity of this program. Remember in those days there were no personal computers. The early computers that were available read information hand-punched on cards; 1.8 million of these cards were coming from all over the United States.

Fourteen doctors were asked by the people heading up this program about the percentage of immunization required to prove the vaccine a success. The answers ranged from 15 to 25 percent showing the antibodies without resulting polio to consider the vaccine a success. They believed that an immunization of this percent would be significant for a disease as widespread as polio. Meanwhile, as the large program was initiated, people across the country fell into one of several categories: some were anxious, some pessimistic, some nervous, some optimistic, and some who thought the program would result in data that couldn't determine anything. Of course there were those pushing to cancel the program because they feared many children would die.

The day when the data would be analyzed drew near, and invitations went out from the University of Michigan to many doctors and other high-profile people across the United States, inviting them each to attend a scientific meeting at Rackham Lecture Hall in Ann Arbor, Michigan, on April 12, 1955. The results of the reports on the efficacy of the poliomyelitis vaccine used in the field study sponsored by the National Foundation for Infantile Paralysis that was initiated in the spring of 1954 would be shared. Of course many members of the media would be there also. By this time, television had spread across the country since its beginning in about 1949; so many people would be watching their TVs. In addition, closed circuit TV broadcasts would be made available to 54,000 doctors across the country. Of course, Salk was to attend, along with several of his co-workers from the University of Pittsburgh; there would also be many medical dignitaries and thousands of people interested in the results, especially the parents of the children who had been inoculated.

When the day arrived and guests began arriving at the lecture hall, they saw a large stage that had been specifically built for this scientific meeting. On the stage was a large white screen for showing slides. Salk and about fourteen other dignitaries were seated in the first two rows. After a few comments about the program Dr. Thomas Francis Jr. (remember I mentioned that he had worked with Salk on a flu vaccine while they were both at the University of Michigan) was introduced to the crowd. He was responsible for collating the information being received from all the locations around the states. The crowd was expecting to see slides and was shocked when Dr. Francis went immediately to the results. He stated that the results on the two worse types of Polio were completely positive and that the results on the less dreadful phase of polio was positive but not as good as the other two more dreadful stages. The people were sort of overcome by the briefness of his report and seemed stunned into silence. Dr. Francis then stated that the Salk Vaccine was a complete success. There were signs of relief in the crowd from the people who had children who had received the vaccine. Meanwhile there were shouts of joy among the crowd and the newspaper reporters ran to their phones. Salk, who had been expecting these results sit quietly as he hugged his wife who was so excited she was crying. The less positive results on the milder stage of Polio were found to be due to the incorporation of Merthiolate into the vaccine by some pharmaceutical companies and Salk had never used this chemical. In fact he had heard they were going to incorporate it into the vaccine and he violently opposed this. He was thankful that most of the companies had not included it and this result showed how detailed he had been about what was to be done to provide this vaccine.

This data brought to a conclusion the dramatic effort by a doctor who was persistent, patient, thorough, and convinced of the eventual outcome of his research. Jonas Salk was vindicated. The dead virus approach worked and was safe for use. In 1952, 57,879 cases of polio were reported in the U.S.; in 1961, only 1,312 American children contracted polio. In 1969, there were twenty, and in 1974 there were nine. In 1979 there was one case. The impact was just as great around the world in countries that would use the Salk vaccine. Children (and adults) could begin to swim again in public pools. Russia did not benefit at all for several years due to their inability to use the Salk vaccine and they later used the Sabin pill.

Jonas Salk established the Salk Institute for Biological Studies in Southern California in 1962. This institute's primary objectives related to the study of genetics and molecular biology. Later it turned much of its research on finding a cure for AIDS, Under the direction of Jonas Salk, this institute has done significant work in its areas of focus. Jonas Salk died in June 1995 at the age of eighty.

Here was a doctor who ignored his critics and almost single-handedly defeated the dreaded polio disease. Not only that, but he opened another door to fighting various illnesses through the use of killed viruses.

When I think of Salk, I think of the times when I was a kid and my parents wouldn't allow my twin brother and me to go to a public swimming pool because they were afraid we would get the dreaded polio disease. My mother was born crippled in her left leg and limped badly all her life. I think this made her extra cautious about this disease. It took years for people to allow their children to go swimming in a public pool.

Another significant result of all this was that the side effects that were predicted for people taking the Salk vaccine never developed. To my knowledge, not one person was affected by any side affect of this vaccine.

One more comment about polio. I read a report that was in the paper in November 2007 that 808 people in the world had contracted polio the previous year. All of these victims lived in four countries that had never received the Salk vaccine. These countries would be given inoculations before the next polio season. Isn't that a fantastic result? Worldwide, this disease has been nearly extinguished.

THE CONTINUED SEARCH FOR THE SECRETS OF LIFE

The Importance of Human HygieneScientists puzzled over the nature of life and the work done by Gregor Mendel, which was rediscovered early in the twentieth century. The work by Thomas Hunt of Columbia University on chromosomes in 1915 reopened the subject matter. (88) Hunts work on chromosomes, heredity and what controls life became very important because he essentially proved Mendel's work. Still scientists were puzzled about what in the chromosomes dictated a person's traits. The answers were not obvious, and many were discouraged and gave up on the hunt for life's secrets. So this subject went dormant from lack of success. It reminded them of the "fountain of youth" that Ponce de Leon searched for, only to meet with failure. They felt looking for what created us—where "us" means not only human beings, but all life—would be a long, desperate search that would only end in failure.

Work seemed to progress in the physics of what was happening, with the works of Einstein and Bohr. Major jumps occurred in understanding how the inner parts of an atom worked. As much as we know now about the atom, it always shocks me when I realize that we didn't know that a neutron was inside the center of an atom until 1932—the year I was born. The lack of basic knowledge about the atom bothered me when I found out years later, while attending college, that they had just recently discovered this fact. I was studying to be an electrical engineer and was under the pretence that we had known this for many years, only to find it was discovered only one generation ago. Major advances in quantum physics were made by Einstein and Bohr and various others, and these discoveries, though not medical in nature, helped to open the eyes of those studying medicine.

Scientists thought they knew everything there was to know, and they had a hard time with quantum physics because science had always believed that every motion was continuous—that is, no breaks in the continuity of actions. If you throw a ball in the air, it goes up until it reaches a peak and begins to fall. It may, for a very minute period, stop at the top of its motion before it comes back to Earth, but this was believed to be continuous motion that could be easily explained by mathematical analysis. It shocked the scientific community to realize that atoms worked discontinuously. Things didn't just keep on flowing in a nice, even flow with quantum physics. Movement occurred in quantum jumps. The electrons inside an atom didn't move from one shell to another on a continuous basis, but leaped forward to a higher energy shell, or fell backward to a lower shell, in quantum amounts. The more that the physicists worked on this issue, the more they realized it was true; things can jump from one level to another, but nowhere in between. There was no energy level in between. In 1905, one of Einstein's papers had shown this. He received the Nobel Prize in physics in 1921 for the paper he had written some sixteen years before. It took that long for scientists to believe it. So, the scientists that were working on the biology of life, including the chemists, the physicists, the biochemists, the bacteriologists, and the medical doctors, found many things to keep them busy without being bothered about failing to discover what life is and where it came from.

The dormancy on looking for the secrets of life began to loosen up in the World War II. Between 1939 and 1945, there were many discoveries that brought man some tools that would allow him to make progress. The work on the atomic bomb, as deadly as it was, generated advanced knowledge of the basics of the atom and radioactive material.

The bomb contributed an important tool: radioactive material to aid in research. With this material researchers could mark a protein or various other things within the human body that would allow them to observe what happened to it within the body. It gave them a sort of roadmap. The biochemists borrowed this tool from the physicists and took responsibility for finding how the body works. Earlier I had mentioned that the scanning electron microscope was invented during the twentieth century. Here was an electronic tool that allowed the biochemists to see things magnified up to 10,000 times over what the microscope was able to provide. Here was a super tool to provide a new set of eyes for scientists; and they put it to work.

Cells of Prokaryotes and Eukaryotes

With the microscope advances of the 1800s, scientists were able to see that every form of life they researched was made up of cells. This was true of plants, animals, humans, and even the bacteria and viruses. The shapes of cells are quite varied, with some, such as neurons, being long stick-like figures and some round like our blood cells. Cells vary in size as well as shape. A woman's eggs in her ovaries constitute the biggest cells in a human, and the man's sperm cell is the smallest. It was easy for scientists to observe some animal cells, such as a chicken or a bird egg. However, there is one commonality among man and animals that is not common in the bacteria or virus. This returns us to the subject of prokaryotes and eukaryotes, two completely different cells, and our general way of defining forms of life.

Eukaryote is a generalization for the type of cells that humans, animals, plants, and fungi have. The word eukaryote is derived from the Greek, where *eu* means "true" and *karyote* means "nut," referring to the nucleus; so it means "true nucleus." The most characteristic thing about eukaryote cells is that they are made up of an outer membrane and an inner shell called the nuclear envelope, which contains the nucleus. Between these two membranes are many other compartments with many functions. The purpose of this book is to cover the generalities of such things as cells without the detail that would require another book. Therefore I won't discuss the many things that transpire between the nucleus and these other compartments within the cell. I believe it is sufficient to say that the nucleus contains the chromosomes that contain the genetic material of life. I will cover these in a later, separate section of this book.

In contrast, the prokaryotes relate to bacteria and viruses and their cells. The word prokaryote is also derived from Greek; *pro* means "before" and *karyote* means "nucleus." So the word means "before nucleus." This originates from an historical standpoint, since prokaryotes were on Earth before eukaryotes and they have no nucleus. Remember the section where I described the birth of the world and man's eventual appearance on Earth. The prokaryotes were here almost from the beginning of Earth four and a half billion years ago. Plants and animals came billions of years later. When man became educated enough and observed this difference between the cells of bacteria and those of man, he decided to call one *pro*, meaning "before," since historically the prokaryotes were here before the eukaryotes and they had this difference related to the nucleus. It's as simple as that. Prokaryotes have a single cell, whereas the eukaryotes are multi-cellular.

I intend to spend most of the discussion on the cells that make up man and will only take a little time to discuss the cells of the bacteria. Both types of cells reproduce and create new cells by dividing into two cells, which divide into four cells and so on. I believe it is one of the wonders of life that there are only two types of cells in the world. When you consider the vast number of animals, plants, fungi, and humans here on the Earth and that they have only one type of cell while bacteria have another, that's a marvel.

Cells of animals, plants, and man

Humans have an estimated 100 trillion cells, or 10^{14}, cells, with a typical cell size of 10 microns (25 microns equal a thousandth of an inch). A normal cell weighs approximately one thousandth of a gram. All cells come from preexisting cells, which relates to my comment on how they divide. Of course this division had to start somewhere, and that's where the discussion of life begins. Within the nucleus of the human cell (and all eukaryotes) are the chromosomes that contain the genes that determine our heredity and how each of us developed. To find out how the first cells started this whole thing in humans, plants, and animals, one has to begin with sex. When I discuss how the first cells are formed, I am not discussing how the very first cells appeared on Earth. I will take a stab at that later. I am relating to the first cells of a newborn, but more specifically at the very beginning when the child to be is still in basic, undefined form.

Sex and Mating: The Chromosomes

In the human case, a man has sexual intercourse with a woman. During the culmination of sexual intercourse, the man releases sperm cells in the millions. If a sperm cell makes contact with the woman's egg, fertilization of the egg occurs. Once the male sperm reaches the egg, normally no other sperm can also penetrate the egg. The woman's egg contains the equivalent of female sperm plus food to feed the embryo that has been produced and will become a male or female baby. The female has twenty-three chromosome pairs; each half of a pair is called a chromatid. Sperm also contains twenty-three chromosome pairs. The last two pairs of chromosomes (chromosome 23) determine the sex of the new embryo. The female has two X chromosomes as the last pair in her set, and the male has either two Xs or an X and a Y as his last two pair. These combine in the newly conceived embryo to provide a complete set of twenty-three chromosome pairs; a chromatid of the male contributes one half and the chromatid of the female makes up the other half of each new pair. If the Y chromosome combines with the woman's chromosomes, the baby will be a boy. If the X chromosome combines with the woman's chromosomes, the baby will be a girl. Below is an illustration of the male and female chromosomes that will combine and result in a normal pregnancy.

Genotype specificity

Each individual is identified by a relatively unique combination of nucleotides found in long, coiled strands of DNA, organized as chromosomes, in a cell's nucleus. The number and arrangement of chromosomes in an organism is characteristic of that organism and can be represented as a karyotype, which is derived by arranging the chromosomes in pairs by size. The karyotype can be used to show a difference in genetic makeup (genotype), which determines the features that a baby will have from this combination of the chromosomes between the male and female involved. (48)

Genotype Specificity (48)

Each individual is identified by a relatively unique combination of nucleotides found in long, coiled strands of DNA, organized as chromosomes, found in a cell's nucleus. The number and arrangement of chromosomes in an organism is characteristic of that organism, and can be represented as a karyotype, which derived by arranging the chromosomes in pairs by size. The karyotype can be used to show differences in genetic makeup (genotype), which determines the features that person has (phenotype). Karyotypes of various humans are shown.

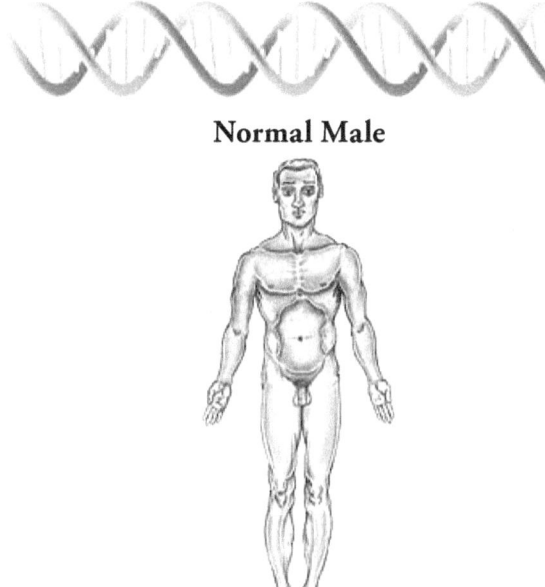

Normal Male

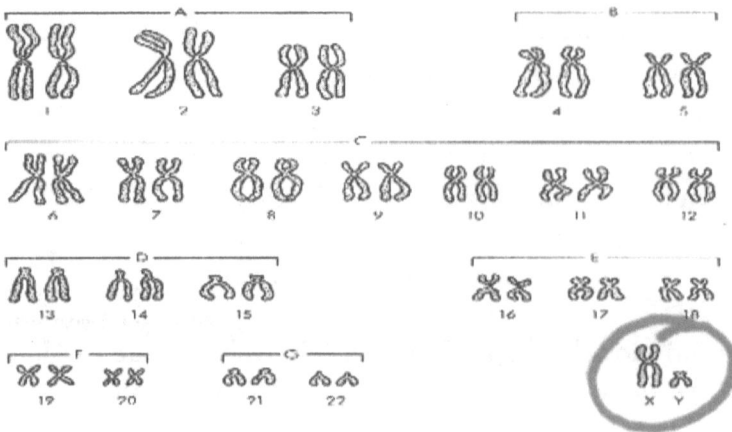

Twenty-three pairs of human male chromosomes. Twenty-two pairs are called autosomes. Autosomes determine the heredity traits of the embryo. One pair is called the sex chromosome—XY in a male. Males are associated with secondary sexual characteristics—abundant facial hair, voice, etc. Differences are also evident in the genitalia.

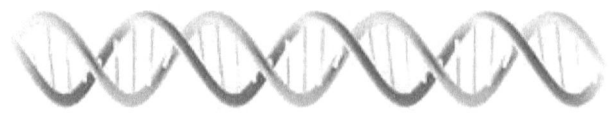

Normal Female

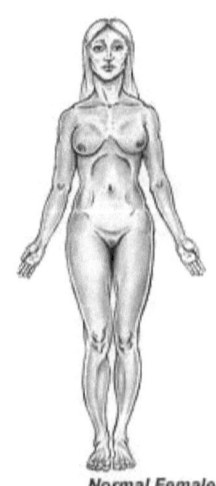

Normal Female

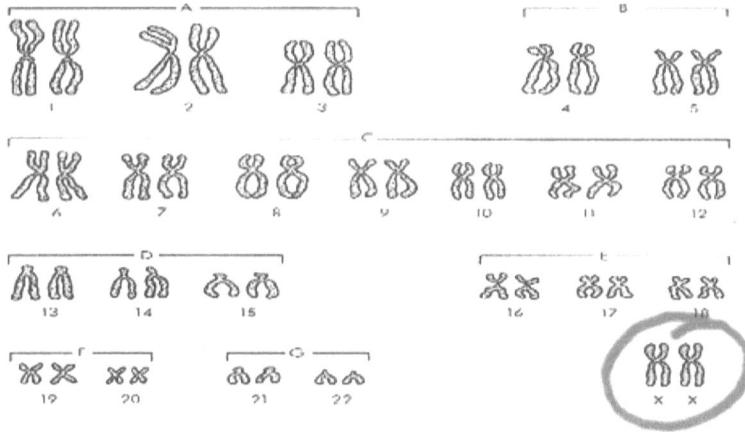

Twenty-three pairs as in the male, but instead, sex chromosomes are represented by XX. Female physical features differ from males. A Barr body is also present in cells of the female, representing an inactivated X chromosome.

On rare occasions, abnormalities occur as a result of certain irregularities in either the male or female chromosomes when the egg is fertilized. One such irregularity, known as *Klinefelter's syndrome*, is due to the male having a twenty-third chromosome that contains three chromosomes, including an extra Y, resulting in an XXY in the twenty-third position. This will result in a male with some breast tissue development and little body hair. An affected person is normally tall, with or without evidence of mental retardation. Males with XXXY, XXXXY, and XXXXXY karyotypes have a more severe presentation, and mental retardation is expected.

Turner's syndrome results when a female has only an X in the twenty-third chromosome position. The second X chromosome is missing. Turner syndrome is associated with underdeveloped ovaries, short stature, a webbed or bull neck, and broad chest. Individuals are sterile and lack expected secondary sexual characteristics. Mental retardation is typically not evident.

Down syndrome is normally associated with three copies of chromosome number 21 (trisomy of chromosome 21), rather than the two found normally. Down syndrome is characterized by differing degrees of mental retardation, a skin fold over the eye, short stature (typically), and a short hand with a deep crease in the palm. Down syndrome is also known as mongolism.

Several other chromosomal deviations have been recognized over time, but I will not cover them in this book.

These factors had been discovered fairly early in the search for what causes heredity; and people believed in them. Still scientists couldn't decide what determined inheritance—the characteristics of a child. They were ninety-nine percent positive that inherited characteristics were determined by the chromosomes, but how; they didn't know. Of course they returned to the work of the monk Gregor Mendel and read through his work again and again; they reviewed the work of Hunt as mentioned. They concluded that Mendel's laws of inheritance were right, but still they sought the chief ingredient that carries inheritance. This work continued throughout the 1900s. They agreed that one parent might have the dominant hair color and the other the dominant eyes color, since these characteristics were visible, but what caused the hidden ones to be what they were. The good news, they all agreed, was that the culmination of the human sex act resulted in a human. The newborn didn't happen to have four legs like a horse—it was human.

Early in the twentieth century, the unknown element that resulted in a child being born with certain characteristics like from his parents was called *genes*; which is derived from a Greek word that meant "giving birth to." The science concerned with the manner in which genes are inherited and in which the characteristics they determine are displayed was named genetics.

Late in the nineteenth century, bioscientists had begun to study, via the microscope, the cells that I have described as prokaryotes and eukaryotes. Differences were distinguishable. Eukaryotes had a nucleus and prokaryotes did not. It was during this time that cell division was being studied by a German biologist, Walther Flemming. His studies showed that the nucleus could be observed by adding a red dye, which allowed him detailed views. This dye was called chromatin, from a Greek word for color.

During the process of cell division, he observed that the chromatin collected into pairs of threadlike bodies, which he named chromosomes because of this association with the chromatin. As he observed the splitting of the cells and the chromosomes within the nucleus, he also saw the cells line up in a thread like position, a phase he referred to as *mitosis,* from the Greek word meaning thread. During the splitting of the cells, pairs of the cells separated, with half of each pair going to one side and forming a string of half cells (we will call this string A) and the other half of the pair going to an opposite side and forming a string of half cells (string B). This resulted in two half-cell strings—A and B—of chromosomes. These strings appear identical to the halves they came from in the original coupling that was made up of AB, and they are not identical to each other. After lining up and just before pulling apart, each half forms a replica of what previously was the half that it is now missing, which then looks like AB on one side and AB on the other side. This is called *replication,* since the original chromosome has now been replicated. When cells complete the pulling apart phase, mitosis is complete, leaving two chromosome cells that are exactly like the original cell. How this happened was a mystery to Flemming, but he wrote about it. How the cell that split into two halves that don't look identical could then have transferred to each half the identical part each half had missed was a mystery.

This process offered an explanation for what happened during conception between man and woman with only one set of twenty-three chromosome pairs. It explained how one set of twenty-three chromosome pairs became many sets that have exactly the same genes as the original set. The genetic code had been retained and eventually produced a boy or girl, but it didn't explain how this was accomplished. One thing that was sure, when the original act of conception took place, the man only provided a sperm, the smallest of all cells in the human body. Since it had nothing in it that could contribute to any other act besides this magic mating and provide his twenty-three chromosomes;

then inheritance had to be included within the chromosome pairs of the man and woman.

This became one of the big mysteries that were to be pursued for many years. Since there was only a single set of twenty-three chromosomes originally, then each of them must carry some characteristic in each of the sets. But since there are only forty-six chromosomes and there must be thousands of genes in every human body, the question was: how did these forty-six chromosomes carry all the genetics of the human body?

As the embryo that constitutes a new child grows in the mother's womb, this splitting of the chromosomes via replication and mitosis continues hundreds of thousands of times. Every cell in the body has a nucleus that contains these chromosomes, whether it is located in the arm or leg or anywhere in the body. Remember that the adult human body has one hundred trillion (1×10^{14}) cells. You can see that there are going to be many mitosis acts occurring over time, producing cells exactly like the originals.

However, many of the scientists that were working in the 1940s on finding the genetic code for inheritance believed the chromosomes were the key. However, twenty-three could not contain all the information required for the total number of genes in a new human. Scientists believed that in order to accomplish the task that had to be carried out, each chromosome carried many thousands of genes somewhere in the nucleus of each cell. So the search was on to find the genetic information carried in the chromosomes. This search for the genes and how they performed their function was labeled genetics, and what was to follow was the search for the genetic code. Just changing the name of what they were looking for gave a great emphasis to this work. Many biology scientists in the labs that were doing research on chromosomes got excited about the name "genetic code."

Later a Dutch botanist named Hugo de Vries was to show that inheritance doesn't always proceed smoothly. There are strange characteristics that appear every so often. He called this *mutation*, from the Latin word that meant change. Earlier I gave examples of issues in children due to a missing or extra chromosome. These are only a few of the recognized mutations; if you will. De Vries felt there were too many replications and mitosis events within the body, as well as many outside events, that could cause a change, even slightly, that results in mutations in the genes that must be within the chromosomes. Time was to prove he was correct.

Studies showed that chromosomes were very delicate and could be affected by heat, radiation, and even by vibration. It is a wonder of life that something so delicate would find a home here on Earth where there were solid forms of matter that could take all kinds of punishment without any variation. Here, the problem was just the opposite, and their fragility made it difficult for the scientists and bioscientists that worked with these fine, delicate forms of life.

ORGANICS, PROTEINS, AND NUCLEIC ACID

Much earlier in the evolution of biology, it was determined that there were organic substances and inorganic substances. At the time all organic substances fell into one of three categories: carbohydrates (e.g. sugars and starches), lipids (oil and butter), and proteins (gelatin and egg whites). Early research focused on the proteins, the most complex of these three organics, which appear in the body in many places. Proteins were complex and fragile and appeared related to discoveries in the study of the chromosomes. It didn't take much of an argument to convince biologists and bioscientists that protein must be the thing that makes up the source of life. Because they were the biggest of the organic molecules, logic dictated that proteins would be responsible for determining the inherited factors. A protein can become denatured—unable to carry out its tasks—with heat, acids, bases, vibration, and other things that can snuff out delicate life. The chromosomes and all the work done on them showed that they were definitely delicate organic substances. Further investigation of chromosomes showed they were mainly made up of water and proteins. Since the name protein means "of first importance," why wouldn't it be first in importance relative to carrying the inheritance of the human race forward?

However, in 1869, Friedrich Miescher isolated a substance from tissue that was not carbohydrate, lipid, or protein. Since he had recovered it from the nucleus of a cell, he called it nucleic acid, due to its acidic nature. (50) At the time of his discovery it was not considered a major finding. Who cares that some scientist happened to find something that was not one of the three organic families? The discovery of nucleic acid lay dormant for many years. Eventually, many years later, the answer would come for his findings. This substance was found to be joined to the protein of the chromosomes and was given the name *nucleoprotein*. I will cover nucleoproteins in a later section of this book. The work of Miescher would be appreciated many years later.

A considerable time passed without any major contributions to solving how the chromosomes worked and from where we inherited our characteristics. Many of the scientists and doctors were tied up with the fighting for the life of man during the first thirty-odd years of the twentieth century. I described the major issues—plagues, flues, small pox, infection and wars that we were involved in—and how they each sapped man's time for doing studies on other things, like chromosomes. These problems sapped, not only their time, but, in many cases, the actual lives of many of the people that would have been involved in further research. And so, time passed without much in the way of advancement on this search.

A virus to show the way

An odd occurrence in 1935 started providing new clues into how nature worked. American biochemist Wendell M. Stanley isolated the tobacco-mosaic virus. This virus caused a disease that affected the tobacco leaf. His studies showed the virus to be crystals that were protein in nature. This virus was not composed of cells, but rather was a fragment no larger than a chromosome. The comparison that Stanley made related to the ability of this virus to duplicate itself once it got inside the cell of the tobacco leaf—the same capability as the chromosome. This virus was also like the chromosome in that it was protein in nature, and it contained nucleic acid as well. It was therefore what was previously described by Miescher as a nucleoprotein. This finding would be followed by more discoveries over the next few years. All viruses were found to be protein and to have nucleic acid in their cell. Thus chromosomes within a cell and these viruses outside the cell were shown to replicate themselves in exactly the same manner and were nucleoproteins. This gave direction to the scientific community at a time when their energies should be directed toward the study of nucleoproteins as the possible answer to what caused life. Up until this tobacco virus was found, the direction of energy was focused on proteins. Now the focus of discovery would be nucleoproteins.

Nucleoproteins

However, as the biochemists studied the nucleoproteins, their main focus returned to the proteins, since the nucleic portions were rather straightforward and the proteins were very complex. Take for instance hemoglobin, which was not even all protein. The goblin portion was a protein and the hemi portion was a form of iron that is in the blood to take on oxygen. This molecule was large and rather complex, but it could be split and was easy to work with. There were many other proteins that the body can take in and chemically deal with, without problems, but those proteins did not react the same way in a test tube outside the body. Not being able to study these proteins in a test tube had bioscientists looking for why. Further study found that the body deals with this issue in a different way. They found that enzymes make reactions occur readily with the proteins taken into the body.

An enzyme is a catalyst that speeds up a chemical reaction within the body. I like one of the examples that Isaac Asimov gives in one of his books. He relates enzymes to the fact that when one wants to tie his shoe laces, he bends over; it takes an effort to get this done. However, if you put your foot on a stool, it is quite easy to tie the laces. In this example Asimov says that the stool acts like an enzyme, in that it allows the process to proceed easier and faster. When you are done, the stool looks just like it did before the procedure. This is how an enzyme works; allowing the action to be accomplished easier and faster, without the enzyme changing during or after the process is completed. The body has an enzyme for every one of these complex actions. The unusual thing about an enzyme is that it works for one thing and nothing else. As many complex proteins that exist and are taken in the body, there are that many specific enzymes to provide the action required, and no other. Each reaction has its own enzyme; and every enzyme is a protein, a different protein than the one it facilitates. This phenomenon became known as "an enzyme for every protein."

Therefore, it is almost impossible to re-create the actions outside the body that happen in the body. This is true for all living things, not just humans. In fact, some of the same enzymes exist in a horse or pig that exist in man, helping speed up the actions in the processing of proteins. Some children are born with an enzyme deficiency of one type or another, and they have difficult times doing things that are simple for the average child. They can be helped if the diagnosis is able to determine which enzyme is deficient and if that enzyme is provided to the child with the deficiency. In time, bioscientists would discover how to synthesize many of the enzymes and re-create the action as the body does.

To give you an idea of the catalytic action of enzymes and how fast they accelerate chemical reactions in the body, we only have to look at the reaction of orotate decarboxylase as an example. Without the enzyme, it would take 78 million years to complete the reaction—with the enzyme, it takes 18 milliseconds (18 thousandths of a second). Isn't nature wonderful?

There are other sources of proteins that come from outside the body and invade the body. Whenever there is a strange source that enters the body, the body considers it an invader and treats it as an antigen. An antigen is an invader of the body. When the body recognizes an antigen, it goes into action to protect the body. It forms antibodies. These antibodies are man's early protection system. It turns out that antibodies are proteins that come from the white blood cells of the body and act just as the enzymes work; antibodies can only work against one disease that happens to invade the body.

At times the body and its first line of defense is not sufficient to overcome an antigen, and a doctor will provide a medical solution to the problem. In many cases the medical world has developed vaccines that protect us before the invader arrives. The purpose of the vaccine is to have the body develop antibodies specifically for a given antigen (or disease). If that antigen tries to invade the body, the immune system has already developed the antibodies to combat the invader. However, an antibody can only work against one particular antigen. If a person gets a flu shot, the body generates antibodies against the strain of flu for which the shot was developed. If a different strain of flu happens to hit the person, the antibodies will not protect it against that strain of flu.

This is why each year biochemists have to develop a different flu shot than the year before. Each year the World Health Organization (WHO) determines which strains of virus are reaching parts of Asia at a certain time of the year, and then they develop a flu shot that will encourage antibodies against that particular strain of flu. When it reaches North America, we are prepared for it. We are fortunate in this country that this is found out early enough in the cycle of flu to allow us to develop a specific flu shot before it hits the United States, Canada, and other countries of the world. The development of the flu vaccine is not a quick process. A culture must be prepared and put in chicken eggs six months ahead of time to allow the antibodies to develop prior to being useful in this yearly cycle. Just to supply the United States, this has to be done in over 100 million eggs each year;.

I am spending considerable time on the subject of proteins to give the reader an idea of the extent of the number of proteins in the body, including the number of enzyme proteins, antibody proteins, nucleoproteins, and normal proteins. There are millions of them. I want each reader to get a feel for the extent of the problem that scientists were faced with when they tried to narrow down the elements that might be involved in the creation of life. The genetic code was the end result being sought by the scientists. The genetic code was like the Holy Grail that was sought many years before. What is it that allows characteristics to be carried on from one generation to the next generation and to the generations that follow? What is the secret miracle in the body that has brought us from the several humans and several animals that existed only about ten thousand years ago to this period in time, when there are over 6.5 billion humans on Earth and more animals by far than the number of humans? What is it that allows us to breed dogs that are almost exactly alike—except for maybe a little different personality? When we want a German Shepherd dog that is exactly like thousands of German Shepherd dogs before it and has the same mannerisms that are considered a part of this species, we can get one. It turns out that each living being, whether human, animal, or plant, has its own particular species of proteins, enzymes, and antibodies and specific reactions to various invaders. This is what was being sought for the last one hundred and fifty years. This is one of the wonders of life that we so diligently sought.

Man's problems to solve: the genes

Among all the creatures, plant life, bacteria, and viruses, only man is capable of determining the answer to this puzzle. While man is best-suited for this task, it wasn't until recently that he became educated enough in life's sciences and life's mysteries to approach the answer. Equipment became available that would allow him to take steps that couldn't be taken before. When one considers that through the 1800s we didn't know what made up all the elements and didn't know there was such a thing as an atom, let alone what constitutes an atom; it's a wonder we got as far as we did.

Work was performed by chemists on molecules during the 1800s and during the first twenty or twenty-five years of the twentieth century. The atom was first described in one of Einstein's four magnificent papers in 1904. It took another twenty years or so before it became clearer how an atom's electrons spin about the center of the atom and then how they jumped quantum leaps to go from one energy level to another. It took till 1932 before the neutron was discovered in the center of the atom. Physicists had data showing that there was something there, but it took many years to determine what it was. So, when you take that ignorance into account one can readily see why it took so long to decipher where genes came from and how they performed their magic. Keep in mind that there were no light bulbs in most of these labs till after the nineteenth century. Likewise there were no bulbs in microscopes till Edison invented the light bulb. In addition, microscopes had taken us to their limit of magnifying 270 times the size. It wasn't until fifty years later that a commercial scanning electron microscope was available that allowed scientists to see some of what I am discussing.

The chemists had done a wonderful job working with molecules and staining them so they could be observed in the limited light a candle or oil lamp would provide. The chemists, biologists, medical doctors, physicists, and engineers of the time did a fantastic job of carrying the technology as far as possible without many modern tools. But time and man's persistence led to an understanding of and solution for many of these problems.

Now I will continue on the trail of the genes and the genetic code.

Thomas Edison

I felt that I should bring Tomas Edison's name into this writing since he contributed several things that would help scientists and doctors and all the people in the world. Around 1877, as a fairly young inventor, Edison invented the phonograph. This was just the start of an advance in communication. Now someone could make music on a record and listen to it for months. The first ones he made didn't last long. I believe they were made on a thin piece of tin. Later he improved this, adding a wax coating to a cardboard-type material. People couldn't get over this ability to hear sound from a piece of material, although it was crude relative to what was to follow. This invention set the stage for many happy times for people over the years. Here was an invention that was practical for certain applications and marvelous for entertainment as the years passed.

As important as phonograph player was, the big hit for Edison and the world was the light bulb. Others had actually invented the basics of a light bulb before Edison, but their approaches resulted in novelties. Earlier versions worked for a couple of hours before burning out; and they were expensive. Only the rich had them, and they used them like a novelty. But after many hours of work, Edison came up with a high-resistance filament made of carbon that worked for several hundred hours. Later he was to make production light bulbs, using an improved vacuum and a better filament, that lasted for 1,500 hours. I don't know if he was the one who eventually came up with the tungsten filament, but if he didn't do it, he at least set the stage for it.

Edison wasn't just an inventor, he was a production addict. He tried to find ways to produce things in high volume so costs went down and prices went down, so many people could use these inventions. Can you imagine what life would be like when it was dark outside and the only light was an oil lamp or candle inside the house? Compare this to what we have now. There is light any time that we want it. The first town that had street lights was Menlo Park in New Jersey; Edison was the producer.

What about microscopes? Can you imagine looking at things under a microscope using only a candle off to the side? We owe a lot to the engineers and scientists that have helped to make the world a better place to live in. If we so desired, it could be void of wars.

It took men like Edison to provide bioscientists another tool to help them on their way. One thing we can say about the twentieth century: it was a great century for discovery. I could write a book about the discoveries during the twentieth century, but I only bring this to this book as a reminder for those of you scientists, engineers, biologists, medical doctors, biochemists, and bioscientists to keep working on your science, since it brings more weapons to the people that work on the elements that make up our lives.

Amino Acids

Early in the 1800s, a French chemist named H. Braconnot heated a protein gelatin in acid and obtained crystals of a sweet-tasting compound.

Eventually, this was given the name *glycine*, from the Greek word meaning sweet. (49) The structure of the glycine molecule was mapped out, and it proved to be simple. Eventually it was determined to have ten atoms, less than half the number in glucose. The molecule consists of a central carbon atom, which is attached by one bond to an amine group and by a second bond to a carboxylic acid group. The remaining two bonds are occupied by hydrogen atoms. This was eventually called an amino acid. Braconnot went further and obtained a second amino acid which he called *leucine,* from the Greek word for "white," because of the crystal's color. Additional amino acids were found as the years passed, and in 1935, a new and important amino acid was discovered after a protein molecule was broken down by heat and acid. This special amino acid is called *Cystine,* and you will see why it was so important.

It was determined that amino acids were the building blocks of the protein molecules. Additional amino acids were found, but as far as the biochemists, in their search for what makes up the proteins that they see related to the chromosomes in the nucleus of the cell, were concerned, there were special ones. These special ones, Cystine, were found in every protein and added up to twenty-one. However, another one was found that was only in one protein, so this made twenty-two amino acids that related to the makeup of the various proteins. At this point in time there was no other macromolecule found or synthesized that was made up of so many different units. This discovery of the ability of the amino acids to build the various proteins is like finding a brick with which one could build a house. The brick stays the same, but the house can look completely different from all the houses you look at, even if made with the same brick. This finding during the time leading up to World War II was fruitful in establishing what the biochemists and bioscientists thought was one stage of the building block of life.

I am going briefly discuss the atomic structure of an amino acid and then provide information on how the twenty-two amino acids provide different connections to the proteins that the biochemists were interested in. Don't get nervous! The information will be supplied in a simple and easy to understand way, even if the reader is scared of trying to understand atomic structures.

Remember: At that time in history, it was felt that proteins were the key to what determines genes and the inherited characteristics provided by the genetic code. As you will see, the amino acids were rather simple, and their lack of complexity, plus the large number of proteins that could be constructed from them, led many biochemists to believe they were the key to the proteins and the key to the genetic code. Shown in figure #2 below is Cystine, the foundation of the amino acids. (49) As you can see by its atomic structure, this amino acid is made up of a central carbon atom, called the alpha carbon, and it is tied to the amine group of nitrogen and two hydrogen atoms on the left and to the carboxylic acid group shown attached to the carbon atom on the right. Notice that there is an "R" connected to the bottom of the alpha carbon. This "R" represents the side chains that can be attached at this position to give the twenty-one other amino acids besides Cystine. So, every amino acid has Cystine as its base. What attaches in the "R" position makes up the twenty-one other amino acids. Simple, right?

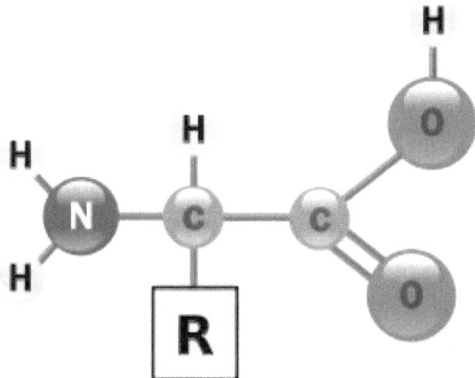

Figure #2 Cystine

The general structure of an alpha amino acid, with the amino group on the left and the carboxyl group on the right. Note; where the R is placed relates to where the twenty one other side chains would be placed to determine the full complement of the amino acids that become the building blocks to fabricate all proteins.

You can see how simply this amino group is built up with the side chains. Each of these twenty-two amino acids, as a result of these side chains, can be part of a multiple number of proteins. With the twenty amino acids and the large number of proteins, the combinations could form over 40,000 different proteins. This gave the bioscientists a stronger feeling that, with large number of different selections to choose from, the amino acids must be where the genetic code was stored.

The magic paper

The story of how many of these amino acids were discovered is interesting. In 1944, a sheet of absorbent paper came to the rescue. In that year two English biochemists, A.J.P. Martin and R.L.M. Synge, devised a technique in which a mixture of amino acids, obtained by breaking down a particular protein molecule, were placed on porous filter paper and allowed to dry there. The edge of the paper was then dipped into an organic liquid that slowly moved up through the fibers by capillary action. As the liquid passed the dried area of mixed amino acids, these amino acids found themselves pulled along. Each amino acid was pulled at a different rate, and before long, each had been separated from all the others. Methods were easily devised thereafter for identifying each amino acid as it took up a characteristic position on the sheet of paper and for estimating the relative quantity of each.

This technique, *paper chromatography*, for the first time made possible accurate identification of all amino acids in a particular protein. This was the first stage of the solution to the problem of finding amino acids. Through the late 1940s and thereafter, many exact identifications of the amino acids in one protein or another were performed. Martin and Synge were awarded the 1952 Nobel Prize in Chemistry.

As soon as the Martin-Synge technique had been developed, another British biochemist, Frederick Sanger, solved the problem of amino-acid order. (50) His method of attack was to only break down the protein molecule part way. Instead of reducing it to individual amino acids, he stopped at short lengths of peptides, each containing no more than two or three amino acids. He separated these small peptides by paper chromatography, isolated each, and worked on it separately. Carefully, he worked out the exact order of the amino acids in each of these small peptide chains and then slowly deduced the manner in which all the amino acids must have been fitted together in long chains so that, when the latter were broken down, just those small peptides that he had detected would be produced, and no others. By 1953 he had worked out the complete amino acid order of a protein molecule called *insulin*; a hormone formed by certain cells in the pancreas. It controls the body's breakdown of sugar for energy; its deficiency results in sugar diabetes. Further work with animals determined that insulin supplied from pigs and cattle could be administered to people suffering from sugar diabetes.

This is one of the wonders of life that I am writing about. Isn't this exciting that a person could have the diligence and patience to work long and hard on something and use a piece of paper to provide him much of the answer? Do you realize how long it would have taken to find this answer without that little piece of paper and a person creative enough to invent this process and another creative enough to work out all the amino acids and discover one that saves many lives year in and year out? It not only saves lives, it make life bearable for many people in the world with sugar diabetes.

The American biochemist Vincent du Vigneaud used Sanger's methods to work out the exact structure of two other protein molecules, called oxytocin and vasopressin. (50)

Oxytocin is a hormone produced by the hypothalamus (part of the brain) and stored in the pituitary gland. It is used to help start or strengthen labor in a woman during birth and to reduce bleeding after delivery.

Vasopressin is a manmade form of an anti-diuretic hormone. Vasopressin is normally secreted by the pituitary gland. In the body, vasopressin acts on the kidneys and blood vessels. It is used to treat *diabetes insipidus*, which is caused by a lack of this naturally occurring hormone. Diabetes insipidus is a disorder in males that cause them to urinate frequently. Vasopressin taken by affected people allowed them to retain their urine longer and made life more comfortable for them.

These two protein molecules turned out to be rather simple molecules, and du Vigneaud was therefore able to put together amino acids in the order he had deduced from his experiments. In that way, he was able to produce synthetic molecules that possessed all the properties and performed all the functions of the natural proteins. This was the strongest proof of the correctness of the theories of protein structure that had been developed from Fischer onward. This was so dramatic that du Vigneaud was awarded the Nobel Prize in Chemistry in 1955, the very year of his discovery; Sanger had to wait three more years for the reward for his more general labors. It is amazing that by changing only two side chains, two completely different hormones were produced that worked on two completely different functions in the body.

To give you another example; the hemoglobin molecule contains 547 amino acids, distributed among four polypeptide chains held together by electrical attraction and by disulfide links. There are three types of hemoglobin: type A, type S, and type C. Type A is normal; people with type A with C or S they will live a normal life. Those who can only manufacture type C or S will not survive long. The difference is that normal blood has glutamine; if the glutamine happens to be replaced by a valin or a lysine to make type S or C respectively, then survival is not likely. This demonstrates that where only one amino acid out of 574 is wrong, results will be a major problem.

The number of proteins the twenty-two amino acids can form according to where they are located in the given molecule turns out to be an almost infinite number. This discovery gave rise to a question; do the proteins or amino acids or a combination of these determine heredity? The larger the number, the more complex the problem of how genes can control the proper combinations and locations becomes. Maybe it isn't the proteins. Maybe it isn't the combination of amino acids, peptides, and proteins that determine heredity.

Keep in mind that out of 40,320 possible vasopressin combinations, the body chooses just one. Out of eight octillion (1×10^{18}) possible combinations for one of the insulin polypeptides, the body chooses just one. How can that be controlled? We are talking about probabilities. The probabilities decrease as the number of possibilities goes up; and we are only discussing insulin and vasopressin here. What about all the other proteins and hormones that seem to beat all these odds? When one considers how many people are born and have been born since the first couple were around and that, in most cases, they came out fine and normal, what are the probabilities for this to be so if the number of choices for failure is so high? So bioscientists started thinking that there must be instructions coming from the chromosome's nucleus. However, how does this take place? All it takes for scientists to get excited is to tell them there is a genetic code that determines heredity, and they can't wait to experiment and find out why. Here they were, searching for the wonders of life.

IT ISN'T THE PROTEINS

Scientists the world over continued their research into these complex subjects, still trying to determine if the key to inherited characteristics was the proteins, the amino acids, or some combination. The answer had been there waiting, so it seems now. Pneumonia-causing bacteria come in two strains, one smooth and called S, the other rough and was called R. In 1928 it was reported that a batch of S bacteria killed by boiling could be added to living R bacteria to bring about the production of live S bacteria. It was guessed that the S bacteria contained a gene that controlled an enzyme that was responsible for the smooth surface and that this was still active and changed the R (rough) bacteria to S (smooth).

In 1944 this experiment was repeated when three biochemists working at the Rockefeller Institute, Oswald T. Avery, Colin M. MacLeod, and Maclyn McCarty, were able to show that the gene was in the solution of nucleic acid; without any protein involved in the experiment. (50) Other experiments were performed using nucleic acid, and the results pointed definitively toward the nucleic acid as containing the genetic code. The bioscientists were confused by this situation. How could nucleic acid hold the key to heredity?

After so many years of research on how proteins determine the genetics of a person, the sudden shift from "It's the proteins" to "Maybe it isn't the proteins" was like a truck hitting a brick wall. That's how fast the pursuit of proteins came to a halt when these three men from the Rockefeller Institute provided their findings.

Now came a quest for what was in the nucleic acid that might be the key to the genetic code. Study of the history of nucleic acid began in 1919 by a Russian-born American.

DNA and RNA

We have to go back in history to 1919, when Russian-born American biochemist Phoebus A. T. Levene first identified ribose as a component of nucleic acid. (50) Later Levene discovered that not all nucleic acid contained ribose, which is a sugar, but some had another sugar that was only different because it didn't have an oxygen atom in the molecule. He named this type *deoxyribose acid*, where "deoxy" meant "without oxygen." Over time biochemists started calling them RNA for ribonucleic acid and DNA for deoxyribonucleic acid. These two are the only nucleic acids that contain a sugar.

Further investigation showed that DNA was only found in the nucleus of the chromosomes and nowhere else in the body. Most of the RNA is found in the chromosomes just outside the nucleus. Every cell tested showed this to be true. Further investigation showed that human chromosomes had RNA both inside and outside the nucleus and the DNA just inside the nucleus. This led to reviewing the tobacco mosaic virus's makeup once more. It was found that the tobacco mosaic virus only had RNA. Previous data had shown that nucleic acid is an acid because it contains phosphorus. Some proteins were known to contain some phosphorus, but nucleic acid contained nine percent phosphorus, which is about three times the amount found in the white of an egg. This made it fairly heavily acidic.

Now we know that DNA and RNA are made up of acids—courtesy of their phosphorus content—and sugars, through the ribose or deoxyribose content. There is more to it than just the sugar and acid contents. (51)

DNA

DNA uses deoxyribonucleic acid as its sugar. Each nucleotide consists of a nitrogenous base, deoxy sugar, and a phosphate acid.

Next it was found that DNA contained a base pair of *purines* (pronounced pure-eens) that are acids and a base pair of *pyrimidines* (pie-rim-a-deens) that are acids.

The purines are made up of a class of double-ringed chemical structures. One ring is made up of a six-sided hexagon, and the other ring is made up of a five-sided pentagon sharing one side of the six ringed structure; there are two purines, *adenine* (add-a-neen) (A) and *guanine* (gwa-neen) (G). These are shown below in figure 3.

The pyrimidines are made up of a single ring of six sides in the form of a hexagon. There are two pyrimidines; *cytosine* (si-toe-seen) (C) and *thymine* (thi-meen) (T); they are shown below in figure 3.

A purine is only complementary with a pyrimidine. By this I mean that a purine such as adenine (A) or guanine (G) must be connected to a pyrimidine (C) or (T). This is called *complementary base pairing*.

To make things easier, biochemists started to refer to them only by their first letter and used capitals. So the allowed paired connections for DNA are A to C or A to T, or G to C or G to T. These connections can all be in the reverse order; for example, A to C could be C to A. In complementary bonding there is always the big double-ringed structure tied to the smaller single-ringed six-sided structure of the pair through hydrogen bonding. These are shown in figures 3 and 4 below.

Hydrogen bonding and stability

Figure 3 shows a GC base pair, purine (G) hydrogen bonding to pyrimidine (C) through three hydrogen bonds.

Figure 4 shows an AT (adenine and thymine) base pair, demonstrating two hydrogen bonds connecting the purine A to the pyrimidine T.

Hydrogen bonding is the chemical mechanism that underlies the base-pairing rules described above. Appropriate geometrical correspondence of hydrogen-bond donors and acceptors allows only the "right" pairs to form stably. The GC base pair has three hydrogen bonds, as shown in figure 3, whereas the AT base pair has only two, as shown in figure 4; as a consequence, the GC pair is more stable.

Paired DNA and RNA molecules are comparatively stable at room temperature, but the two nucleotide strands will separate above the melting point, which is determined by the length of the molecules, the extent of mispairing (if any), and the GC content. Higher GC content results in higher melting temperatures. (51)

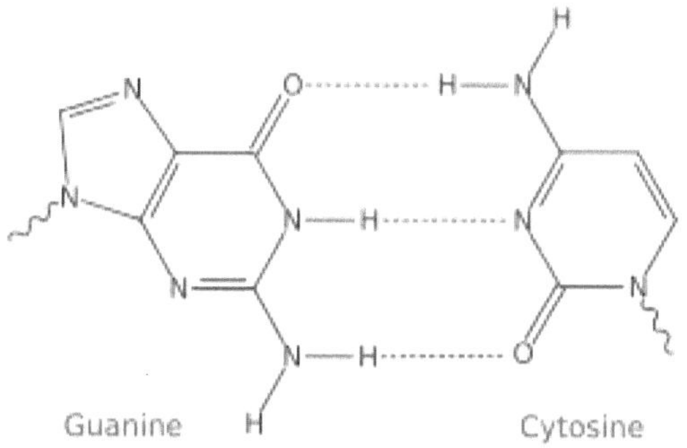

Figure 3. Base pair GC

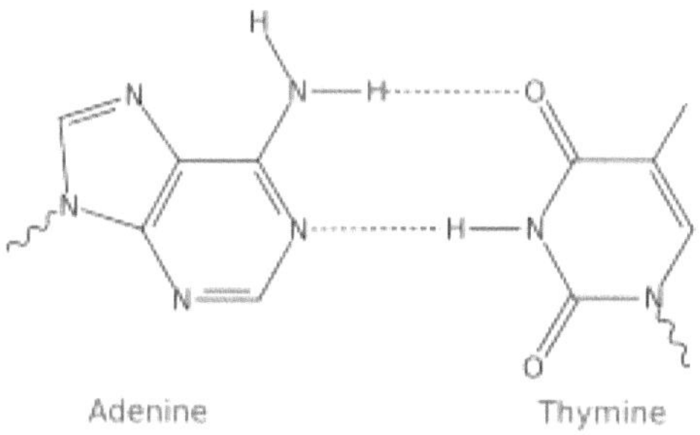

Figure 4. Base pair AT

RNA

Ribonucleic acid or RNA is a nucleic acid. RNA nucleotides contain ribose as their sugar. RNA uses the uracil base in its composition, instead of thymine, which is present in DNA. So if you review the base pairing shown above for DNA, and specifically the one containing thymine (figure 4), if you were looking at RNA the uracil would be in the position of the thymine with everything else remaining like DNA. So, instead of GCAT as the nucleotides of DNA there would be GCAU for the RNA, with the U replacing the T of the DNA. Uracil looks exactly like thymine. DNA is inside the nucleus and never comes out of the nucleus, while the RNA is single-stranded and outside the nucleus, so uracil performs the task in place of the thymine. As we review this further you will understand how important it is that the RNA is single stranded and has the uracil.

RNA is very similar to DNA, but differs in a few important structural details. RNA is usually single-stranded, while DNA is double-stranded. This is a very important difference. RNA is transcribed from DNA enzymes called *RNA polymerases* and is generally further processed by other enzymes, some of them guided by non-coding RNA,s. Each nucleotide consists of a nitrogenous base, a ribose sugar, and phosphate acid. RNA plays several important roles in the processes of translating genetic information from deoxyribonucleic acid (DNA) into proteins. One type of RNA acts as a messenger between DNA inside the nucleus and the protein synthesis completed in structures known as ribosomes that are located outside the nucleus in the chromosome. Others form vital portions of the structure of ribosomes, act as essential carrier molecules for amino acids to be used in protein synthesis, or change which genes are active.

When I think of DNA and RNA, I think of the way that bees or ants behave. In each there is a queen bee or queen ant, and the other bees or ants are the workers. They go out and find food for the queen. So they are in and out of the hive or ant hill on a continual basis. You will see that this is the modus operandi of DNA and RNA. The DNA is like the queen who stays in the hive (in this case the nucleus inside the chromosome), and the RNA is like the working bees moving in and out of the nucleus and doing something at the DNA's instructions. You will soon see how this works in the cells of a human. This analogy may help you to envision the methodology of the DNA/RNA actions.

Austrian-American biochemist Erwin Chargaff broke up the DNA molecule until all the purines and pyrimidines were loose. (50) He then analyzed the mixture of the two purines (adenine and guanine) and the two pyrimidines (cytosine and thymine) to see how much there were of each. In 1948 he showed that in the entire DNA tested, the total number of purine molecules was always equal to the total number of pyrimidine molecules. This meant that adenine plus guanine was always equal to cytosine and thymine (A + G = C + T). He also found the number of adenine molecules was always equal to the number of thymine molecules (A = T), and the number of guanine molecules was always equal to the number of cytosine molecules (G = C). This became a valuable clue to information found later that would provide the information needed to solve the genetic code.

In 1951, American chemist Linus Carl Pauling worked on protein structures, using of x-ray diffraction and his own previous studies of the way in which atoms fit together. He showed that chains of amino acids would twist into the shape of a helix (like the shape of a spiral staircase). This gave another important clue as to how a DNA molecule was shaped, and bioscientists began to seek the final shape of the DNA, keeping this helix in mind. (53)

FOUND, THE SOURCE OF LIFE - THE DOUBLE HELIX AND THE HUMAN GENOME

Two scientists who were particularly interested in the possibility of DNA helixes were an Englishman, Francis Harry Crick, and his American co-worker, James Dewey Watson. They tried different types of helixes, but none seemed suitable. A helix had to twist according to the natural way in which the atoms fit together. It had to be the kind of helix that would explain the x-ray diffraction images. What they needed were good x-ray diffraction images of pure DNA, but those weren't easy to obtain. (52)

As it happened, at the place where Crick and Watson were working there was a New Zealand-born biochemist, Maurice Hugh Frederick Wilkins. He prepared pure DNA fibers that would be expected to produce particularly good x-ray diffraction images. Working for him was English chemist Rosalind Elsie Franklin, who used Wilkins' DNA fibers to make the very best x-ray diffraction images that had yet been taken. Franklin was a very cautious scientist and didn't wish to hurry in figuring out the meaning of her images. She did not want to make any mistakes, nor did she want anyone else to see them while she was thinking out their meaning.

Wilkins, however, showed her images to Watson and Crick without asking her permission. They (Watson especially) were much less cautious than Franklin, and the images gave them a remarkable idea almost at once.

Watson and Crick decided that whereas a protein molecule was made up of a chain of amino acids, a DNA molecule was made up of a double chain of nucleotides. This became known as the famous double helix. The two chains of nucleotides were so arranged that the purine and pyrimidine portions faced each other and pointed toward the center of this double chain. This is shown below in figure 5. (Isn't it beautiful?)

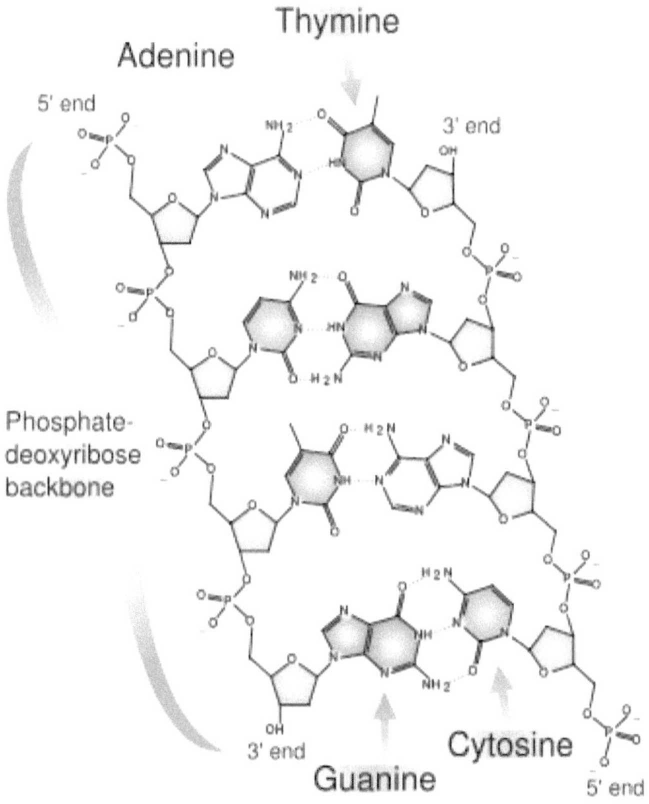

Figure 5 shows the chemical composition of the Helix

Notice in this structure that the G to C and A to T are held together by the hydrogen bonds as previously discussed. (51) The hydrogen bond is much weaker than the ordinary bonds that hold atoms together in a molecule. It is strong enough to hold the two nucleotide chains together under ordinary circumstances, but at crucial moments, the two chains can be pulled apart. This is ideal for replication. The two chains are, in fact, like the opposite teeth of a zipper. The zipper usually holds together under the proper conditions, but when you pull down the slide, the two sides of the zipper pull apart easily. This analogy will help you to envision what happens during replication (the function of splitting apart and producing two cells where there was only one).

In order to even the space between the nucleotide chains, a double-ring purine on one side must always be opposite a single-ring pyrimidine. This makes the space between the nucleotide chains just wide enough to hold three rings together at every position. If a purine faced a purine with their two rings each, there wouldn't be enough room, because there would be a total of four rings across and this would be too big. If a pyrimidine faced a pyrimidine, with their single rings each, they wouldn't reach across. Either way, the two chains wouldn't cling together properly at those points. (50) These observations were brought forth by Watson and Crick in their findings.

Hydrogen bonds hold adenine and thymine together quite well, and they also hold together guanine and cytosine. On one nucleotide chain, the order can be anything, but on the other side, there must always be a matching (complementary) set of purines or pyrimidines; C for G, T for A, and vice versa. If the arrangement on one nucleotide is A, G, A, T, T, C, G, G, G, C; then on the other it must be T, C, T, A, A, G, C, C, C, G. It's as simple as that—just match the complement of the arrangement seen on one side (just like the zippers mentioned). As we discuss how these codes are passed, you will understand how these complements work.

This explains why Chargaff (previously discussed) had found that in DNA molecules there were always equal numbers of adenines and thymines and equal number of guanines and cytosines.

Finally, the two chains were twisted in such a way as to produce a double helix. They were like two spiral staircases, twisting together, with the banister of one just fitting between the curves of the other. See figure 6 below.

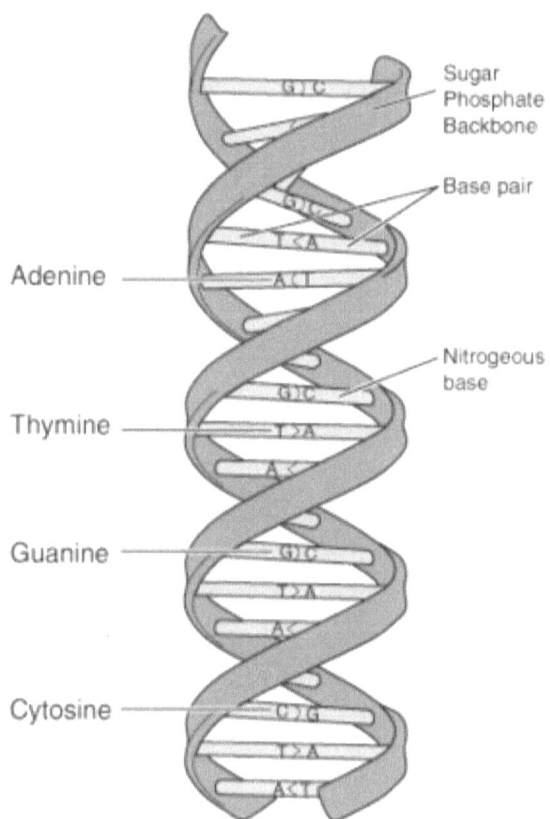

Base pairs, of a DNA double helix

Figure 6 Double helix, showing A to T and G to C pairs and showing the base pairs of adenine, thymine, guanine, and cytosine between the two "banisters."

The backbone of the DNA strand is made from alternating phosphate and sugar residues. (62) The sugar in DNA is 2-deoxyribose, which is a pentose (five carbons) sugar. The sugars are joined together by phosphate groups that form *phosphodiester bonds* between the third and fifth carbon atoms of adjacent sugar rings. These asymmetric bonds mean a strand of DNA has a direction. In a double helix, the direction of the nucleotides in one strand is opposite the other nucleotide strand. This arrangement of DNA strands is called anti-parallel. The asymmetric ends of DNA strands are referred to as the 5' (five prime) and 3' (three prime) ends. (23) Two of the major differences between DNA and RNA are the sugar previously mentioned and uracil in place of thymine. Also review figure 4; of course, RNA is not in a double helix but is a single strand.

Watson and Crick described this double helix structure of DNA in 1953, and it made a sensation at once. (62) Watson, Crick, and Wilkins all shared the Nobel Prize for medicine and physiology in 1962. Franklin might have been honored too, but she had died four years earlier, and the Nobel Prize is never presented posthumously.

Watson and Crick not only described the double helix structure, they worked out many of the features of this double helix and how the base pairs worked. They described the directions of the backbones and the anti-parallel structure of the backbones of the structure.

The structure worked out by Watson and Crick explained how DNA molecules produced replicas of themselves when cells divided. Because each DNA molecule can produce another just like itself, skin cells can divide into two skin cells, liver cells can divide into two liver cells, and so on. It's why egg cells have DNA molecules like those of the mother, sperm cells like those of the father, and resulting young have DNA molecules and characteristics like those of both parents.

Replication

Here's how it works. When a cell is ready to divide, the two chains of the double helix begin to pull apart at the hydrogen bonds. This is made easy, as mentioned earlier, due to the hydrogen bonds, which are fairly weak. (51) Here are figures 3 and 4 again so you can see the bonds.

At top, a **GC** base pair with three hydrogen bonds. At the bottom, **AT** base pair with two hydrogen bonds. Hydrogen bonds are shown as dashed lines.

As hydrogen bonds are not covalent (covalent bonding is when two atoms share one or more of their valence electrons. The valence electrons are the ones in the outermost shell of the atom. This forms a strong bond.), they can be broken and rejoined helix can therefore be pulled apart like a zipper, complementarity, all the information in the double-stranded sequence of a DNA helix is duplicated on each strand, which is vital in DNA replication. Indeed, this reversible and specific interaction between complementary base pairs is critical for all the functions of DNA in living organisms.[1]

The two types of base pairs form different numbers of hydrogen bonds, AT forming two hydrogen bonds, and GC forming three hydrogen bonds (see figures). The GC base pair is therefore stronger than the AT base pair. As a result, it is both the percentage of GC base pairs and the overall length of a DNA double helix that determine the strength of the association between the two strands of DNA. Long DNA helices with a high GC content have stronger-interacting strands, while short helices with high AT content have weaker-interacting strands. Parts of the DNA double helix that need to separate easily, such as the TATAAT Pribnow box in bacterial promoters, tend to have sequences with a high AT content, making the strands easier to pull apart. In the laboratory, the strength of this interaction can be measured by finding the temperature required to break the hydrogen bonds, their melting temperature (also called T_m value). (89)When all the base pairs in a DNA double helix melt, the strands separate and exist in solution as two entirely independent molecules. These single-stranded DNA molecules have no single common shape, but some conformations are more stable than others.]

Look at figure 4 above. The hydrogen bonds are shown between the purines and the pyrimidines, and you can see where it is easily detached, one side from the complementary side. The nucleotides along each chain quickly pick up single nucleotides that are present in the cell fluids (the fluid is made up of many purines and pyrimidines) of the chromosome nucleus. It picks up its complement, as previously discussed, so as to maintain not only the integrity of the code, but also the spacing between the backbones of the double helix that are made up of the sugar molecules. It is important that this spacing remains constant as well. When a guanine-cytosine base pair pulls apart, the guanine picks up a new cytosine from the nucleotides in the nucleus fluid almost immediately; the same action occurs when an adenine-thymine base pair pulls apart. They therefore complete the replication. This occurs throughout the whole DNA structure as the chromosomes split and form two identical chromosomes. In this way two complete chromosomes result, and after the pulling apart and splitting, the DNA within each is identical. Keep in mind that this occurs in all the cells of the body. This is a miraculous undertaking.

The other unique feature of this double helix structure is that it can fold like an accordion into a short pile in the small nucleus of each chromosome, taking up very little room while achieving the tasks it is to perform. The DNA chain is 22 to 26 Angstroms wide (2.2

to 2.6 nanometers), and one nucleotide unit is 3.3 Angstroms (0.33 nanometers) long. Although each individual repeating unit is very small, DNA polymers can be enormous molecules containing millions of nucleotides. For instance, the largest, chromosome number 1, is 220 million base pairs long. Think of a chain as a long word. Remember, the DNA is responsible for the entire genetic code. This means it has to be able to "write" many words, all of different lengths. Each of these words will mean something relative to what the DNA wants to happen in the body. These words represent instructions to produce certain amino acids and compose certain proteins. Keep in mind that all the cells of your body are alike and the entire nucleus and their DNA are alike. This means the cells in your heart are the same as the cells in your muscles. However, they have to perform quite differently. It's amazing to me that after conception these cells must make all the parts of the human body and somehow know which ones will be heart cells and which are going to be muscle cells. The wonder of life.

The nucleotide repeats (in the double helix the same base can be repeated, such as CA, CA, CA tied to the backbone and to its complement on the complementary side of the double helix) contain both the segment of the backbone of the molecule, which holds the chain together and a base, which interacts with the other DNA strand in the helix, its complementary nucleotide. In general, a base linked to a sugar is called a *nucleoside,* and a base linked to both a sugar and one or more phosphate groups is called a *nucleotide.* If multiple nucleotides are linked together, as in DNA, this polymer is referred to as a *polynucleotide.* The backbone of the DNA strand is made from alternating phosphate and sugar residues. The sugar in DNA is 2-deoxyribose, which is a carbon sugar. The sugars are joined together by phosphate groups that form phosphodiester bonds between the third and fifth carbon atoms of adjacent sugar rings. These asymmetric bonds mean a strand of DNA has a direction. In a double helix, the direction of the nucleotides in one strand is opposite to their direction in the other strand. This arrangement of DNA strands is called antiparallel.

Although scientists recognized the structure of the DNA as distinct from RNA, it was unclear how it worked and how it related to the genetic code. It was understood how this busy nucleus caused certain proteins to be formed. So, the question became What's the code, and how does it work?

We have covered how replications occur and affect all the chromosomes in the body, but we haven't discovered how DNA controls the generation of amino acids and the structuring of the proteins in the body: the sought-after secret.

The order of the nucleotides that we just reviewed is different for every human being. It is so representative of an individual that we now use it to like fingerprints; we now use DNA to solve mysteries. It is better than fingerprints, but how does it work? Bioscientists wanted to solve that also. The order of the nucleotides, with their Gs and Ts and As and Cs, must be the key. This key must control the order of the amino acids required to provide the proteins needed by the human body.

There are four different nucleotides (adenine, guanine, thymine, and cytosine). Can they determine the information to select the amino acids? There are twenty-two amino acids, and we have four nucleotides. In order to solve this problem, think about today's personal computers, or all computers for that matter. They work using just ones and zeros. However, these ones and zeros can do much more than the twenty-six letters of the alphabet. It's just a matter of how the ones and zeros are generated and sequenced. With one sequence they mean one thing, and with another sequence they mean something quite different.

But maybe more important than the number of nucleotides and their codes is how they get out of the nucleus of the chromosomes. The nucleus of the human chromosome has DNA inside, and the nucleus shell that surrounds this core of DNA is impervious to DNA passing through it. But remember that I told you that the chromosome of the eukaryotes (humans, animals, plants) has an outer membrane that we can call one enclosure; between it and the shell that surrounds the nucleus are other structures that I told you I would discuss later. Well, this is later. I'll discuss what's in between these two walls. However, I won't go into it in too detailed a matter or it would take up another book. So I will cover the basics.

In 1956, Romanian-American biochemist George Emil Palade found the place where the enzymes are located. Using an electron microscope, a tool that could magnify structures about a thousand times more than a microscope, he found tiny structures within the cytoplasm; the sea of material between the outer membrane of a cell and the nucleus shell, in which many small structures are located. There are upwards of 150,000 of them in every cell, and this is where the enzymes are produced. He found each of these structures also contained RNA, and he called these structures ribosomes. Palade received the Nobel Prize for physiology and medicine in 1974. (50)

To learn about the ribosomes and their locations within a cell, review the diagram below in figure 7. (63)

Eukaryotic Cells

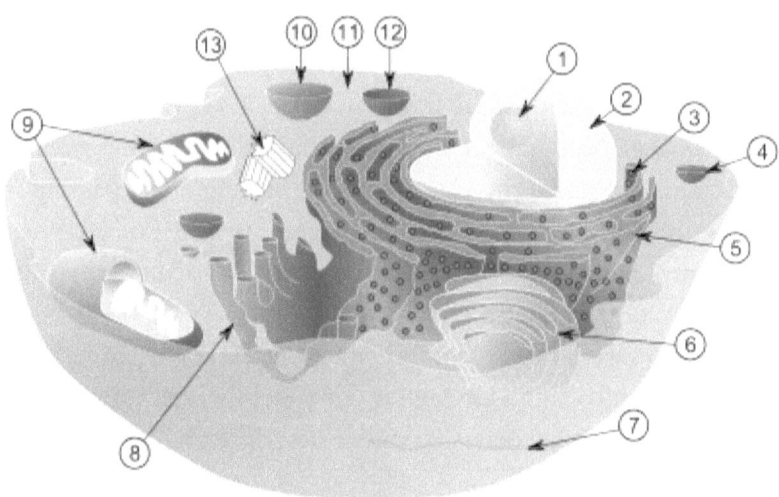

Diagram of a typical eukaryotic cell, showing subcellular components. Organelles: (1) nucleolus; (2) nucleus; (3) ribosome; (4) vesicle; (5) rough endoplasmic reticulum (ER); (6) Golgi apparatus; (7) Cytoskeleton; (8) smooth ER; (9) mitochondria; (10) vacuole; (11) cytoplasm; (12) lysosome; (13) centrioles within centrosome. (63)

Eukaryotic cells are about ten times the size of a typical prokaryote (bacteria or virus) and can be as much as a thousand times greater in volume. The major difference between prokaryotes and eukaryotes is that eukaryotic cells contain membrane-bound compartments in which specific metabolic activities take place. Most important among these is the presence of a cell nucleus, a membrane-delineated compartment that houses the Eukaryotic cell's DNA. It is this nucleus that gives the eukaryote its name, which means "true nucleus."

The diagram of a typical eukaryotic cell (Figure 7 above) shows what would be found in animals, humans and plants—all have a similar cell. The key difference between the eukaryote cell and the prokaryote cells found in bacteria and viruses is that the eukaryote cell has a nucleus. It's within this nucleus that the chromosomes and DNA are located. There are twenty-three chromosome pairs within the nucleus. The parts diagrammed in figure 7 that we are interested in now are: (1) nucleolus, (2) nucleus, (3) ribosome, and (11) cytoplasm. These relate to where the DNA is located in the nucleus. The RNA are located within the ribosome, with some in the nucleus. The cytoplasm is the material between the outer membrane of the cell and the nucleolus shell. Cytoplasm contains the various other organelles, comparable to organs in our bodies like the heart, lungs, etc. Organelles, likewise, perform organ-like functions in the cytoplasm. To discuss them fully is beyond the scope of this book.

If you want to learn more about the functions of the various sections of the eukaryote cell, visit the following Web site: (http://en.wikipedia.org/wiki/Cell_Biology), where a complete description is given.

Palade's work provided information about the ribosomes, without answering how the information gets from the DNA to these ribosomes. Palade's findings, along with information determined by Watson and Crick and the Russian-American scientist George Gamow (who I personally believe was a genius in many areas of science), began to reveal the answer. Gamow suggested that it was not the individual G, A, T, or C that determined the code, but a group of them. He used great logic in reviewing this. He claimed that if you used only these four, the most codes DNA could offer would be sixteen. Any two of the four nucleotides such as TA, GA, etc., would only create sixteen combinations. He knew that sixteen was not enough to decode to produce twenty-two amino acids. He suggested that three nucleotides at a time would create sixty-four combinations that could then be decoded to provide more than enough to produce the enzymes and amino acids. So, his solution was triplets, and that's how the genetic code must be passed from the DNA in the nucleus. What Palade showed in 1956 was not only where the enzymes were located, but also where significant amounts of RNA were located.

THE WAY INTO THE NUCLEUS

In 1961, two French biochemists, Jacques Lucien Monod and Francois Jacob, suggested that RNA was the answer to that question. After all, RNA is found both in the nucleus and in the cytoplasm and in the ribosomes in particular. (53) RNA has a structure just like DNA, except that it has ribose instead of deoxyribose and uracil instead of thymine. When a DNA molecule replicates, it might, every once in a while, form an RNA nucleotide chain, instead of another DNA nucleotide chain. The RNA nucleotide chain would have its nucleotides in the exact order of the DNA nucleotide chain except that uracil (U) would be found where thymine (T) had been. Since the RNA is not a double helix, it must take the nucleotides off the DNA in a series. But how would a single strand of nucleotides represent the double helix with the nucleotide pairs. This would be reviewed and answered. The molecule of RNA would slip out of the nucleus and would serve as the messenger, carrying the DNA information to the ribosomes. This molecule of RNA came to be known as *messenger RNA* (mRNA).

It is important to remember the other things about RNA that are different than DNA. The RNA is not in a double helix formation but in a linear one. Whereas the DNA has two base pairs between the two backbones of the DNA, the RNA is not limited. It is a linear molecule and therefore can continuously take the base pairs and line them up on the ribose sugar backbone in single-file order. (Later it was determined that it would take half pairs from one of the backbone strands for the

RNA messenger.) As an example, if ten base pairs were be taken off the DNA, they would be shown in order one after the other as ten nucleotides in series on the RNA ribose single backbone. This is very important; remember that Gamow had said that the code had to come off as triplets. This is not possible with DNA, where only pairs come off. The series of nucleotides on the RNA could be taken off in triplets; its just a matter of nature providing a method of cutting these single strands every third nucleotide.

Another major difference is that the RNA can pass through the nucleus shell and the DNA cannot. The DNA stays within the nucleus shell almost like this is the way to protect it from changing. It's possible the DNA with its double backbones cannot pass through the semipermeable shell because it has a broader and more complex structure than the single backbone RNA; perhaps the fluid of the deoxyribonucleic acid is blocked whereas the ribonucleic acid is not. There is also a difference of one nucleotide, where uracil (U) replaces thymine (T). However, it turns out that this is not what is intended by Mother Nature, and you will soon see why.

Both Monod and Jacob received the 1965 Nobel Prize for medicine and physiology. Prior to Monod and Jacob's work, Spanish-American biochemist Severo Ochoa had discovered an enzyme that acted to tie nucleotides together to form an RNA chain. This made it possible to make synthetic RNA. Ochoa received a share of the 1959 Nobel Prize for medicine and physiology. This played a part in the progression of successes in solving the riddle of the DNA/RNA issue. Using the information that Ochoa, Monod, and Jacob had developed concerning the messenger RNA, American biochemist Marshall Warren Nirenberg manufactured synthetic messenger RNA. By choosing which nucleotides to start with, he could make messenger RNA with particular triplets. He would then find out which particular amino acids would be produced in an nucleotide chain by these triplets. He knew if he could convert these triplets into an amino acid, then he could determine which amino acid it represented and eventually the protein it produced. This was all done by known chemicals in test tubes. In this way, Nirenberg began to break the genetic code. He started with a polyuridic acid and added it to several systems containing other known enzymes, ribosomes. Eventually out of one of the mixtures came a known protein. By carefully choosing several known nucleotides he arrived at all the amino acids and their related proteins. He discovered which nucleotide triplet, called a codon, produced which amino acid. By 1967, every nucleotide codon was tied to a particular amino acid, and the genetic code was completely worked out, although the method of it still was not complete. (53) Nirenberg and Indian-American chemist Har Gobind Khorana received shares of the 1968 Nobel Prize for medicine and physiology.

While Nirenberg was working on the genetic code, another American biochemist, Mahlon Bush Hoagland, was locating small RNA molecules in the cytoplasm (material between the nucleus wall and the outer membrane of the cell). (53) These were double-ended molecules. At one end was a nucleotide triplet (anticodon) that would fit a particular codon on the messenger RNA (like a zipper, as I previously mentioned). On the other end was a portion that attached itself to a particular amino acid located in the cytoplasm. Because they transferred the information from the anticodon triplet to the amino acid, such molecules are called *transfer RNA* (tRNA).

Putting these pieces of information together, bioscientists could determine the complete function. It is the sequence of these four bases along the backbone that encodes information in the form of codons on the messenger RNA. This information is read using the genetic code, which specifies the sequence of the amino acids within proteins. The code of the DNA is read by copying stretches of DNA into the related nucleic acid RNA, in a process called *transcription*. Transcription forms the messenger RNA (mRNA). Compare this to writing words. You take the letters of the alphabet and you combine them into words. The process of transcription is the same within the cell. The codons are like the letters of the alphabet. A combination of codons forms a word coming from the nucleus. This is the message emanating from the nucleus via the messenger RNA.

Transcription and mRNA

RNA polymerase (an enzyme) opens the part of the DNA to be transcribed. This is like the action of unzipping a zipper. This RNA polymerase acts to unzip the double strand into single strands. Keep in mind that the base pairs are held by the double backbone of the double helix. These backbones are called the strands. (54) There are two of them with the information between them in the pairs we discussed. By unzipping, the two backbones are split from a double helix to single strands with each strand having one backbone and combined with half a pair formed one half of the information in the strand. This can be seen in the figure number 8 below. Remember, the backbone (strands) move in opposite directions, so the top backbone comes off as the mRNA as shown in figure 8.

Notice when the triplet comes off as ATG it is now coming out as AUG since there is no T outside the nucleus and it is replaced by the U as we discussed, as uracil.

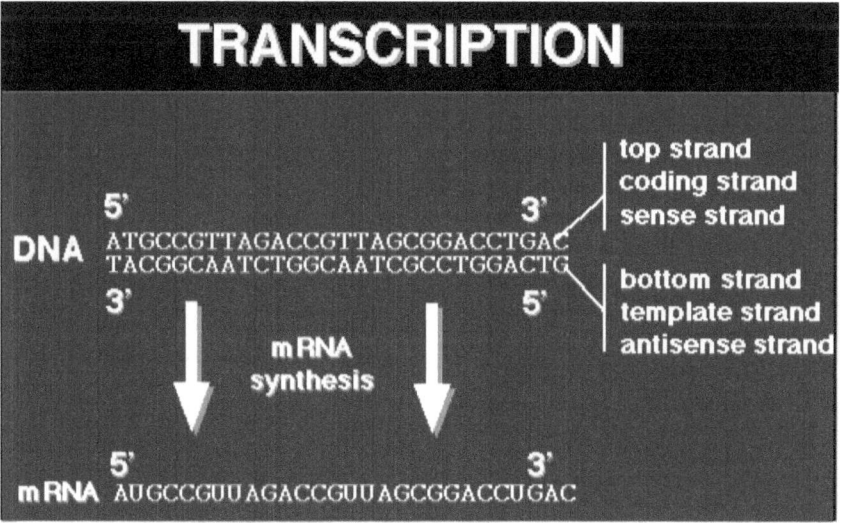

Figure 8 shows the double strand DNA going off as a single strand on the messenger RNA (mRNA)

As mentioned, the code consists of at least three bases, according to astronomer George Gamow. To code for the twenty essential amino acids, a genetic code must consist of at least a three-base set (triplet) of the four bases. If one considers the possibilities of arranging four things three at a time (4x4x4), there are sixty-four possible code words, or codons (a three-base sequence on the mRNA that codes for either a specific amino acid or a control word). With the mRNA coming off in a serial fashion, it can form codons, such as AUG or CCG, for example.

One strand of the double-stranded DNA is called the *bottom strand*, or *template strand*, or *antisense* strand, as shown in figure 8. This strand is tied to one-half of the base pairs, or codons, that are transcribed into the messenger RNA (mRNA). The other strand is called the *top strand*, *coding strand* or *sense strand*, as shown in figure 8. This contains the other half-pairs called the anticodons, which become the transfer RNA (tRNA). The anticodons are therefore the complements of the codons, just as they were when they were together as base pairs in the double helix. Only one strand of DNA (template strand) is transcribed as shown in the figure 8 and comes off as the mRNA (messenger RNA). RNA nucleotides are available in the region of the chromatin (this process only occurs during interphase) and are linked together similarly to the DNA process.

As can be seen in figure 8, the codons are no longer associated as base pairs but become a string of mRNA. This allows them to be decoded in triplets as mRNA.

Likewise the transfer anticodons are no longer associated as base pairs but become a string of anticodons that were taken from the opposite strand of the DNA than the mRNA took; so, it's the complement. Like the mRNA, the tRNA anticodons can move through the nucleus shell and do so in another direction. Each of these streams of codons and anticodons move through the nucleus shell at different points.

These are done in series on the messenger RNA shown in figure 8. (54) Note that wherever there is a T on the coding strand (top strand), there will be a U on the mRNA strand. (Refer to figure 8 again, since recognizing the U in place of the T makes it easier to see what is happening.) This is because the RNA does not have thymine but has uracil in its place, as discussed previously. The messenger RNA is transcribed as indicated with the copy of a section of the DNA molecule. The mRNA travels through the nucleus shell to the ribosome where tRNA has transferred amino molecules that attach themselves as the various anticodons of the messenger RNA. The anticodons formed in the transfer RNA were from the coding strand and are the complements of the template strand and therefore form a perfect mate.

To summarize the cycle that occurs: the DNA contains the code. The code is unzipped into two strands. The messenger RNA (mRNA) reads the code and therefore contains the blueprint for construction of a protein. The complement other half of the unzipped code, tRNA, is transferred out of the nucleus. The mRNA moves through the nucleus shell to the ribosome. The ribosomal (rRNA) is the construction site where the protein is made; and transfer RNA (tRNA) is the truck delivering the proper amino acid to the site at the right time. From this a protein is generated. The mRNA and the tRNA are the complementary half's of the DNA and make their way out of the nucleus with their information for manufacturing the amino acids which eventually produce the proteins.

Transfer RNA,s (anticodons) were studied carefully by American chemist Robert William Holley. He purified several varieties in 1962. By 1965, he actually put the proper nucleotide together and synthesized one of them. In 1968, he shared the Nobel Prize with Nirenberg and Khorana. Nirenberg's group was able to determine the sequences of fifty-four out of sixty-four codons. Subsequent work by Har Gobind Khorana identified the rest of the code, and Holley determined the structure of transfer RNA, the adapter molecule that facilitates translation.(53) Each anticodon gets the transfer RNA molecule that happens to fit that particular codon and no other. Amino acids attach to the other end of each transfer RNA, but only the amino acid that specifically fits that end of that particular transfer RNA. The amino acids then all hook together to create a particular enzyme molecule. The DNA has done its duty of sending a message via the mRNA and the complementary transfer tRNA to complement the mRNA and pick up the proper amino acids called out by the DNA.

You can now envision the DNA in its shell passing out instructions one after the other determined by the genetic code that is held within its genes. This is amazing enough, but you have to remember that DNA was present at the conception of the new baby. It handles the building of the baby from time zero until the time of death. It even has encoded within its genes when that child will go into puberty and eventually become a grown man or woman. Isn't this a wonder?

THE GENETIC CODE: TRANSLATION OF RNA CODE INTO PROTEIN

The genetic code was broken by Marshall Nirenberg and Heinrich Matthaei a decade after Watson and Crick's work. Nirenberg discovered that RNA, regardless of its source organism, could initiate protein synthesis when combined with contents of broken E. coli cells. (54) By adding poly-U to each of twenty test tubes (each tube having a different "tagged" amino acid), Nirenberg and Matthaei were able to determine that the codon UUU (the only one in poly-U) coded for the amino acid phenylalanine (see figure 9).

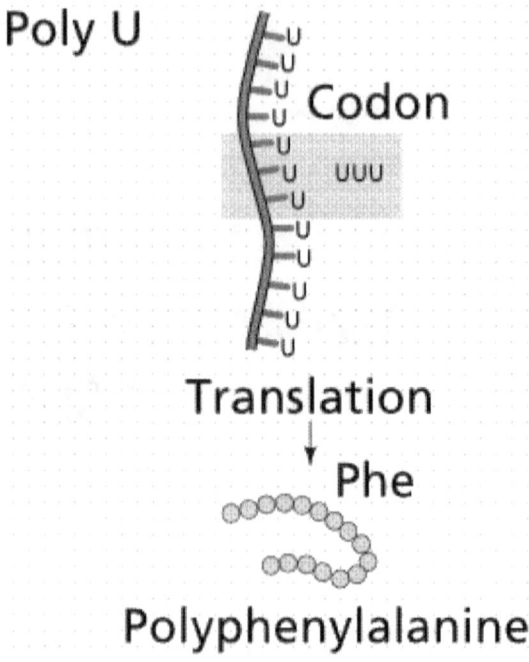

Figure 9: Steps in breaking the genetic code: the deciphering of a poly-U mRNA.
Image (90)

Likewise, an artificial mRNA consisting of alternating A and C bases would code for alternating amino acids histidine and threonine (figure 10). Gradually, a complete listing of the genetic code codons was developed. (54)

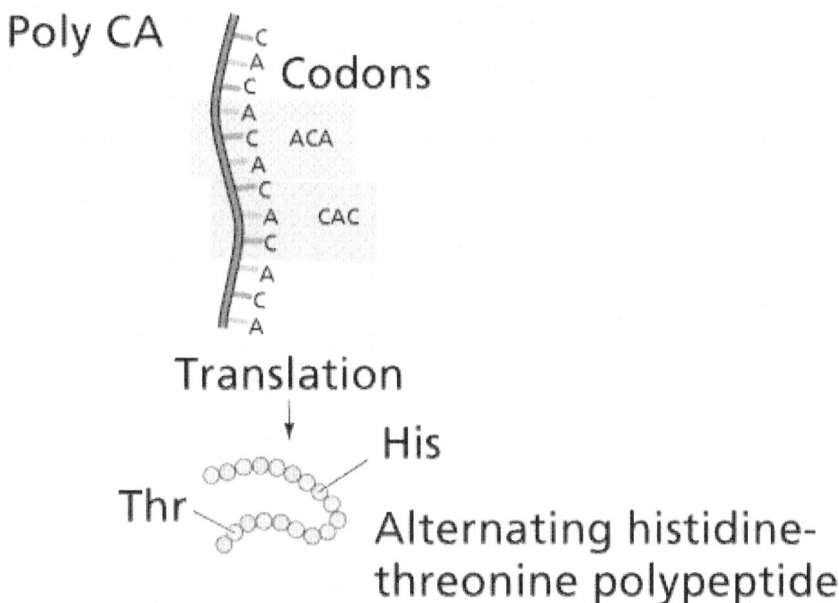

Figure 10: Deciphering the code: poly CAC to histidine-threonine polypeptide. (90)

The genetic code consists of sixty-one amino-acid coding codons and three termination codons, which stop the process of translation. The genetic code is thus redundant (degenerate in the sense of having multiple states amounting to the same thing), with, for example, glycine coded for by GGU, GGC, GGA, and GGG codons. If a codon is mutated, say from GGU to CGU, is the same amino acid specified?

The genetic code has redundancy but no ambiguity. (57) For example, although codon GAA and GAG both specify glutamic acid (redundancy), neither of them specifies any other amino acid (no ambiguity). Only two amino acids are specified by a single codon; one of these is the amino acid methionine, specified by the codon AUG, which also specifies the start of translation; the other is tryptophan, specified by the codon UGG. The degeneracy of the genetic code is what accounts for the existence of silent mutations.

Review the complete code of sixty-four codons shown below in figure 11. Inside the squares is marked the amino acid that will be picked up by the code. This is how twenty two amino acids are picked which will then be used to generate the proteins. Note on the left side is the letter that will appear as the first letter of the triplet code (Codon). The second letter is determined by the horizontal U, C, A, G. at the top of the chart. The third letter of the codon is determined by the letters going down the right side of the chart; amino acids formed by each code are shown. (54)

First letter	Second letter: U		Second letter: C		Second letter: A		Second letter: G		Third Letter
U	UUU UUC	Phenyl-alanine	UCU UCC	Serine	UAU UAC	Tyrosine	UGU UGC	Cysteine	U C
	UUA UUG	Leucine	UCA UCG		UAA UAG	Stop codon Stop codon	UGA UGG	Stop codon Tryptophan	A G
C	CUU CUC CUA CUG	Leucine	CCU CCC CCA CCG	Proline	CAU CAC	Histidine	CGU CGC CGA CGG	Arginine	U C A G
					CAA CAG	Glutamine			
A	AUU AUC AUA	Isoleucine	ACU ACC ACA ACG	Threonine	AAU AAC	Asparagine	AGU AGC	Serine	U C
	AUG	Methionine; initiation codon			AAA AAG	Lysine	AGA AGG	Arginine	A G
G	GUU GUC GUA GUG	Valine	GCU GCC GCA GCG	Alanine	GAU GAC	Aspartic acid	GGU GGC GGA GGG	Glycine	U C A G
					GAA GAG	Glutamic acid			

Figure 11. The Genetic Code (91)

tRNA carries the proper amino acid to the ribosome when the codons call for them. There are sixty-one different tRNAs, each having a different binding site for the amino acid and a different anticodon. For the codon UUU, the complementary anticodon is AAA. Energy for binding the amino acid to tRNA comes from ATP's conversion (adenosine triphosphate, which we discussed early in the book as the universal energy element in the human body) to adenosine monophosphate (AMP).

THE WONDER OF LIFE

The illustration below (figure 12) is from Genentech's Access Excellence site The drawing is available at http://www.gene.com/ae/AB/GG/protein_synthesis.html

Protein Synthesis

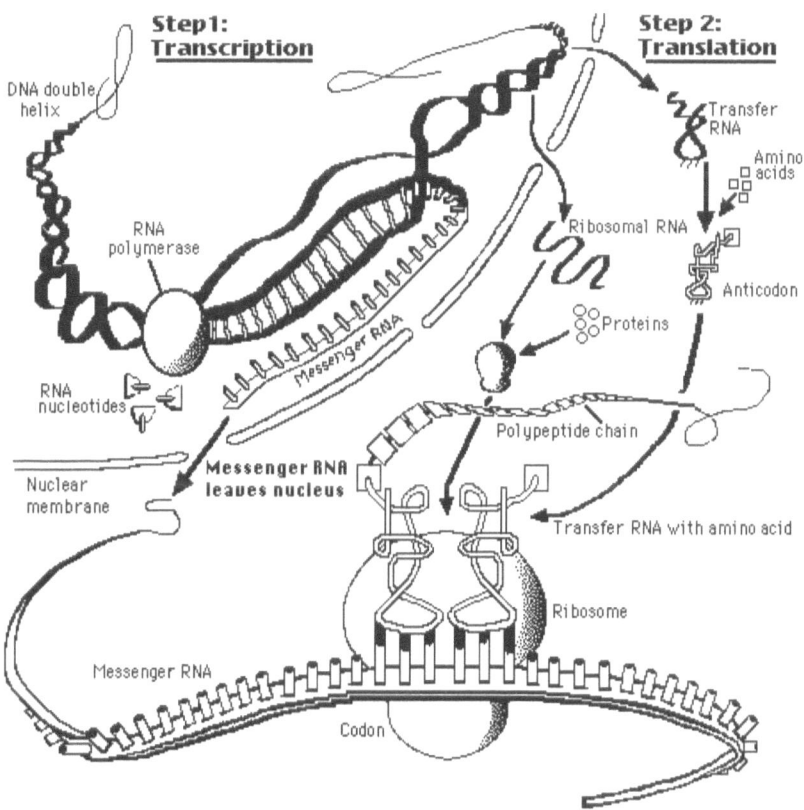

Figure 12. Protein Synthesis "http://www.estrellamountain.edu/faculty/farabee/biobk/protein_synthesis.gif" * this diagram shows how proteins are synthesized. (54)

Start from the upper left part of the schematic. Step 1 is the transcription, which is activated by the RNA polymerase. The messenger RNA transcribes the DNA by taking one-half of the pairs from the backbone of the double helix. Notice, as mentioned, that the mRNA only takes half pairs of the nucleotides and, as codons, transports them in series rather than the complementary pair in the double helix. While the mRNA proceeds through the nuclear shell on the one path that carries the codons to the ribosome, Step 2 shows the tRNA (upper right hand corner of the schematic) and its anticodons passing through the nuclear membrane, picking up the amino acids and taking them to the ribosome to meet with its particular codon. The ribosomal RNA passes through the nuclear membrane and arrives at the ribosome where the proteins are manufactured. (28).

Number of Genes in the Human

Human cells have twenty-three pairs of large linear nuclear chromosomes, for a total of forty-six per cell. Sequencing the human genome over the past few years has provided a great deal of information about the number of genes in each of the of the chromosome pairs. Below is a table (figure 13) compiling statistics for the number of genes, the total bases, and the sequenced bases. (55)

Chromosome	Genes	Total bases	Sequenced bases
1	3,148	247,200,000	224,999,719
2	902	242,750,000	237,712,649
3	1,436	199,450,000	194,704,827
4	453	191,260,000	187,297,063
5	609	180,840,000	177,702,766
6	1,585	170,900,000	167,273,992
7	1,824	158,820,000	154,952,424
8	781	146,270,000	142,612,826
9	1,229	140,440,000	120,312,298
10	1,312	135,370,000	131,624,737
11	405	134,450,000	131,130,853
12	1,330	132,290,000	130,303,534

13	623	114,130,000	95,559,980
14	886	106,360,000	88,290,585
15	676	100,340,000	81,341,915
16	898	88,820,000	78,884,754
17	1,367	78,650,000	77,800,220
18	365	76,120,000	74,656,155
19	1,553	63,810,000	55,785,651
20	816	62,440,000	59,505,254
21	446	46,940,000	34,171,998
22	595	49,530,000	34,893,953
X (sex chromosome)	1,093	154,910,000	151,058,754
Y (sex chromosome)	125	57,740,000	22,429,293

Figure 13. Chromosomes and Number of Genes per Chromosome
http://en.wikipedia.org/wiki/Chromosome

Keep in mind that there are twenty-two amino acids, but there are an infinite number of proteins that can be made from the combinations of the amino acids. The table above shows how the codons provide the twenty-two amino acids. The sequencing of the different amino acids determines the action that takes place to generate the proteins. The amino acids are like words and the proteins are like sentences. There is a complete paragraph that determines how the various proteins are generated and sent to do their service in the body.

    I am an electrical engineer by education. This method that the chromosome's DNA uses to send out codons via the mRNA to provide given actions is quite similar to how a microprocessor works. The microprocessor has a CPU in its center, which is like the DNA inside the nucleus. The CPU—Central Processing Unit—can add, subtract, multiply, divide, and do logic. However, it needs an operating program to tell it how to do the functions it does. This is done by programming ROM (Read Only Memory) codes that provide the operating program for the CPU. These ROM codes are built into the microprocessor and do not change. In that respect they are like the DNA which one is provided at birth and doesn't change. We will learn later that the DNA can be changed by a retrovirus, but this is a disease. Likewise a ROM code in a computer is not supposed to change, but accidents happen to it like they do to the DNA. The ROM code provides the program for the CPU to do the various functions as it receives information from the input to the microprocessor. This program of the operating system is like the genetic code of a human. It will only do what it has been coded to do. The program is a sequencer of sorts. It tells how to handle various sequences. Meanwhile, while the functions are being carried out, the CPU sends messages to the memory and recalls messages back from the memory, depending on the function that has been programmed. The CPU makes decisions based on what has been programmed into it, relating to the information (data) coming in.

In a living cell, the genetic code is the code that is built in and won't change (unless a mutation occurs). It is similar to the program built into the microprocessor. It sequences through the various codons via the mRNA and completes the buildup via the tRNA of the proteins. However, it doesn't keep putting out the same information all the time. The body is a dynamic system, and it may need changes, depending on the stresses placed on it. These stresses depend on which of the millions of alleles (code addresses, which are sort of like the random access memory (RAM) of the microprocessor) are called upon for a response. The alleles are the like the addresses within each chromosome. See the table 2 above, which shows the number of genes in each chromosome.

Conclusion on cells and DNA/RNA

I tried to achieve the difficult task of describing the way the chromosomes, genes, and genetic code works as simply as possible for the layman to understand. I am not a bioscientist, so in that respect I am a layman, and I presented it as I understand it. I am a professional electrical engineer who has been involved in the development of integrated circuits over the past forty-five years, including the solid state physics involved, and I understand technical information. From this background, after much research I have tried to supply the reader with my interpretation of the events. I find it truly amazing that a difficult a problem that took so many years for scientists to track down could be tied together in a manner that is fairly easy to understand. Isn't that the way of life? That is, when something as complicated as this is established, it looks easy when looking backwards in time. This was probably the toughest puzzle for the bioscientists and chemists to put together, yet once they got the basics done, it is presented in fairly simple form. I added the names and the countries of the people that made significant contributions toward this complex picture; they look like a football team that is working together for one purpose; and they came up with it. Of course the details I left out of this book are too complex to try to cover in this book, so I provided enough to give an understanding of the process. It would take another book to go into the details.

THE HUMAN GENOME

Even when scientists reached this level of understanding toward determining the genome of man, it took many years and computer hours to put that whole genetic code (genome) together. The federal government had a program to decipher the code, and a private concern headed up by Craig Venter, head of Celera, both raced to beat each other. (56) It didn't start out that way. It started with the government program, and then the private concern worked to do it faster with their approach. I believe in the end that each helped the other. It was about a fifteen-year venture to reach as far as I have discussed. The completion of the human genome led to mapping other genomes to see how they compared with humans. They tackled the mouse and found it was almost the same genome as man. Isn't that something?

As complex as the cell is, with its DNA and RNA and the resultant amino acids and the building of proteins, it's even more complex when one considers that every cell in the human body is exactly the same, yet none carry out functions the same way. For example, a cell in the skin is the same as a cell in the brain and a cell in the arm muscle, yet the neurons in the brain do not act like the arm muscle or the skin tissue. Here is a key secret. Although the cells are the same throughout the body, they are controlled by some kind of switches in their location that makes them work the way they do for that location. It's like the cells in the muscles see different switches for turning on special sections of the chromosomes and only use those to perform their functions. In that respect it's comparable, as I mentioned earlier, to the microprocessor, which functions so similarly to the workings of the nucleus and the various parts of the cell to perform a task. Microprocessors are used for many tasks. It's a matter in many cases of how the human addresses the microprocessor as to how it performs a given function. If the operator wants one thing, he provides data to certain portions of the processor. If he wants it to be used differently, he puts a different code into the same processor, and it performs that task. Most of the time it only requires one different button to be chosen for a completely different function. Likewise, each cell in its physical position performs a completely different function than if it were in some other place in the body. But it isn't anywhere else—it's wherever it is, and the thing that changes is the code or human function switch at that location.

We know that, although identical at every location, the cell controls the amino acids and the construction of the proteins that are probably different for each physical location of the cell. For example, the cells in the brain do not have to do the functions that the muscle in the arm does, so different amino acids and proteins are generated in the brain. The question that I have as a layman is what is it that allows the cell to identify its location and what is required of the cells at that location?

In the beginning, when an embryo is just a set of chromosomes made up of the male and female contributions, it begins to replicate while in the mother's body. As this replication expands and cells are formed, the embryo grows. From the embryo to the formation of a complete child, it is a wonder that each of these replications become a different part of the body and begin to function as individual parts of the body while taking food from the mother. This continues while in the mother's body and after birth. However, after birth, there are no new things that grow; the ones already there begin to take on growth. Somehow, the body knows that it doesn't have to add any more new things, just take in nutrition and let the body grow.

Males and females both go through puberty, bringing changes to their bodies and their lives. Sex organs change, and both voices change, the male more than the female. His voice transforms to a deeper tone; this is another thing that differentiates the male from the female. This transformation within the male and female is the first step in becoming an adult and makes it possible for starting another human being; which more or less begins the sequence all over again.

Prior to reaching this stage, neither males nor females are able to reproduce. The male has no sperm to generate, and although the female has eggs, they are not released until puberty is reached. Then each month the female body releases an egg. If it is not fertilized, it leaves the female in the form of blood. This is sometimes called "the disappointment of the uterus." But eventually most females have their egg fertilized by male sperm, and the chromosome combination becomes the start of a new life. The wonder of life.

This reaching of maturity or adulthood reminds me of the Mendel experiments with self-pollinating pea plants. They eventually flower and produce pollen, which contains the male gametes, which fall on the female parts of the plant, which are not yet prepared to accept this sperm. But the pollen grain grows a pollen tube, which allows the sperm to travel through the stigma and style to reach the pea plant's ovary. The ripened ovary wall becomes the fruit, or pea pod, of a new plant. In this case the pea plant is self-pollinating and the female has nothing to say about when it is ready; whereas with humans, the male and female have to consent to mate (most of the time) to carry on their expansion of the human race. Whether with a pea plant or a human being, the change is dramatic. How those genomes know what to do after that is amazing.

Back to the discussion about the human genome and what that will bring to mankind. The completed genome, either accomplished by Craig Venter and/or the government program, gave many bioscientists a look into many possibilities. They believed that this insight should show what causes various diseases and what results in different functions between genes in the body. One good thing—they found the genome was smaller than expected. It originally was believed that the human genome was on the order of 150,000 to 200,000 genes. It was found that there are actually 30,000 to 45,000 genes, which can make the problem easier to solve.

Every person is made up of three billion chemical combinations. It took thirteen years and cost about $450 million to finish the first-ever complete detailing of the human genome in 2003, using a fleet of genetic analysis equipment. Today it takes only weeks at a cost of abut $5 million, mainly due to obtaining this base. I would take a wild guess and say it will be down to half a million dollars five years from now (2007).

It was found that several mutations can occur, resulting in certain diseases, but to date there has been no progress on finding out how to prevent the disease. I am sure this will be resolved the more we work on it. Many of these things are found by inputting data into a computer as we find new things, and eventually a program will be written to tie things together. Sometimes this is done by trial and effect. This is much easier with a computer than done if by human effort.

By helping chart the entire human genome, machines for the first time have provided a clear view of the three billion chemical combinations—the nucleotide base pairs we discussed—that make up a human. And since the mapping of the human genome, the power of DNA analysis equipment has steadily increased, making it easier to answer age-old questions about who we are and where we come from—and hopefully how to live longer. Comparisons are being done by the National Geographic Society to trace human migratory routes over the past 150,000 years, and they show how closely related we are, like a big family. The current technology helps us to look backwards in time and allow us to determine the evolution of life.

The resolving of the human genome has shown that there are times where more than one gene is responsible for an action. They are somewhat related. We should have realized this, since we found early in the hunt for the genetic code that there is one protein that results in the generation of insulin and another from the same protein that results in the female's organs being better moisturized to allow for easier function during certain female functions. We have to keep in mind that the genome is made up of contributions from both the male and female during conception. Therefore the resulting chromosomes and their genes aren't always those that are just from the male or the female. This being a fact, there are probably times when part of the genome is not used by the male and likewise for the female. I guess that is why for certain diseases one takes several types of medicines that affect different parts of the body.

I have suffered from a dramatic case of high blood pressure since I was eighteen. In 1966 I was told that if I didn't take care of the problem that I had five years to live. This was due to having a very high reading on the systolic and diastolic readings. What was done to lower the systolic didn't lower the diastolic, and the difference between these two is the pulse pressure. Lowering the high reading without changing the low reading resulted in a drop in pulse pressure, and I could pass out. Eventually over the course of a year of trial and error, three medicines were found to help. Ten years later, a doctor in California weaned me off of these and changed me over to three different medicines that worked quite well. During this transaction, I was told to keep taking Aldactone, which is a hormone diuretic, but only one a day instead of the three I had been taking. I asked him why I should take this one pill, and his comment was, "Most of the time a person is given medicines to lower their blood pressure and it goes down. However, there is a gland on the kidney that controls certain aspects of blood pressure. After a time it recognizes that the blood pressure has changed since last it controlled it, so it takes an action to bring the blood pressure back to where the gland was controlling it before. The diuretic action of adactone is to keep the kidney busy so it won't push the blood pressure back up." Evidently he was right. The point is, the other two medicines he gave me had nothing to do with the kidney gland—one controlled my heart rate and the other was a beta blocker.

However, now that the genome is "known," studies will lead to information about how the various genes work and which share duties with other genes. Having the genome on a computer allows one to agitate one gene and see if there is a response elsewhere in the system. The interplay will provide valuable information about how the body's immune system works. Since each person is different in some way, doctors will be able to compare the codes of a group of people that have a given disease against a group of people that do not have the disease. Then they will compare what is common to the diseased group and isn't common on the disease-free group's code. This should lead them to a faster resolution of what it is that causes the disease. This would be fantastic information, since we know that the immune system works throughout the body. It reacts when you get a prick from a needle, and it works when a pathogen enters the body. It should be able to show us how the pathogen gets past the immune system and causes a disease that requires an antibiotic or some other response. Cause and effect is easier to study with a computer model containing the human genome. This is another wonder of life.

Late News!

Genome from one bacteria to another. As reported in the December 2007 article "Biologists Perform Genome Transplant" by Jocelyn Rice in the magazine *Discovery*, the J. Craig Venter Institute announced that they had successfully transplanted the genome of one species of bacteria into another bacterial species. "This was the ultimate identity theft," says Venter, a biologist well known for his private sector contribution to the sequencing of the human genome. "The chromosome (genome) that we put in took over the cell completely, and any characteristics of the original species were lost."

The transplant team took several steps to be sure the transfer was complete. First, they added two genes to the donor species' chromosome: one that made the cells resistant to the antibiotic tetracycline and one that made them turn blue. By dosing all the post-transplant bacteria with tetracycline and looking for blue colonies, the scientists could identify which cells contained the donor DNA. Next, they tested all the blue, tetracycline-resistant bacteria for any traces of the recipient species' genome. When they found none, they knew the bacteria must contain only the donor species' genome. Finally, they found that all the proteins manufactured by the new bacteria were characteristic of the donor species.

This is a critical advance in Venter's quest, which he has been pursuing for a decade: to create a fully synthetic life form. Now, he say, it could be just a matter of months before a living cell stocked with a synthetic genome becomes a reality.

HIV AND AIDS

When reviewing earlier the various diseases and ailments that man has endured, I didn't include HIV (human immunodeficiency virus) and AIDS (Acquired Immune Deficiency Syndrome) because of the nature of this disease. I felt that it was important for the reader to have a firm understanding of human DNA and RNA before reviewing the HIV virus and the related AIDS. These terrible diseases work almost like DNA and RNA, but in reverse. I talk about them separately, but they are both related.

A person acquires HIV before it turns into AIDS. In fact, the time from infection by HIV till a person is hit with AIDS is from two weeks to twenty years. On average, a person has the HIV virus for ten years before it degenerates into full-blown AIDS. You will be able to realize why this takes so long as we describe the method by which one acquires HIV and it eventually becomes full-blown AIDS.

Realizing that AIDS may not show up for ten years gives you a feeling of why it was so hard to track down what was happening when AIDS first began its assault on mankind. In the early 1980s, people began arrive at medical facilities around the world with symptoms that were like flu, or a bad cold, or pneumonia, and with sores and sicknesses that normally are more an irritant and not so persistent. Doctors found they could not relieve the symptoms with normal medications and treatments.

The fact that it appeared in various parts of the world at about the same time and with the same dire effects resulted in a great amount of research in looking for the cause of this pandemic. The first thing that made the sickness hard to isolate was that antibodies weren't found in the victims. Usually with the types of illness that were showing up, a medical exam would identify antibodies that the body generates to counteract the invader. The medical people and bioscientists test for antibodies; by identifying the antibody they can determine the antigen. After much time and research the doctors that were in charge of this type of research in the United States and France began to believe that the illness was caused by a retrovirus. (58) A retrovirus can remain in the body in an inactive role for a long length of time before having an effect. There is another problem that prevailed at the time of this invasion, as I remember reading in the paper at the time.

A retrovirus possesses a RNA-type system as opposed to a human DNA genome. A person can carry the HIV virus for days or weeks or years before showing any signs of antibodies in their system. A retrovirus is made up of an RNA which enters the person's system. It then invades the DNA by passing its RNA through the protective shell surrounding the nucleus. Remember how I discussed, with regard to a human, the messenger RNA's transcription of the DNA inside the nucleus and then the mRNA passing out the nucleus? This works just the opposite. The RNA of this retrovirus passes through the nucleus shell into the nucleus. Then a reverse transcription changes them from RNA to DNA, and that new DNA becomes a part of the person's DNA genome. This is a defective DNA genome. It replicates just like the original DNA, so it spreads into all the cells of the body.

At the time this was thought to be a retrovirus, the scientists of France and United States worked long and hard to determine the culprit. Each found the result at about the same time through different techniques. It was difficult to pinpoint using normal medical techniques because in most cases the DNA of an infected individual was not reviewed.

Years before, there had been another outbreak of a sickness in San Francisco, in the late 60s or early 70s. The head doctor who was in charge of the identification program for our country, Dr. Robert Gallo, called to see if the doctors in San Francisco had any samples of blood from that earlier event. They did, and they forwarded them to Washington, D.C. A review of the blood showed that indeed there was evidence of the same problem. However, in this case the antibodies were in the blood. Finally it was diagnosed by bioscientists in the U.S. and in France, and it was determined to be a retrovirus that invades the person's genetic material. Additional information at the time determined that this was a retrovirus that entered the system of a person through various rough sex acts; it was given various names, but finally the acronym AIDS—Acquired Immune Deficiency Syndrome—stuck. (59) The individual who acquired this disease acquired it through some misdemeanor of their own. It wasn't just a random disease that hit based on statistics, but it hit specific people in the various countries due to stretching the sex act too far. It was later determined that HIV is transmitted by infected body fluids. This included using needles previously used by others with the infection. Dope addicts were transmitters of this disease by injecting dope into an HIV infected body and then using the same needle to inject others. It was found that AIDS is transmitted by fluid transfer such as when a person is being operated on and a transfusion of blood is used. At the time blood banks were not screening the blood for this retrovirus. The original source of AIDS appeared to be through male homosexual sex acts. This, initially, was identified as the main cause of the disease, because the sex acts between two males were quite violent in nature. Anal sex acts could result in the tearing of the tissues and bleeding. For this reason the gay community in the U.S showed the effects of this problem early. Recent information indicates that the first carrier of this disease came from Haiti in 1969. So, this probably started the sickness that sometimes takes ten years to show up. As time passed, the HIV disease in the United States and other developed countries became prevalent in females also and eventually in newborn children who were infected by the disease.

As indicated, the HIV virus enters the person's system. He may not even show symptoms. In many cases infected persons don't realize they are infected and continue having sex. A person can carry HIV without any signs of infection for as long as ten to twenty years. Some people are actually immune to this disease due to some characteristic of their genome and other body functions. However, eventually, in most cases the HIV and the subsequent AIDS hits the person and hits them hard.

One of the other major factors relates to people using drugs that they inject using other people's needles. If the other person has HIV, it can be transferred via the needle into the person's blood. Since this mode of infection was brought to the world's attention, some locations in the United States and other countries have programs where they supply needles to drug users, so that they will not continue the practice of using infected needles. This program has helped. Another major cause was due to transfusions. Since this retrovirus was unknown and wasn't easy to find, blood donated by people with HIV would be used in operations on people who no risk factors for this disease; and they would end up suffering through no fault of their own. An African American tennis star, Arthur Ashe of the United States, was operated on for some minor problem and acquired the disease from tainted blood and eventually died of AIDS. This brought the problem to a high visibility because of Arthur Ash's popularity.

The main issue at the time was learning how to screen for the problem, especially a way of reviewing blood in the blood banks to determine the purity of the blood. The doctors had to find the virus so they could take samples and try various techniques for finding and eliminating the sources for it. The problem was that there were no good ways to obtain enough of the virus to work with. I remember reading twenty-five years ago about how they solved a part of this problem. The doctor in charge of the U.S. program, Robert Gallo, was trying to determine the nature of the disease and a possible cure, but couldn't find how to get enough of samples to work with. He and his assistants were not successful in finding a way to generate a significant number of the pathogens. Gallo had to leave to attend a conference in France concerning the subject matter. The French had done considerable work on this issue, and it was hoped that the combined inputs from each would result in a plan of attack Gallo left instructions with his lab assistants to try to find ways to generate enough of the virus so they could do battle with it. After Gallo left and they began to work on a method for generating large numbers of the HIV virus, the male technician remembered some effects he had seen on people with leukemia. He decided to try an experiment where he used this leukemia blood as the soup for the small sample he had of the HIV virus. The two prepared a broth of the leukemia blood and the HIV virus and placed it in an oven to keep the temperature constant. By the time they came back the next day and reviewed the results, they were shocked to see an enormous amount of the live virus on the microscope slide. They were excited by the results but didn't want to contact Dr. Gallo in France and excite him over something that may have just been a bit of good fortune. Gallo was a stickler on details and exact results and they didn't want to disturb him while he was in conference.

So they decided to try again. They set up the culture and had another go at it, and the next day they had the same results. They then decided to contact Gallo. They sent him a telegram and he got word in France that they had some success. He finished some immediate things he had to do and then flew back to Washington, D.C. He went directly to the lab where his technicians had set things up again, because they knew he was so thorough that he would have to see for himself. They discussed their method and what the results were and, sure enough, he wanted to see for himself. The next day the look through the microscope showed they had found the right recipe. Gallo was surprised by this rapid result from his two assistants. This now provided a method for producing enough of the virus to work on. It was under this framework that more was learned about the virus and how to screen for it in the blood held in the blood banks. Ever since that time, advances by bioscientists provided methods for screening of blood. Problems with the blood bank supplies have been very rare in developed societies over the last twenty years. During the 1980s and 1990s, many people would have a pint of their own blood set aside every six months and stored for any future problems that might occur; such as the need for an operation where they might need blood transfusions. Although this was a good idea for those wealthy enough to afford it, it was no longer needed as the blood banks became reliable.

When a retrovirus becomes part of a person's genome and is stored in the DNA of their chromosomes, it can be passed on to the next generation. The pregnancy of a woman results, as we have discussed, in a chromosome that is some mixture of the chromosomes of the two individuals involved. This means the DNA of the child may be infected. These are called endogenous retroviruses. Of an estimated 2.8 million lives lost to AIDS in 2005, 570,000 were children as a result of this scenario.

Sub-Saharan Africa remains by far the worst affected region, with an estimated 21.6 to 27.4 million people currently living with HIV. (61) Approximately two million of them are children under fifteen years of age. More than 64 percent of all people living with HIV are in sub-Saharan Africa, as are more than three-quarters of all women living with HIV. In 2005, there were between 10.6 and 13.6 million AIDS orphans living in sub-Saharan Africa

South and Southeast Asia are the second-worst affected regions, with 15 percent of the total. AIDS accounts for the deaths of 500,000 children in this region. Two-thirds of HIV and AIDS infections in Asia occur in India, with 9.4 million (0.9 percent of population), surpassing South Africa's estimated 4.9 to 6.1 million (11.9 percent of population) infections, making India the country with the highest number of HIV infections in the world. (34) In the thirty-five African nations with the highest prevalence, average life expectancy is 48.3 years—6.5 years less than it would be without the disease. [61]

There is no cure for HIV. There has been tremendous progress made in relieving the distress from this disease, especially in developed countries, where certain high-priced drugs are available. Because reverse transcription lacks the usual proofreading of DNA replication, this kind of virus mutates very often. This enables the virus to quickly grow resistant to antiviral pharmaceuticals and impedes the development of an effective vaccine against the retrovirus HIV. Two of the places in the body that become a major target for this disease are the tonsils and adenoids. I personally would recommend that, where medical treatment is available, that young people should have these removed. Perhaps the people affected with HIV should also have their tonsils and adenoids removed to at least eliminate this target area and reduce any discomforts in these areas.

There are other diseases that the HIV person can pass on other than HIV. People suffering from AIDS contract many other diseases due to their immune system's lack of response. Because of this, the victims may contract such diseases as tuberculosis, which could be passed on to a partner. Tuberculosis can be treated and cured, but it's not an easy battle. Acquired immune deficiency syndrome results in damage to the immune system that cannot be reversed. As the virus works its bad medicine on the immune system, the victims are hit with infections of all sorts. There are terrible flu-like symptoms, pneumonia or pneumonia-like symptoms, tumors, rashes, sores, breathing problems, eyesight problems—and the list goes on.

The only good thing about AIDS is that people without AIDS are now aware of how powerful their immune system must be to be able to counter and to keep all these illnesses at bay. The natural immunity that a body builds up is tremendous. People think they can't get rid of a cold, but they do. Once a cold has hit and the body builds up its immunity and the cold is conquered, the virus that caused that cold will not cause it any longer in the future. However, there are many viruses that cause colds, so they keep coming, especially in the winter each year. (People don't suffer from many of these illnesses in the southern hemisphere where it is warm. There are much fewer illnesses like colds and flu. In fact the word *flu* comes from the word *influenza,* which means "during cold weather.) Time after time, a person gets colds as he grows older. Many people at ages above fifty-five find themselves free of the colds they used to get. It's because they are immune to many strains, and they no longer have children bringing the new strains home from school. So, that is probably one advantage of old age.

Treatments for AIDS and HIV exist to decelerate the virus' progression in its victim, but with no known cure. The word is out as to how to prevent AIDS. The HIV virus is transmitted through bodily fluids. This includes anal, vaginal, or oral sex, blood contact to exposed wounds to the body, blood transfusion, contaminated hypodermic needles, and these types of antics. The best method to avoid the problem is not to have sex with anyone that is known to have the problem. The next best thing is not to have sex with someone you don't know or haven't known long enough to know their sex habits. There are steps to be taken to prevent exposure even if the sex partner is not known well enough, such as the use of condoms by men and condones made for women. Although not perfect, barrier methods are estimated to be 90+ percent perfect. In cases where consistent and correct use of condoms are maintained, couples where one partner is infected show that the HIV infection rate for the uninfected partner is less than 1 percent. Women are taught to carry condoms in case the opportunity arises and the male doesn't carry condoms. Women that happen to be promiscuous wear a rubber diaphragm inside their vagina and dispose or clean it after any intercourse. Being faithful is a strong course of action. This mostly applies to the male member of the marriage or partnership who is normally the one that feels the urge and doesn't want to take the time to put on a condom.

The use of clean needles and methods to ensure zero risk has changed in hospitals as well as by drug addicts. Different methods for extracting the needles to be used for a blood sample are not as casual as they once were. Needles are discarded religiously in the medical areas. Rubber gloves are worn in more places. A scratch occurring on a nurse is treated immediately. In basketball games if a player is injured and bleeds, he is removed from the game until the problem is corrected. I find that this scourge that has come in the form of HIV has resulted in techniques to prevent the spread of the disease and, probably more importantly, provided a higher level of hygiene throughout the medical and non-medical communities that did not prevail before this problem. This is probably the most encouraging progress, since it helps for all diseases, not just for HIV. There are additional steps taken, such as mothers who have HIV are told not to breastfeed their child so as not to pass this problem via this fluid.

UNAIDS and the World Health Organization estimate that AIDS has killed more than twenty-five million people since it was first recognized in 1981, making it one of the most destructive epidemics in recorded history. Despite recent improved access to antiretroviral treatment and care in many regions of the world, the AIDS epidemic claimed an estimated 2.8 million lives in 2005. Globally, between 33.4 and 46 million people currently live with HIV. In 2005, between 3.4 and 6.2 million people were newly infected, and between 2.4 and 3.3 million people with AIDS died, an increase from 2003 and the highest number since 1981. (59)

The development of highly active antiretroviral therapy (HAART) as effective therapy for HIV infection and AIDS has substantially reduced the death rate from this disease in those areas where these drugs are widely available. This has created the misperception that the disease has vanished. In fact, as the life expectancy of persons with AIDS has increased in countries where HAART is widely used, the number of persons living with AIDS has increased substantially. In the United States, the number of persons with AIDS increased from about 35,000 in 1988 to 220,000 in 1996. The life expectancy of those that are treated has increased to 32.2 years. In the absence of antiretroviral therapy, the median time of progression from HIV infection to AIDS is nine to ten years, and the median survival time after developing AIDS is only nine months. (59)

There was a recent short article in the New Yorker section of the *Wall Street Journal* by Michael Specter entitled, "A Look Back May Push AIDS Fight Ahead," which I thought was applicable to the subject I am covering here.

"The body's past battles against retroviruses such as HIV having been a major engine of evolution and perhaps lies behind some of the most important steps in human development," writes Michael Specter.

Scientists are gaining these insights by reconstructing extinct forms of retroviruses. Retroviruses reproduce by imprinting parts of themselves onto a cell's DNA. In some cases, this means they become a part of a species' DNA. The damaged remnants of retroviruses make up about 8 percent of the human genome. Many of those viral fragments are shared with chimpanzees and monkeys.

Scientists around the world have recently been reconstructing the original viruses from these fragments, careful to ensure the reborn diseases are able to reproduce themselves only once.

This has been sufficient to show the role retroviruses have played in human development. For instance, they seem to have led mammals to form a placenta, which makes it possible to produce offspring with larger brains than egg-laying animals.

Another reconstructed virus might provide a clue as to why HIV, which infects chimpanzees as easily as it does humans, doesn't harm them.

A recent experiment showed that humans have developed an effective defense against an extinct retrovirus, called PtERV (pronounced "pea-terv"). Chimpanzees haven't. The experiment suggested that this lack of a defense against one retrovirus actually makes chimpanzees immune to the effects of another, HIV.

This approach is still decades away from creating a cure for AIDS, Mr. Specter says, but already has suggested new lines of attack.

Each of these types of experiments going on all over the world are bringing a learning curve to the scientists trying to find a cure for AIDS or finding a means of preventing the virus.

The impact of AIDS on the world is evident when one looks at the median ages of the various countries of the world. The median age in Africa is nineteen years, which is the youngest of any continent. The country with the lowest median age in the world is also found on the African continent: Uganda. The landlocked East African nation of Uganda has a median age of fifteen years, meaning that half the country's population is younger than fifteen years old and half is older. In contrast, Mauritius, an island off East Africa, with a median age of thirty-one years, has the highest average in Africa. (59)

The median age in India, the world's second most populous country, is twenty-four. In comparison, the median age in China is much higher, at thirty-four years.

HIV and AIDS are hard to get!

It's important that the reader understands that HIV and AIDS are impossible to contract. What do I meant by that? I mean just as I say. Humans have to go out of their way to get AIDS. With proper attention, HIV and the resultant AIDS is very hard to acquire. You can't get it from kissing, even though there's an exchange of fluids in this act. You can't get it from tears in the eyes from one to another. You can't get it from the door knobs of men's or women's bathroom facilities. If a person with these two diseases leaves a bathroom facility after relieving themselves or having masturbated and put their hands on the doorknob, you won't get HIV or AIDS if you place your hand on that doorknob. You won't get it from the commode seat in the bathroom. You won't contact HIV from urine. The HIV virus is very weak under normal conditions. The HIV virus cannot retain its potential under normal living conditions, such as being exposed to everyday air. It doesn't lie around waiting to infect a person like some bacteria do. Chances are you won't even get it from semen from a person unless it involves sexual intercourse that is rough in nature. The biggest risks come from blood transfusion in those countries or areas where blood is not screened or there is a transfusion directly from a person who has the disease. From direct transfusion from a person with the disease, the estimated risk is 90 percent. Childbirth by an infected mother has a 25 percent risk. From here, the risk factor drops to less than 1 percent for the widely distributed list of potential sources, such as oral sex and anal sex—less than one percent out of 10,000 incidents.

So, what does this mean? It means that after learning about this disease for about twenty-five years, the data shows it is hard to acquire HIV and the related AIDS. It is not contagious. It is not like any other disease that you might think about and worry about contracting, diseases like cancer, tuberculosis, influenza, infection, staphylococcus, pneumonia, streptococcus, malaria, and many other diseases that may come your way no matter how well you live. It's not like other illnesses that are a function of your age and cause heart failure, or hardening of the arteries, or liver failure and those things that eventually will happen to each of us if we live long enough. Having any of these normal illnesses when and if they come your way is a matter of statistics, your basic health, where you live, surgery, heredity, accidents that lead to other complications, your environment; and so on. You will die from something.

However, you will not get HIV and the eventual AIDS no matter what, as long as you live a natural, healthy life away from unprotected sex—at least in this country. You can't get it from breathing right next to a person with AIDS. If you could, there would be many doctors and nurses in this world with the infection. It's almost impossible to acquire HIV if you live a normal life. AIDS is what it says it is; Acquired Immune Deficiency. You have to go out of your way to acquire HIV and the resultant AIDS.

Late News on Advances on HIV

Wake Forest Scientists Find Way To Short-Circuit Initial HIV Invasion

ScienceDaily (Oct. 14, 1997) — WINSTON-SALEM Scientists at Wake Forest University Baptist Medical Center announced a finding on how to stop HIV invasion

In a report in the Oct 14 issue of the *Proceedings of the National Academy of Sciences*, **Si.-Yi Chen, M.D., Ph.D.**, assistant professor of cancer biology, and his colleagues describe how they have inactivated the most frequently used co-receptor—docking site—for HIV-1 viruses on the surface of both macrophages and lymphocytes, resulting in immunity of those macrophages and lymphocytes to HIV-1 infection.

Two weeks ago, the same team reported in *Nature Medicine* that they had found a way to inactivate a different co-receptor—CXCR4—which is the docking site for late stage HIV-1 virus, known medically as T-cell tropic virus.

In the late stage of AIDS, HIV-1 viruses change their infectivity to T-cell tropic, and use the CXCR4 receptor to get into the lymphocytes.

So, blocking entry of that type of virus into the cell blocks the late stages of AIDS.

The approach described in *Nature Medicine* could be utilized to treat AIDS patients and late stage HIV-1-infected individuals, while the approach described in *Proceedings* could be used to treat early-stage of HIV-infected individuals and may be some day be used to prevent HIV-1 infection Chen said that the intrakine approach avoids technical problems facing many current gene therapy approaches. In treating people Chen envisions that, in the near future, human macrophages and lymphocytes from an infected patient's peripheral blood can be genetically modified with the appropriate intrakine, and periodically reinfused back into patients to delay the disease progression.

His group is now in the stage of pre-clinical study to further evaluate the efficacy and safety of this intrakine approach, and clinical trials in humans are a year or more away.

As you read the following portion of the book on stem cells, you will find that as you approach the end of the subject it starts to fit in the curing of, or the preventing of AIDS by other methods. That's my personal look at it.

STEM CELLS AND RESEARCH

And now we come to the great hope: the hope to cure many of the sicknesses that are not promiscuous-type illnesses or illnesses spread by bacteria; but are sicknesses of statistics —100 percent statistics. All of us are going to die, some at early ages. In the developed countries the average age of death is going up, but when people become sixty or older, they start to wear down. Those cells we discussed are starting to have problems. Some start having Parkinson's disease at the age of fifty; or if not fifty, sixty or seventy. Some will die of heart problems also starting at about the age of sixty or so. Some will die of hepatitis, at almost any age. Some will die of liver failure, starting at around sixty years of age. Some will die of kidney failure, usually at the upper ages. Some become crippled for life at any age due to accidents or other precocious events. The list goes on. Most people would like to live to the age of ninety or so, but if one of the above gets hold of you, your chances go down rapidly. How about senility, or the advanced cases of Alzheimer's diseases, where you don't know who you are and should be dead because you have become a burden to those closest to you?

When you look at the above list, you should think about how well life has treated you and be thankful for the increased longevity we now enjoy. At the start of the twentieth century, the average life span was forty-two years. It is now around seventy-six years. That's remarkable. That's what this book is about. It's about the diseases man has met and defeated. It's about how man became educated, and how the added knowledge from his own experiences or the experiences of others has led him to the present-day wonders of man's inventiveness. Many bacterial diseases were overcome with the advent of the higher power microscopes and electron microscopes; along with anti-bacterial medications developed since the mid-1800s and during the first half of the twentieth century.

Our more recent battles have been against viral-type sicknesses. This story has been about the learning curve we have been on and how we have learned. Of course, we learned from of the dead bodies that preceded us and the hard-working doctors, scientists, bioscientists, physicists, nurses, and many others.

When I graduated as an electrical engineer, I was very proud. I became even more proud when I developed new things that made life easier, happier, or better for mankind in some way. Later I became disenchanted. The integrated circuits I had invented and helped to make manufacturing success stories were turning out television sets, improved cars, games for people to play, reducing the power required for the technical achievement of an event through the use of transistors and integrated circuits compared to vacuum tubes and the many other technologies we zipped past.

One day I visited an RCA plant in Indiana. This was in the middle sixties. After touring the plant that made television sets, I stood on a hill that overlooked the plant and talked to the plant manager. I looked out at the land and said, "You know what, I am not proud of what I do. As I look out over the land surrounding your plant and I see bees flying around on the flowers along this hillside, I think they do more than I do for people. They bring food and color to people. All I bring are television sets and other electronic elements that allow man to have fun, and nothing else do I add to mankind." He didn't know what I was talking about. I knew. If I stopped making these things, man would not suffer one bit less because they don't bring anything vital to man. I went away and returned to work in a couple of days. But what I meant stuck with me.

Later in life I was to be operated on for a blockage of blood in my carotid artery. When I entered the operating room flat on my back and was waiting for them to put me to sleep and begin the operation, I looked around at the fantastic equipment they had. Then the surgeon began to fidget with an oscilloscope that they were hooking up to me, and he couldn't get it to work properly. He called for help, and a technician in a white coat and face mask entered the operating room and looked at the hookup. He said, "Oh, I see that you are using the red cable; it's supposed to be the blue one," which he proceeded to change. I began laughing as I lie looking up from the operating table, and the doctor said, "What are you laughing about? I said "This reminds me of being back at work, where the same types of things happen with the electronic equipment, and it hit me as funny." He smiled and began to insert the needle into the IV drip inserted into my arm. As he was doing that I said, "You know, as I look around and see all the electronic equipment you now use to help safe people's lives, I feel good about what I do. What I do provides the electronics that allows doctors to see things better through electron microscopes and hear things better through electronics, and measure things better," and I mentioned several other things. Before he put me to sleep I felt good about myself and what I do for people and people's lives.

Why do I mention this? How does it relate to stem cells and stem cell research? I provide the reader with my experience because I believe it could and should provide readers with better insight into how their work might someday relate to the total experience that provides a better understanding of things you are not aware or aren't familiar with. You won't know how what you know might connect to some other work and allow people to solve a problem they haven't been able to solve. It may help solve the eventual use of stem cells in medicine. Remember the discussion about the microscope and how it helped to see bacteria and then they were able to find something to eliminate the bacteria. When the electron microscope came along it allowed the scientists to see the workings of the DNA, the amino acids, the proteins and much more. The MRI is an invention that allows one to see the internal organs by magnetically causing them to resonate and then a computer puts the pieces together and you see a picture of your brain or some other organ. The fight against disease, organ failure, infection, and many

THE WONDER OF LIFE

other things is an easier battle when you can see what you are working with and against. So, it isn't only the bioscientists and doctors that are fighting these phenomena, it's the engineers of the world as well – and probably many others that are not engineers but have innate intelligence that helps to solve the problems.

This is not just a medical issue; it requires invention in all forms of equipment that can allow better analysis of stem cells and their application. Remember that the solution of the genome came down to computers and their speed, which allowed the genome to be resolved to the level it has been resolved. Without the computer they would have been working on the solution for decades. As I mentioned in my case, one does the best he or she can in their chosen fields, not knowing what impact it can have on other fields of endeavor, or, in this particular case, how it could impact stem cell research and improve the life of mankind. You can help. What you do may have an impact. The equipment you produce could help in many ways to reduce illnesses, or reduce the effect they have on a person. Each of us should strive to do the best we can in the work we produce, not knowing where it will be used.

Now, let's look into stem cells and what is known at this time. The section on normal human cells should have provided a good base for understanding stem cells. Stem cells have three basic characteristics that are different than the standard cells I discussed:

> *They are **uncommitted cells**: That is, they are not the standard cell that one finds at the fertilizing of a female egg by a male sperm that contains chromosomes that are within the original cell and are a mix of the twenty-three chromosome pairs from the male and female. That first cell is a committed cell. It cannot change. It may be different than either of the parents (and is). Likewise as the cells replicate, they do so as duplicates of the initial cell and its inherited characteristics.

> *Like a standard cell, stem cells divide like regular cells and **continue generating new cells**. Therefore, they

can carry out continual replications, like a standard cell. This is a paramount requirement.

*The stem cell has **no identifying tag.** (They are undifferentiated.) They can be, it is believed, any part of the body that requires cells; whereas the cells that form in the human body soon after conception become tagged for providing functions of certain areas of the body and providing that function. Stem cells are in a position to be tagged later in their cycle to become a muscle, a heart part, a pancreatic insulin supplier, or other things not suggested at this time in its development.

It has been proven experimentally in mice and other animals that the stem cell can be used to become cells with these special functions, such as heart cells, skin cells, and probably many other cells. In this case they would be tagged to do that special function one wants to occur.

So, what do we have here? The one thing we hope we have is the same ability found when we were able to achieve bone marrow transplants successfully using stem cells. Yes, you read that right. Stem cells from a donor's bone marrow transplant were the way certain ailments were overcome many years ago. Let's review what occurs during bone marrow transplant.

Bone marrow transplant using stem cells
Hematopoietic stem cell transplantation (HSCT)

Bone marrow transplant has been around for over thirty years. The reason for bringing it to your attention in this book is to make you aware that a stem cell procedure has been in effect for this long. Many of the readers will understand the reason for this remark since today there is a pro and con battle going on about stem cells. Most of it relates to conjecture about whether stem cell technology will actually be effective in curing many of the problems with organs and illnesses such as Parkinson disease and many others. At the same time there is a battle going on about whether it is ethical to take stem cells from the birth of a new baby. These are embryonic stem cells and some believe they represent life and should not be used for research. This is a philosophic discussion and beyond the scope of this book.

Before discussing bone marrow transplant it helps if you understand that *HLA* stands for human leukocyte antigens before you start reading. Also remember that antigens turn on the body's immune system. That's when our antibodies become initiated to fight the antigens.

Hematopoietic stem cell transplantation (HSCT) is the transplantation of blood stem cells derived from the bone marrow (that is, bone marrow transplantation) or blood. Stem cell transplantation is a medical procedure in the field of hematology oncology, most often performed for people with diseases of the blood, bone marrow, or certain types of cancer.

Stem cell transplantation was pioneered using bone-marrow-derived stem cells by a team at Fred Hutchinson Cancer Research Center from the 1950s through the 1970s, led by E. Donnall Thomas, whose work was later recognized with a Nobel Prize in Physiology and Medicine. Thomas' work showed that bone marrow cells infused intravenously could repopulate the bone marrow and produce new blood cells. His work also reduced the likelihood of developing a life-threatening complication called Graft-versus-host disease. With the availability of the stem cell growth factors GM-CSF G-CSF, most hematopoeitic stem cell transplantation procedures are now performed using stem cells collected from peripheral blood, rather than from the bone marrow. Collecting stem cells provides a bigger graft and does not require that the donor be subjected to general anesthesia to collect the graft. (92)

Hematopoietic stem cell transplants remain a risky procedure with many possible complications; it has always been reserved for patients with life-threatening diseases.

Many recipients of HSCTs are leukemia patients who would benefit from treatment with high doses of chemotherapy or total body irradiation. Other conditions treated with stem cell transplants include sickle-cell disease, myelodysplastic syndrome, neuroblastoma, lymphoma, Ewing's

Sarcoma, Desmoplastic small round cell tumor Hodgkin's disease, and multiple myeloma. More recently non-myeloablative, or so-called "mini transplant," procedures have been developed that require smaller doses of preparative chemo and radiation. Mini transplants remain in the experimental domain of medicine as of May, 2007. (92)

Allogeneic HSCT involves two people: one is the (healthy) donor and one is the (patient) recipient. This is the method that was used for many years before newer approaches were used. You probably have heard of someone with leukemia and they were looking for bone marrow transplant donors. They would test the potential donor and see if certain criteria was met and if it was then they would allow that person to donate their bone marrow. This worked at a very low percentage till more was found about how the body worked and before they found other methods of obtaining Allogeneic HSC donors must have a tissue (HLA) (human leukocyte antigens) type that matches the recipient's. Matching is performed on the basis of variability at three loci of the (HLA) gene, and a perfect match at these loci is preferred. Even if there is a good match at these critical alleles (alleles are gene locations on a person's chromosome, similar to addresses. Certain alleles are known to possess certain capabilities for controlling specific events in the body), the recipient will suffer rejection and immunosuppressive medications will be taken for life to eliminate graft-versus-host disease. Allogeneic transplant donors may be related (usually a closely HLA matched sibling) or unrelated (donor who is not related and found to have very close degree of HLA matching). Allogeneic transplants are also performed using umbilical cord blood as the source of stem cells.

Donor selection to graft-versus-host disease. The donor should have the same human leukocyte antigens (HLA) as the recipient. About 25 to 30 percent of potential HSCT recipients have an HLA-identical sibling. Even so-called "perfect matches" may have mismatched minor alleles that contribute to graft-versus-host disease.

Autologous HSCT involves isolation of haematopoietic stems cells (HSC) from the patient and storage of the harvested cells in a freezer.

This is the more modern approach since the discovery of stem cells located elsewhere in the body that could be used. (See the following section on adult stem cells) The patient is then treated with high-dose radiation, with or without radiotherapy, in the form of total body irradiation to eradicate the patient's malignant cell population. This is at the cost of also eliminating the bone marrow stem cells, before returning the patient's own stored stem cells to their body. This is a tricky situation also since the person after this radiation has a low immunity to diseases until his body has recovered its immune system. Autologous transplants have the advantage of a lower risk of graft rejection and infection. However, the recovery of immune function is quite rapid and the patient is soon able to resume his normal body functions. The incidence of a patient experiencing graft-versus-host disease is close to none, as the donor and recipient is one and the same.

Sources of HSC. Peripheral blood stem cells are now the most common source of stem cells for HSCT. They are collected from the blood through a process known as apheresis. The donor's blood is withdrawn through a sterile needle in one arm and passed through a machine that removes white blood cells. The red blood cells are returned to the donor. The peripheral stem cell yield is boosted with daily subcutaneous injections of Granulocyte-colony stimulating factor, which mobilizes stem cells from the donor's bone marrow into the peripheral circulation. (92) Umbilical cord blood is obtained when parents elect to harvest and store the blood from a newborn's umbilical cord after birth. (This is the same as embryonic stem cells that will be discussed, but is done on the live newborn baby to be kept in storage for any future medical use.) Cord blood has a higher concentration of HSC than is normally found in adult blood. (Keep this in mind to tell your children so when they have their children, they can take advantage of this step. Of course, by the time this event happens I would hope that technology has advanced to the point where on the birth of a baby, they do a fairly easy test to tell if the baby has any issues. A more distant time from now [Nov. 27, 2007], and they may know it while the baby is still in the mother and know what to do then in situ or immediately after birth. We will see.)

Storage of HSC. Unlike other organs, bone marrow cells can be frozen for prolonged time periods (cryopreserved) without damaging too many cells. This is necessary for autologous HSC because the cells must be harvested months in advance of the transplant treatment. In the case of allogeneic transplants, fresh HSC are preferred in order to avoid cell loss that might occur during the freezing and thawing process. Allogeneic cord blood is stored frozen at a cord blood bank because it is only obtainable at the time of childbirth. HSC may be stored for years in a cryofreezer, which typically uses liquid nitrogen because it is non-toxic and it is very cold (boiling point: -196°C.) It is my personal understanding that this is not a well known procedure to "about to be" parents and therefore this is not usually a method chosen due to ignorance. It is also my understanding that the "about to be" parents don't know enough about any deficiencies their newborn will have that would require this procedure. Hopefully, by the time of a birth in a reader's life; the medical level will have advanced to the point that this option is academic. I hope so.

Non-myeloablative (or "mini") allogeneic transplants, because of their gentler conditioning regimens, are associated with a lower risk of transplant-related mortality and therefore allow patients who are considered too high-risk for conventional allogeneic HSCT to undergo potentially curative therapy for their disease. These new transplant strategies are experimental, for the most part, and available at academic research centers.

After several weeks of growth in the bone marrow, expansion of HSC and their progeny is sufficient to normalize the blood cell counts and reinitiate the immune system. Donor-derived hematopoeitic stem cells have been documented to populate many different organs of the recipient, including heart, liver, and muscle—a phenomenon known as stem cell plasticity.

HSCT is associated with a fairly high mortality in the recipient (10 percent or higher), which limits its use to conditions that are themselves life-threatening. Major causes of complications are veno-occlusive disease mucositis, infection-sepsis, and graft-versus-host disease.

Get the picture?

The fact that bone marrow transplants have been around for years and have proved to be successful leads today's bioscientists to be optimistic that we could have the same, if not better, success in the future. Experience has shown in many cases that the use of one's own stem cells eliminates the effect of the body's rejection, as can happen when there is a donor involved. (I will be discussing new stem cell breakthroughs in a later part of this book which should start making inroads on many medical problems.)

I hope this overview gives the reader a better picture of a traumatic procedure where stem cells were the only chance for life for many people suffering from what were then called irreversible diseases. Now take into account that this is a procedure established over many years, the first where stem cells were used as the cure for a sure death. This hopefully prepares the reader for the discussion I will now pursue concerning stem cell research and, more specifically, embryonic stem cell and other promising new types of stem cell research. You can see that bone marrow transplants began with one approach, but experience led to other approaches, some based on boundaries set by the physical limits of the recipient. This was a learning process that took time, patience, creativity, and bright minds. For this reason I support the push for several types of stem cell research that have shown promise. It takes a long time from promise to employment on a large-scale basis. I believe that politics and misunderstandings by some religious groups have slowed down progress.

First, some background. Bioscientists prioritize their work on stem cells from animals and humans with embryonic stem cells and adult stem cells, each of which may have better characteristics for specific uses in the near future. It's interesting to know that we owe most of our advances to the little mouse. Their embryos have been studied for over twenty years and resulted in the 1998 findings of how to obtain and isolate stem cells from human embryos. This had lead to further laboratory research . Human embryonic stem cells were created to provide families with infertility issues some means of fertility. This work was done using in vitro fertilization and has been practiced for years.

The Unique Properties of Stem Cells

Stem cells differ from other kinds of cells in the body. All stem cells—regardless of their source—have three general properties: they are capable of dividing and renewing themselves for long periods; they are unspecialized; and they can give rise to specialized cell types. First, let's review the meanings of a few terms you will find in this write up.

Differentiation. This is the process where the cell goes from an undefined option to a defined option. Bioscientists need the stem cell to remain undefined. They want to be able to use it in an undefined state and have it change when they need it to, preferably when injected into a patient. When a cell is undefined it means it has not been programmed, naturally or otherwise. It is like a person's head without a brain. Without a brain, there is no action/reaction to stimuli. It is like a person who is medically brain dead, without a connection to reality or access to mobility. In this case it is a cell without a defined task.

Proliferation. This is the process by which the embryonic cells keep multiplying. Bioscientists would like for the cells to proliferate without differentiation so as to have many of them to work with. Stem cells are capable of dividing and renewing themselves for long periods, while remaining undifferentiated. Unlike muscle cells, blood cells, or nerve cells—which do not normally replicate themselves—stem cells may replicate many times. When cells replicate themselves many times over, it is called proliferation. A base population of stem cells that proliferates for many months in the laboratory can yield millions of cells. If the resulting cells continue to be unspecialized, like the parent stem cells, the cells are said to be capable of long-term self-renewal.

Unspecialized. Stem cells are unspecialized. One of the fundamental properties of a stem cell is that it does not have any tissue-specific structures that allow it to perform specialized functions. A stem cell cannot work with its neighbors to pump blood through the body (like a heart muscle cell); it cannot carry molecules of oxygen through the bloodstream (like a red blood cell); and it cannot fire signals to other cells that allow the body to move or speak (like a nerve cell). However, bioscientists want to use unspecialized stem cells and change them to specialized cells to perform the functions I just mentioned—specific functions, including heart muscle cells, blood cells, or nerve cells.

Scientists are trying to understand two fundamental aspects of stem cells that relate to long-term self-renewal: Why can embryonic stem cells proliferate for a year or more in the laboratory without differentiating, but adult stem cells cannot? (this was a rather old question and bioscientists have found that adult stem cells can proliferate for long periods of time.(I will be discussing this in a later section of this book)? And what are the factors in living organisms that normally regulate stem cell proliferation and self-renewal? We will discuss.

Discovering the answers to these questions may make it possible to understand how cell proliferation is regulated during normal embryonic development or during the abnormal cell division that leads to cancer. Importantly, such information would enable scientists to grow embryonic and adult stem cells more efficiently in the laboratory.

The specific factors and conditions that allow stem cells to remain unspecialized are of great interest to scientists. It has taken scientists many years of trial and error to learn to grow stem cells in the laboratory without them spontaneously differentiating into specific cell types. For example, it took twenty years to learn to grow embryonic stem cells in the laboratory following the development of conditions for growing mouse stem cells. (This long time span is one of the main reasons a great deal of time and effort remains on this subject. The political and questionable moral issues have held these programs back for many years.) Therefore, an important area of research is understanding the signals in a mature organism that cause a stem cell population to proliferate and remain unspecialized until the cells are needed for repair of a specific tissue. Such information is critical for scientists to be able to grow large numbers of unspecialized stem cells in the laboratory for further experimentation.

Stem cells can give rise to specialized cells. When unspecialized stem cells give rise to specialized cells, the process is *differentiation*. Scientists are just beginning to understand the signals inside and outside cells that trigger stem cell differentiation. The internal signals are controlled by a cell's genes, which are interspersed across long strands of DNA and carry coded instructions for all the structures and functions of a cell. The external signals for cell differentiation include chemicals secreted by other cells, physical contact with neighboring cells, and certain molecules in microenvironment.

Therefore, many questions about stem cell differentiation remain. For example, are the internal and external signals for cell differentiation similar for all kinds of stem cells? Can specific sets of signals be identified that promote differentiation into specific cell types? Addressing these questions is critical because the answers may lead scientists to find new ways of controlling stem cell differentiation in the laboratory, thereby growing cells or tissues that can be used for specific purposes, including cell-based therapies.

Embryonic stem cells, as their name suggests, are derived from embryos.

There are two types of embryonic stem cells: The first involves those cells derived from a woman's uterus. Embryonic stem cells are derived from embryos at a developmental stage before the time that implantation would normally occur in the uterus. Fertilization normally occurs in the oviduct, and during the first few days, a series of cleavage divisions occur as the embryo travels down the oviduct and into the uterus. (60) Each of the cells (*blastomeres*) of these cleavage-stage embryos is undifferentiated. Each of these blastomeres has the potential to give rise to any cell of the body.

These cells are removed before the first differentiation event, which occurs at approximately five days of development in humans, when an outer layer of cells is committed to becoming part of the placenta. (This is an interesting fact that I had previously discussed; i.e. that in human being the first task in the development of the baby is the development of the placenta. It is believed that this is why the human has such a large brain; due to the protection this provides while in the womb.) The inner cell mass (ICM) cells have the potential to generate any cell type of the body. But after implantation, they are quickly depleted, as they differentiate to other cell types with more limited potential. If the ICM is removed from its normal embryonic environment and cultured under appropriate conditions, the ICM-derived cells can continue to proliferate and replicate themselves indefinitely and still maintain the developmental potential to form any cell type of the body. They essentially obtain the level of *pluripotency*. These pluripotent, ICM-derived cells are embryonic stem cells (es). Incidentally, I mentioned that cells after the five days would normally begin to develop the placenta. It's interesting that this would have been the first step in the normal process because many scientists believe that the human-evolved placenta is one of the characteristics that makes a human unique and may be the reason the human brain is larger and capable of higher intellect.

The second method relates to embryonic stem cells (es) that are derived from embryos that develop from eggs that have been fertilized in an in vitro fertilization clinic and then donated for research purposes, with informed consent of the donors. These cells were fertilzed in vitro for infertile couples. The female egg is fertilized by sperm donated from the husband, in most cases. Such embryos are not derived from eggs fertilized in a woman's body. In the case of in vitro fertilization, many fertilized eggs remain after the medical procedure is completed, and the resulting embryonic stem cells would be thrown away. With the present understanding of the use of embryonic stem cells for medical research, there are more donors giving their consent.

The embryos from which human embryonic stem cells are derived are typically four or five days old and are a hollow microscopic ball of cells called the *blastocyst*. The blastocyst includes three structures: *trophoblast*, which is the layer of cells that surrounds the blastocyst; *blastocoel*, which is the hollow cavity inside the blastocyst; and *inner cell mass*, which is a group of approximately thirty cells at one end of the blastocoel.

Growing cells in the laboratory is known as cell culture. Human embryonic stem cells are isolated by transferring the inner cell mass into a plastic laboratory culture dish that contains a nutrient broth known as culture medium. The cells divide and spread over the surface of the dish. The inner surface of the culture dish is typically coated with mouse embryonic skin cells that have been treated so they will not divide. This coating layer of cells is called the feeder layer. The reason for having the mouse cells in the bottom of the culture dish is to provide the inner cell mass (ICM) cells with a sticky surface to which they can attach. Also, the feeder cells release nutrients into the culture medium. Recently, scientists have begun to devise ways of growing embryonic stem cells without the mouse feeder cells, because of the risk that viruses or other macromolecules in the mouse cells may be transmitted to the human cells. This is a significant scientific advancement.

Pluripotent /embryonic stem cell line

Over the course of several days, the cells of the inner cell mass proliferate and begin to crowd the culture dish. When this occurs, they are removed gently and plated into several fresh culture dishes. The process of replating the cells is repeated many times and for many months and is called *subculturing*. Each cycle of subculturing the cells is referred to as passage. After six months or more, the original thirty cells of the inner cell mass yield millions of embryonic stem cells. Embryonic stem cells that have proliferated in cell culture for six or more months without differentiating are pluripotent and appear genetically normal; they are referred to as an *embryonic stem cell line.*

Once cell lines are established, or even before that stage, batches of them can be frozen and shipped to other laboratories for further culture and experimentation.

Testing for embryonic cells

At various points during the process of generating embryonic stem cell lines, scientists test the cells to see whether they exhibit the fundamental properties that make them embryonic stem cells. This process, called *characterization*, mainly assesses their ability to continue dividing without differentiation occurring.

As yet (to my knowledge), scientists who study human embryonic stem cells have not agreed on a standard battery of tests that measure the cells' fundamental properties. Also, scientists acknowledge that many of the tests they use may not be good indicators of the cells' most important biological properties and functions. Nevertheless, laboratories that grow human embryonic stem cell lines use several kinds of tests. These tests include:

*Growing and sub-culturing the stem cells for many months. This ensures that the cells are capable of long-term self-renewal. Scientists inspect the cultures on a routine basis through a microscope to see that the cells look healthy and remain undifferentiated.

*Using specific techniques to determine the presence of surface markers that are found only on undifferentiated cells.

*Testing for the presence of a protein called Oct-4, which undifferentiated cells typically make. Oct-4 is a transcription factor, meaning that it helps genes turn on and off at the right time, which is an important part of the processes of cell differentiation and embryonic development.

*Examining the chromosomes under a microscope to assess whether the chromosomes remain undamaged or if the number of chromosomes has changed. It does not detect genetic mutations in the cells.

*Determining whether the cells can be subcultured after freezing, thawing, and replating.

*Testing whether the human embryonic stem cells are pluripotent by a) allowing the cells to differentiate spontaneously in cell culture; b) manipulating the cells so they will differentiate to form specific cell types; or c) injecting the cells into an immunosuppressed mouse to test for the formation of a benign tumor called a *teratoma*. Teratomas typically contain a mixture of many differentiated or partly differentiated cell types—indications that the embryonic stem cells are capable of differentiating into multiple cell types.

As long as the embryonic stem cells in culture are grown under certain conditions, they can remain undifferentiated (unspecialized). But if cells are allowed to clump together to form embryoid bodies, they begin to differentiate spontaneously. They can form muscle cells, nerve cells, and many other cell types. Although spontaneous differentiation is a good indication that a culture of embryonic stem cells is healthy, it is not an efficient way to produce cultures of specific cell types.

So, to generate cultures of specific types of differentiated cells—heart muscle cells, blood cells, or nerve cells, for example—scientists try to control the differentiation of embryonic stem cells. They change the chemical composition of the culture medium, alter the surface of the culture dish, or modify the cells by inserting specific genes. Through years of experimentation, scientists have established some basic protocols, or "recipes," for the directed differentiation of embryonic stem cells into certain specific cell types.

If scientists can reliably direct the differentiation of embryonic stem cells into specific cell types, they may be able to use the resulting differentiated cells to treat certain diseases at some point in the future. Diseases that might be treated by transplanting cells generated from human embryonic stem cells include Parkinson's disease, diabetes, traumatic spinal cord injury, Purkinje cell degeneration, Duchenne's muscular dystrophy, heart disease, and vision and hearing loss.

ADULT STEM CELLS

An *adult stem cell* is an undifferentiated cell found among differentiated cells in a tissue or organ. (60) It can renew itself and can differentiate to yield the major specialized cell types of the tissue or organ. The primary roles of adult stem cells in a living organism are to maintain and repair the tissue in which they are found. Some scientists now use the term *somatic stem cell* instead of adult stem cell. While the origin of embryonic stem cells, which are defined by their origin (inner cell mass of blastocyst) are well known, the origin of adult stem cells in mature tissues is unknown. The adult stem cell was not discovered until recently, except for those for bone marrow use. There are several reasons why they took longer to recognize, but the main one is the lack of pursuing this cell due to ignorance.

Scientists became familiar with the embryonic stem cell, and as their knowledge grew, they began to look throughout the body for some signs of a cell of this nature. It is now known that they can be found in almost every cell location of the body. One had to look hard and know what to look for and how to look. They are minor in number compared to the differentiated cells. The discovery of adult stem cells reminds me of an analogous situation that I wrote about in the early parts of this book related to heavy water. Heavy water is found in every water, but it is hard to find unless one knows what to look for. There is approximately one heavy water molecule for every thousand or so normal molecules. Once you know what to look for, they are easy to find. Evidently adult stem cells exist in every part of the body, and they probably look slightly different to the viewer in the different parts of the body. But they are there, and very recent experience is finding them readily available. This may be the next major impact on stem cell research—in fact, it may be here already.

Plasticity of Adult Stem Cells

Adult stem cells are cells removed from an adult's tissue. They typically generate the cell type of the tissue in which they reside. A blood-forming adult stem cell in the bone marrow, for example, normally gives rise to the many types of blood cells, such as red blood cells, white blood cells, and platelets. Until recently, it had been thought that a blood-forming cell in the bone marrow—called a hematopoietic stem cell (which we have discussed)—could not give rise to the cells of a very different tissue, such as nerve cells in the brain. However, a number of experiments over the last several years have raised the possibility that stem cells from one tissue may be able to give rise to cell types of a completely different tissue type, a phenomenon known as *plasticity*. Examples of plasticity include blood cells becoming neurons, liver cells that can be made to produce insulin, and hematopoietic stem cells that can develop into heart muscle. Therefore, exploring the possibility of using adult stem cells for cell-based therapies has become a very active area of investigation by researchers. This research is not subject to the politics that affect embryonic cell research. No unborn babies are lost when researching adult stem cells for high plasticity.

Research on adult stem cells has recently generated a great deal of excitement. Scientists have found adult stem cells in many more tissues than they once thought possible. This finding has led scientists to ask whether adult stem cells could be used for transplants. In fact, adult blood-forming stem cells from bone marrow have been used in transplants for thirty years. Certain kinds of adult stem cells seem to have the ability to differentiate into a number of various cell types, given the right conditions. If differentiation of adult stem cells can be controlled in the laboratory, these cells may become the basis of therapies for many serious common diseases.

Some history

The history of research on adult stem cells began about forty years ago. In the 1960s, researchers discovered that the bone marrow contains at least two kinds of stem cells. One population, hematopoietic stem cells, forms all the types of blood cells in the body. A second population, called bone marrow stromal cells, was discovered a few years later. Stromal cells are a mixed cell population that generates bone, cartilage, fat, and fibrous connective tissue.

Also in the 1960s, scientists who were studying rats discovered two regions of the brain that contained dividing cells, which become nerve cells. Despite these reports, most scientists believed that new nerve cells could not be generated in the adult brain. It was not until the 1990s that scientists agreed that the adult brain does contain stem cells that are able to generate the brain's three major cell types:

*astrocytes, which are non-neuronal cells
*oligodendrocytes, which are non-neuronal cells
*neurons, or nerve cells

Adult stem cells have been identified in many organs and tissues. One important point to understand about adult stem cells is that there are a very small number of stem cells in each tissue. Stem cells are thought to reside in a specific area of each tissue where they may remain quiescent (non-dividing) for many years until they are activated by disease or tissue injury. The adult tissues reported to contain stem cells include brain, bone marrow, peripheral blood, blood vessels, skeletal muscle, skin, and liver. Here's an analogy: the small numbers of stem cells located in the various parts of the body are like spare car parts. Automotive dealers carry spare parts for their cars because they fail at times and need to be replaced, or the car doesn't move. Maybe the small number of adult stem cells in the various parts of the body is nature's way of helping to resolve some normal failings of our bodies over the years. Maybe parts wear out. I have had an experience that is a perfect example of this. In 1985 I began to lose the ability to taste on the right side of my mouth, and over the next two years I lost all taste. So, eating was done just to fulfill my daily requirements for food. In many cases I suffered from strange reactions to food. For example, I couldn't eat ice cream because it acted like I had placed pepper in my mouth. After eating, my mouth had an odd feeling for a couple of hours. I started a procedure after eating that eliminated this problem. I would take Listerine and wash out my mouth by swishing the Listerine around in my mouth for thirty-five seconds and then expectorated it. After this I gargled water to dilute the Listerine and cleanse my mouth and throat with the diluted listerine. I would do this with water six times. Then I was finished, and my mouth didn't have the funny feeling any longer. This condition was originally believed to be due to a tumor on my brain, but they never found one. Fifteen or eighteen years later, I began to have some ability to taste returning to the right side of my mouth. Over the course of a year I could taste at about a 70 percent level. I went to the doctors, and do you know what they said in 2003? They said that probably some part of my brain that allowed a person to taste had stopped working, and over the years the body finds a way with "stem cells" (it was popular about that time to relate things of this nature to stem cells) to create a new path to the brain. Maybe that's why you can now taste. Maybe their wild guess was right. Maybe it was the spare parts syndrome.

Scientists in many laboratories are trying to find ways to grow adult stem cells in cell culture and manipulate them to generate specific cell types so they can be used to treat injury or disease. Some examples of potential treatments include replacing the dopamine-producing cells in the brains of Parkinson's patients, developing insulin-producing cells for type I diabetes, and repairing damaged heart muscle following a heart attack with cardiac muscle.

Testing adult stem cells

Scientists do not agree on the criteria that should be used to identify and test adult stem cells. However, they often use one or more of the following three methods:

> (1) Labeling the cells in living tissue with molecular markers and then determining the specialized cell types they generate;

> (2) Removing the cells from a living animal, labeling them in cell culture, and transplanting them back into another animal to determine whether the cells repopulate their tissue of origin;

> (3) Isolating the cells, growing them in cell culture, and manipulating them, often by adding growth factors or introducing new genes, to determine what differentiated cells types they can become.

Also, a single adult stem cell should be able to generate a line of genetically identical cells—known as a clone—which then gives rise to all the appropriate differentiated cell types of the tissue. Scientists tend to show either that a stem cell can give rise to a clone of cells in cell culture, or that a purified population of candidate stem cells can repopulate the tissue after transplant into an animal. Recently, by infecting adult stem cells with a virus that gives a unique identifier to each individual cell, scientists have been able to demonstrate that individual adult stem cell clones have the ability to repopulate injured tissues in a living animal.

Hematopoietic and stromal stem cell differentiation

In a living animal, adult stem cells can divide for a long period and give rise to mature cell types that have the characteristic shapes and specialized structures and functions of a particular tissue. The following are examples of differentiation pathways of adult stem cells:

>*Hematopoietic stem cells give rise to all the types of blood cells: red blood cells, B lymphocytes, T lymphocytes, natural killer (NK) cells, neutrophils, basophils, eosinophils, monocytes, macrophages, and platelets.

>*Bone marrow stromal cells give rise to a variety of cell types: bone cells (osteocytes), cartilage cells (chondrocytes), fat cells (adipocytes), and other kinds of connective tissue cells such as those in tendons.

>*Neural stem cells in the brain give rise to its three major cell types: nerve cells (neurons) and two categories of non-neuronal cells—astrocytes and oligodendrocytes.

>*Epithelial stem cells in the lining of the digestive tract occur in deep crypts and give rise to several cell types: absorptive cells, goblet cells, Paneth cells, and enteroendocrine cells.

>*Skin stem cells occur in the basal layer of the epidermis and at the base of hair follicles. The epidermal stem cells give rise to keratinocytes, which migrate to the surface of the skin and form a protective layer. The follicular stem cells can give rise to both the hair follicle and to the epidermis.

Adult stem cell plasticity and transdifferentiation

A number of experiments have suggested that certain adult stem cell types are *pluripotent*. This ability to differentiate into multiple cell types is called plasticity, or transdifferentiation. The following list offers examples of adult stem cell plasticity that have been reported during the past few years.

Hematopoietic stem cells may differentiate into three major types of brain cells (neurons, oligodendrocytes, and astrocytes); skeletal muscle cells; cardiac muscle cells; and liver cells.

Bone marrow stromal cells may differentiate into cardiac muscle cells and skeletal muscle cells. Brain stem cells may differentiate into blood cells and skeletal muscle cells.

Current research is aimed at determining the mechanisms that underlie adult stem cell plasticity. If such mechanisms can be identified and controlled, existing stem cells from a healthy tissue might be induced to repopulate and repair a diseased tissue

Plasticity of adult stem cells

Human embryonic adult stem cells each have advantages and disadvantages regarding potential use for cell-based regenerative therapies. Of course, adult and embryonic stem cells differ in the number and type of differentiated cells types they can become; embryonic stem cells can become all cell types of the body because they are pluripotent. Adult stem cells are generally limited to differentiating into the various cell types of their tissue of origin. However, some evidence suggests that adult stem cell plasticity may exist, increasing the number of cell types a given adult stem cell can become. They can become pluripotent.

Large numbers of embryonic stem cells can be relatively easily grown in culture, while adult stem cells are rare in mature tissues, and methods for expanding their numbers in cell culture are being developed. This is an important distinction, as large numbers of cells are needed for stem cell replacement therapies.

A potential advantage of using stem cells from an adult is that the patient's own cells could be expanded in culture and then reintroduced into the patient. The use of the patient's own adult stem cells would mean that the cells would not be rejected by the immune system. This represents a significant advantage, as immune rejection is a difficult problem that can only be circumvented with immunosuppressive drugs.

Embryonic stem cells from a donor introduced into a patient could cause transplant rejection. However, whether the recipient would reject donor embryonic stem cells has not been determined in human experiments, but this has proven successful in mice.

Potentials of for human stem cells

There are many ways in which human stem cells can be used in basic research and in clinical research. However, many technical hurdles exist between the promise of stem cells and the realization of these promises, which will only be overcome through continued intensive stem cell research. Other than the use of stem cells for bone marrow transplants, embryonic or adult stem cells have not been tried on a human as of this date. All experiments have been done on animals.

Studies of human embryonic stem cells may yield information about the complex events that occur during human development. A primary goal is to identify how undifferentiated stem cells become differentiated. Scientists know that turning genes on and off is central to this process. Some of the most serious medical conditions, such as cancer and birth defects, are due to cell division differentiation. A better understanding of the genetic and molecular controls of these processes may yield information about how such diseases arise and suggest new strategies for therapy. A significant hurdle to this use and most uses of stem cells is that scientists do not yet fully understand the signals that turn specific genes on and off to influence the differentiation of the stem cell. Further trials with mice and animals that are more complex or more like humans, such as monkeys, will be part of the learning curve that scientists must pursue to find the key means of activating this "turn on" signal.

Human stem cells for use in the testing of drugs

Human stem cells could also be used to test new drugs. For example, new medications could be tested for safety on differentiated cells generated from human pluripotent cell lines. It may be possible to test these drugs by applying them to the laboratory Petri dishes where cells are grown. One could determine if there is rejection of a drug by the cells, or an allergic reaction, without applying them to a person. Other kinds of cell lines are already used in this way. Cancer cell lines, for example, are used to screen potential anti-tumor drugs. But, the availability of pluripotent stem cells would allow drug testing in a wider range of cell types. However, to screen drugs effectively, the conditions must be identical when comparing different drugs. Therefore, scientists will have to be able to precisely control the differentiation of stem cells into the specific cell type on which drugs will be tested. "Current knowledge" of the signals controlling differentiation falls well short of being able to mimic these conditions precisely enough to consistently have identical differentiated cells for each drug being tested. I quoted "current knowledge" because there has been significant progress made over the last several months, and signals have been located for certain functions.

Remember earlier information about DNA and how the mRNA carries the triplets called codons out of the nucleus? These codons, along with the anticodons, generate the amino acids that then are used to construct the proteins needed by the body. Scientists have been able to change one nucleotide in a triplet, which results in major changes in mice and other animals. The same type of path that that applied to determining of the genome of man and how this allowed a better understanding of what gene affects what function will be likely followed on the stem cell learning curve. It requires continual work on the issue to develop the learning curve to discover these details about the stem cell.

Perhaps the most important potential application of human stem cells is the generation of cells and tissues that could be used for cell-based therapies. Today, donated organs and tissues are often used to replace ailing or destroyed tissue, but the need for transplantable tissues and organs far outweighs the available supply. Stem cells, directed to differentiate into specific cell types, offer the possibility of a renewable source of replacement cells and tissues to treat diseases including Parkinson's and Alzheimer's diseases, spinal cord injury, stroke, burns, heart disease, diabetes, osteoarthritis, and rheumatoid arthritis.

For example, it may become possible to generate healthy heart muscle cells in the laboratory and then transplant those cells into patients with chronic heart disease. Preliminary research in mice and other animals indicates that bone marrow stem cells, transplanted into a damaged heart, can generate heart muscle cells and successfully repopulate the heart tissue. Other recent studies of cell culture systems indicate that it may be possible to direct the differentiation of embryonic stem cells or adult bone marrow cells into heart muscle cells. In people who suffer from type I diabetes, the cells of the pancreas that normally produce insulin are destroyed by the patient's own immune system. New studies indicate that it may be possible to direct the differentiation of human embryonic stem cells in cell culture to form insulin-producing cells that eventually could be used in transplantation therapy for diabetics. What a wonderful event this would be for the many people suffering from this debilitating disease.

To realize the promise of novel cell-based therapies for such pervasive and debilitating diseases, scientists must be able to easily and reproducibly manipulate stem cells so that they possess the necessary characteristics for successful differentiation, transplantation, and engraftment. The following is a list of steps in successful cell-based treatments that scientists will have to learn to precisely control to bring such treatments to the clinic.

To be useful for transplant purposes, stem cells must be reproducibly made to:

*Proliferate extensively and generate sufficient quantities of tissue
 *Not differentiate during this period of proliferation
 *Differentiate into the desired cell type(s) upon selection
 *Survive in the recipient after transplant

*Probably develop enzymes to hasten the action within the human body
*Integrate into the surrounding tissue after transplant
*Function appropriately for the duration of the recipient's life
*Present no serious side effects

Also, to avoid the problem of immune rejection, scientists are experimenting with different research strategies to generate tissues that will not be rejected. Adult stem cells that are pluripotent may prove to be valuable since the body's rejection criteria will be reduced since they are from the same body.

To summarize, the promise of stem cell therapies is an exciting one, but significant technical hurdles remain that will only be overcome through years of intensive research. The last several months in 2007 have been very encouraging.

Exciting Late News on Adult Stem Cells

There have been several dramatic discoveries recently about adult stem cells. An article appeared in the *Wall Street Journal* on November 15, 2007, written by Gautam Naik, discussing the results of a team of bioscientists under the leadership of Shoukhrat Mitalipov of the Oregon National Primate Research Center. The team reported it had created monkey clones by using a variation of the process that yielded Dolly the sheep, the first cloned animal. This has to this point never occurred and is exciting, due to the similarity of the monkey genome to the human genome. This team wants to test whether fresh tissue derived from rhesus clones can treat diabetes or other diseases in a monkey, a process known as therapeutic cloning. Success in this process could strengthen future tests on humans. The idea is to create an embryonic clone of a patient, and then transplant altered versions of that embryo's cells back into the patient. I think it is important here to have the reader understand that the use of the word "clone" by this group may upset certain individual's who are against cloning. I think it is important to understand that this is a play on words. The other scientists working on embryonic stem cell research and adult stem cell research and those working on programming of cells are doing the same thing but calling it a different name. The group from Oregon actually worked with stem cells to generate their results and deliberately chose to use this wording. Ultimately, they want to create a complete monkey from embryonic stem cells, so as to be able to work with a subject that has been created from altered versions of the DNA of cells taken from this subject.

In their lab, they injected the genetic material from a skin cell of an adult monkey into a monkey egg whose own DNA had first been removed. This led to an early-stage embryo called a blastocyst, from which stem cells were then derived. Finally they put the stem cells in a Petri dish and coaxed them into becoming long, thin nerve cells and beating heart tissue.

To show the difficulty in performing this experiment, the researchers used more than 300 eggs from fourteen rhesus monkeys to derive their cell lines, which is fairly inefficient. I guess they learned as they proceeded, and future work would probably come at a better efficiency.

Reports from Wisconsin and Japan

Two teams of scientists, one from Wisconsin and the other from Japan, have reprogrammed human skin cells so they are similar to embryonic stem cells, creating the promise of stem-cell therapy without the need to destroy embryos. The article I got this information from is the 11/21/07 edition of the *San Jose Mercury News*.

The scientists started with normal human skin cells, hoping to induce them to become like human embryonic stem cells, which have the ability to turn into any type of tissue. Four genes suspected of causing pluripotency—the ability to turn into other types of cells—were implanted in retroviruses, which have the ability to insert genetic material into cell DNA. (See the section on AIDS, which is caused by the invasion of the DNA by a retrovirus that causes the DNA to have a new genetic code.) The skin cells were then exposed to the gene-carrying retroviruses. Within two weeks, the skin cells reverted to an embryonic state, becoming what is known as *induced pluripotent stem cell*, or *iPS cells*. The cells were then injected into mice, and the cells developed into a variety of tissue types, demonstrating that they had become pluripotent.

More research is needed; because retroviruses can cause cancer, researchers will likely need to find a way to insert the genes without the retroviruses.

The Yamanaka (Japan) team and the Wisconsin team that involved Thomson, the first to coax stem cells from human embryos in 1998, emphasized that more study is needed to determine if their re-programmed cells are precisely like human embryonic stem cells. Scientists have long suspected that human embryonic stem cells contain a few key genes that give the cells pluripotency, the ability to become every tissue type. Through tests, the teams each picked four genes that seemed crucial to this capability. Then they added the genes to the skin cells along with a retrovirus, which can insert genetic material into a cell's DNA. After a couple of weeks, the cells became pluripotent. "Nobody has any idea the exact mechanism why these genes can actually turn skin cells back to human embryonic stem cell states" said Junying Yu, who led the Wisconsin team. But she suspects the genes turn on genetic material within the cells that helps revert the cells to an embryonic state.

Although both teams cautioned that more studies are needed to perfect the procedure, other experts proclaimed the accomplishments as a promising way to avoid the ethical debate surrounding human embryonic stem cells, which come from discarded embryos that are four to five days old.

This art of reprogramming seems to be moving fairly rapidly. I have now seen several articles where this method is being pursued—most of them with a great deal of early success. Even critics of stem cell research are endorsing this approach.

Similar to my computer programs

I compare the similarity between this reprogramming method and the methods used in microprocessors and full computers. In computers, the inputs are decoded and re-coded into what the computer wants to see (or is programmed to see). Data that the CPU manipulates is moved to the random access memory while the program is telling the CPU to do the next sequence. When this sequence is done (or many sequences), the information is then pulled from the random access memory (and may be placed in the memory again and fetched out with other data to give the full response needed), and the function is completed. The program for the computer is written in ROM (read only memory), which normally cannot be erased; however, newer computer programs are now using read/write memories. The read is the active program, but certain data can result in the data telling the read/write to change to a write and take on a new program—in other words, create its own program based on data being received. If the data being received maintains a steady flow of similar information that the computer may not be programmed for, the data is then used to rewrite a change in the standard program to accommodate this most recent data.

Here's a rough example. Suppose a computer is programmed to handle information on temperatures being received that are between two temperature points. What if the data coming in continues to be strong enough to reprogram the computer to look at temperatures that are between two narrower temperature points, or if the opposite is true—to change the program to accept temperatures of a wider range of temperature? This is a form of self-programming.

Reprogramming cells requires a similar operation of "erasing" the present cell-stored program and re-writing the program to have the cell act in a different manner. In the case I just reviewed with you, they have essentially erased the DNA of the chromosomes and written in a new DNA code. The fact that a cell is shown to be able to accept this reprogramming and function with the new program is outstanding. The flaw so far is that they are using a retrovirus to do these functions. However, a retrovirus, as far as I can understand, is only a problem because it brings in "bad news," so to speak. I would expect that other means, either a retrovirus or a special RNA such as a coding RNA, will be developed to enter the DNA cell and do the same functions as were done successfully by these two teams. I believe they used a retrovirus because they have already seen that a retrovirus (HIV) can enter a cell and change the code. In other words, this was the most straightforward way for them to try their methods. I believe what they have learned from these results establishes a great baseline for them, and this will place them in a position to go to the next step.

My thoughts

The one thing that remains a question in my mind is how long it would take for this method to take over a function of the body, such as a muscle function, or the function of the pancreas to produce insulin of the correct amount. The reason for my question relates to what you have read in the section on HIV and how it enters the body. It does it by way of the retrovirus, but once done it takes many years for this HIV to replicate and cause the body to have AIDS—in some cases ten to twenty years. I would wonder how long it would take after reprogramming by the method being discussed for the human body to assimilate the new function; for example, take over the function of an arm muscle. I guess we will find out. I believe the key might be enzymes. As discussed, enzymes make things such as this be accelerated—accelerated by a huge margin over waiting for nature to take its course. Some acceleration is in the billions over the normal time for a function to be done. Of course, designing an enzyme to do this function may not be simple. On the other hand, bioscientists have great experience on these types of requirements and may already have an enzyme in mind, based on their previous experiences. Hopefully the enzyme selection will be straightforward. Remember, we learned that for every protein there is an enzyme. Maybe the body will produce the enzyme as the pluripotent; re-programmed cell is placed in the area for which it is designed.

JOHN DURBIN HUSHER

Pluripotent Stem Cells from Adult Skin Cells

The report in the newspapers on November 28, 2007, about the success in taking skin cells and reprogramming them to be pluripotent cells brought about a great deal of excitement. Television programs featured the woman doctor who worked on this procedure, and she was very excited. She said the tests done so far indicate the process works, and the cells were converted from differentiated skin cells to noncommittal cells by "reprogramming the cells." This is the first time this has been accomplished. This has more implications than are obvious. The ability to reprogram cells from differentiated cells to noncommitted cells that are pluripotent could open a very wide field of endeavor. I could assume that the ones for skin cells could definitely be used for providing new skin cells for a person in need of this type of cell, but, more importantly, if pluripotent as indicated, cells could be used for replacing cells in many places and eliminate the need for embryonic stem cells.

Maybe more importantly, remember when we discussed the normal cell and the genetic code and how the mRNA copies the DNA in the nucleus and carries it out to the ribosome to have proteins generated? More recently, scientists have been able to change a codon on the code being carried by the mRNA to create the changed results they desired. Using the procedure just discussed to reprogram skin cells to be pluripotent appears to be an analogous situation. It even has more potential, since the pluripotent reprogrammed skin cells are undifferentiated. In theory, one should eventually be able to eliminate diseased sections of the body and introduce these pluripotent and reprogrammed stem cells into any given section of the body. The cells, since they were derived from the body, shouldn't have the rejection problems of other methods and should behave like a normal undiseased section of the body.

Another area of interest, which I may be way off base in mentioning, relates to AIDS and HIV, which are acquired through a retrovirus. The RNA of the retrovirus enters the nucleus of the cell and transcripts its code into the DNA of the cell. If the deprogramming method of skin DNA described in the newspapers could be directed toward the nucleus and DNA that has been changed by the HIV RNA; perhaps it could be deprogrammed to rid it of the contaminated DNA and convert it back to a healthy DNA. Wouldn't that be wonderful? It would prove out the method of deprogramming demonstrated by the bioscientists of the University of Wisconsin and those from Japan that reported on this method.

Of course we have to keep in mind that the standard programs on stem cells that have been in some level of force for a couple of years may prove to be the winner. These programs do not work on reprogramming standard body cells to become pluripotent. Instead, they work on the assumption that finding embryonic stem cells or developing them in vitro may be the most straightforward method of introducing the cells to the body without secondary problems. Remember, all these programs and various approaches are really fairly new, and an advance in one direction may show what is needed to take it to the next step. The number of steps is not known yet. Whether one has reprogrammed cells that are pluripotent or embryonic cells that are omnipotent or adult cells that are found to be pluripotent; the scientists still have to determine the best way to introduce them to the human body. The first steps will be with mice and other animals. The recent favorable work with monkeys is a great step forward, since they have a genome that is similar to humans.

Scientists Are Meeting Their Objectives

With my limited knowledge, the "big deal" I see is that the programs are having the results that the people handling each of these diverse programs were expecting. This wasn't luck; it was the expected objective. This is significant, because there have been many approaches and all seem to provide the given researchers the results they were looking for. It's hard to ask for more than that from a new scientific program. Since there is so much experience with using stem cells from bone marrow to overcome some patients' leukemia, it would seem that one of these programs mentioned should be used in parallel with the present bone marrow transplant methods to give an informed result on a procedure with a history and determine if stem cells work the same or better. Rather than trying to find a person who can qualify as a donor, make a pluripotent stem cell that matches what is needed. It may show results faster and show where more work is needed. After all, bone marrow transplants are less than 50 percent successful at this time. Using omnipotent or pluripotent adult cells, or pluripotent reprogrammed cells, in place of the standard bone marrow from a matched donor may produce better results, and the people handling them would be more experienced in this transplant.

Late News on new stem cell technique: Cures sickle cell in mice

I read an article in the San Jose Mercury on December 7, 2007, about a new technique developed by a research team from the Whitehead Institute for Bio-medical Research in Cambridge, Mass., and the University of Alabama at Birmingham where scientists developed a new technique for curing sickle cell anemia in mice by rewinding their skin cells to an embryonic state and manipulating them to create healthy genetically matched replacement tissue.

After the repaired cells were transfused into the animals, they soon began producing healthy blood cells free of the crippling deformities that deprive organs of oxygen.

The experiments, published online by the *Journal of Science,* confirmed the therapeutic potential of a new class of reprogrammed stem cells, which can be custom-made for patients without creating and destroying embryos. The strategy should work to treat hemophilia, thalassemia, and severe combined immunodeficiency disease—the "bubble boy" disease—according to researchers. Therapy might also apply to disorders linked to mutations in a single gene, such as muscular dystrophy and cystic fibrosis.

Scientists hope to use a similar approach to create cardiac cells to treat heart attack patients or nerve cells that could cure spinal cord injuries. Finding an abundant source of stem cells that could be used as a personalized biological repair kit is the goal of regenerative medicine.

The technique is a few years away from being used to treat humans, scientists said. Before it could be tried, several rounds of animal experiments would need to be done. But the study is certain to lure more researchers into studying the new class of induced pluripotent stem cells, or "iPS" cells. "There's going to be this "tsunami," said Paul Simmons, director of the Center for Stem Cell Biology at the University Of Texas Health Science Center in Houston. "One would have to predict that the pace of observations made using iPS cells is going to rise exponentially."

This appears to be similar to the approach of making skin cells pluripotent, the work done by bioscientists at Wisconsin and in Japan, which I discussed earlier. This approach, if continued success follows, would leapfrog other approaches, since it works on deprogramming cells and making then "virgins" that haven't been differentiated. If a technique can remove the original DNA from a skin cell and produce pluripotent stem cells that can be used in various parts of the body, this provides super control, essentially depriving the original cell of its programming and allowing a reprogramming. It is like random access memories in computers that can be read and written and erased and rewritten. This means the bioscientists are learning how to communicate with the cells like the body communicates with the cells. Of course the "proof is in the pudding," as the saying goes. It has to be proven in humans. I believe that very shortly this can be tried in humans, perhaps those with no other chance of living. It will be similar to the story of Pasteur and his use of the cure for rabies on a child brought to him with no other chance of life except his serum. Let's hope this is tried on a human and is as successful as on a mouse. Remember, there is not much difference in the genome of a mouse compared to man.

Summary of stem cells

We have seen several significant successful steps taken in 2007 on stem cell research. This has happened across a broad spectrum of research: on embryonic stem cells, on adult stem cells, and on programmed adult cells. Although there have been no major advances on applying the stem cells to humans, the use on different animals has proven very fruitful. As I previously commented, the encouraging thing is that every research experiment has resulted in the expected results. Probably the biggest advance was made in the reprogramming of cells to make them pluripotent. This ability, whether we use embryonic cells or adult cells or normal cells, gives us a major opportunity to deprogram cells and then reprogram them. If this continues to prove out, we may see many of the programs converge toward this approach. Even with available undifferentiated embryonic cells, researchers may not take the approach with these that has been used in the past. The reprogramming ability developed in the adult stem cell program should make it more straightforward to program embryonic cells, resulting from the synergy between programs.

It would appear that science has come up with a number of new weapons that will lead us toward applying the acquired knowledge on DNA and RNA plus the use of stem cells to combine into a broader program. It's one thing to be able to find the methods to obtain and use stem cells, but it will require the knowledge being gained on DNA and RNA to put this knowledge into effect. We may find that the knowledge we have learned during our battles with AIDS will prove valuable. Understanding the methods of rewriting DNA by the retrovirus has given some of the researchers the clues needed to develop stem cell programs that work similarly to the retrovirus. In one case, programming of bacteria used a retrovirus to obtain the results. It would seem the key thing to be pursued in the near future is to figure out how to program RNA to act like a retrovirus and enter the DNA nucleus and become part of the genome of the body, without the concern that the retrovirus might bring HIV with it. Since we have discovered in other battles with cancer that the use of a virus allows us to focus the chemical treatments on the exact location of the cancer, we may find that we can use a virus in the same manner to carry the RNA into the nucleus. Likewise there may be some synergy with the attack on cancer using some of the techniques developed in the stem cell programs. The programs on genetics, stem cell research, AIDS, DNA, and RNA seem to be converging with each bit of knowledge we gain. I am seventy-six years of age and hope that I get to see the fruitful completion of these programs, with some part of a human body being replaced successfully. It's in the cards and just a matter of when.

THE WONDER OF LIFE

I have taken you from the start of life on our Earth onward, through the various phases of Earth's life and its various transformation battles. Earth had to acquire oceans, three atmospheres, plants, oxygen, and fresh water in its growth, as well as eliminate most of the ultraviolet rays of the sun, before animals and humans could make a successful entry into this world. Both Earth and Man have been aided by the sun and its constant energy to provide the elements needed by both to make this a successful journey. Our planet fought long and tenuous battles. Likewise, the battles fought by man to gain a toehold on the planet and then persist against the various elements and the need for food to survive have been just as tenuous. With no methods provided by nature to defend ourselves other than our brains, man has learned how to fight the various battles successfully and to take some control over nature into his own hands. The growing of huge amounts of food, over and above previous generations, through various techniques has allowed the world's population to grow tremendously.

This story has shown that, for man to survive, he had to depend on others to combine their energies and work together to provide the basics needed for life to continue successfully. However, as we have seen, man has been his worst enemy as well, and this resulted in many wars that brought significant loss of human life. However, man took advantage of what he learned during these wars. The fight against many ailments, including infection and those carried by insects or animals, used many

THE WONDER OF LIFE

technologies discovered during the wars and immediately after. There have been many wars, and man has survived; usually profiting from some new advances in technology developed during the wars. Man's ingenuity seemed to increase as he prepared for the various wars, using his brains to fight a new foe under different conditions.

It is in the role of advocate, man to man, that man has made the greatest progress. During the years that passed, man has learned how to educate himself and use this education as his biggest weapon. He learned how to spread this education during wars, during the movements of different religions, and eventually through the written and printed word through the development of the alphabet and the invention of the printing press. Thus began the use of mass communication through books. As man ventured to other parts of the Earth, he carried this education with him as he went on his way.

Early on, many of man's battles were against the silent foes of disease and pestilence. Not having any background or education on the cause of diseases resulted in high percentages of human life being expended. It is one of the wonders of life that man has been able to survive the terrible plagues that struck without his knowing the cause. Man was perhaps fortuitous in many of those plagues, since he had no knowledge on how to overcome them; yet they went away for reasons unknown. At times plagues would return, and man first learned to quarantine the sick from the healthy as the first major advance against the silent killers. The wonder of life carried them during these times and allowed man to become educated on how to fight many of these silent enemies. There have been many learning curves for man as he made his journey through time to the present day.

The nineteenth century proved to be a very powerful century in the battles against bacteria. The advent of the microscope, allowing the genius of man to see the enemy and see what affected these small enemies, was a monstrous achievement; led by a Dutch janitor. We began to see our medical heroes appear. People like Pasteur, Koch, Lister, and many others shared in establishing what caused the various diseases and, in most cases, how to overcome the diseases. In some cases enemies were observed under the microscope, but there were no miracle drugs to help to overcome them. Man found that certain diseases were caused by certain mosquitoes and certain flies, and this allowed for the battle to be fought and generally won by man. Man's makeup allowed for survival in many cases. Implementing the methods of improved hygiene began to prevent certain diseases. Documentation became a valuable asset; as we learned more and more about the microbes that could cause us harm, how to overcome them could be recorded.

As the nineteenth century came to a close, there were many technical advances besides medical ones. Man's ingenuity began to be asserted. The steam engine provided a power source for transportation and equipment. Rail lines were installed across the United States, allowing locomotives to ship supplies across the country, as well as providing a means of travel for people. Steam-driven boats carried the many supplies needed for such things as the production of steel. These steam-driven beauties floated across the Great Lakes and down the many rivers of America to their final destination to delivery their goods. Steam was king.

Then came a new king—oil. The first oil wells were drilled for commercial use by Drake in Titusville, Pennsylvania, in the mid-nineteenth century. Man used this energy to create new power tools and equipment. Then the first automobiles were built in small numbers at the end of the century. Tesla and George Westinghouse gave the United States the AC power needed to power machinery and provide man with a source of energy. Electric power initially came from places like Niagara Falls, with its natural drop to the river below, which was converted into a source of electrical power. Long transmission lines began to be laid to provide access to electric power to remote locations. The telegraph gave us a means of long-distance communication. Edison invented mass production and use of the light bulb, one of the wonders of life that helped to extend man's day. Now man could see during the dark of evening and gained additional time to solve problems or produce needed materials. Edison's phonograph gave many the chance to listen to sounds they had never heard before.

At the turn of the century, many of man's contributions were involved in the Industrial Revolution. The Wright Brothers flew the first airplane in 1903 and worked out the bugs on advanced designs that were used by the military in the years that followed. The evolution of the airplane was swift; many were produced in the years to follow. Henry Ford introduced the automobile production lines that would allow the average person to own an automobile. This provided many new outlets for man in his search for entertainment, as well as another transportation option for factory materials.

Albert Einstein produced four amazing papers in 1904 that gave man a better view of the world and the universe. Several scientists were involved in the development of the basic knowledge of how atoms work, with Neils Bohr being one of the main contributors. There was World War I, which again pitted man against himself. The wonders of life became the weapons of war and meant death to many—but not all by bullets. Many were claimed by infectious diseases caused by staphylococcus and streptococcus bacteria. We have discussed the development of the sulfa drugs that allowed man to battle these two bacteria, to almost a complete victory. When the sulfa drugs began to lose their potency, English scientists and American pharmecutical companies did significant work to provide penicillin to fight these diseases and others. These truly were the wonders of life.

And then in mid-century came another traumatic war—World War II, which saw almost the whole world involved in some way in this war. During the war arrived many technical achievements, including the first jet airplanes near the end of the war. Synthetic materials were invented and developed throughout many industries, providing man sources of new materials. These would yield added warmth in the cold weather, improved tires for automobiles and airplanes, lighter materials for certain applications, easier materials to mold into new forms, material that wouldn't rust, and new fabrics for clothes to wear. The synthetics would also provide man with other means of developing medicines for fighting germs in one way or another. DDT was used to nearly rid the world of malaria until man learned of its side effects.

Near the end of the war the atomic bomb was developed, which magnified the early-century genius of Einstein into a horrendous form of energy to both help and hurt mankind. We learned how to use atomic power for energy to supply electricity and to develop some forms of it to provide radioactive markers for mapping the happenings going on inside our bodies. Commercial jet planes that had twice the speed of the propeller-driven planes and flew at almost twice the attitude took over worldwide transportation and provided means of supplying materials and food to many parts of the world. To the people of the world, the planet started looking like a smaller place. The world began acting as one community, with each country realizing its capabilities and spreading them the world over. Now each country was a resource, and the other countries recognized this capability to contribute, either through uniqueness or the ability to use its resources in a better fashion. The world got smart relative to the rules of supply and demand.

The genius of man then brought television to the people of the world, first in black and white, and then in color. Now we could watch the people in all parts of the world or watch a ballgame instead of affording to buy a ticket to a game. About this time Jonas Salk developed the polio vaccine that essentially eliminated poliomyelitis (polio) disease from the world and made swimming in public pools by children the world over possible again. The flu vaccine was developed, which has to be renewed each year to provide immunity for the annual seasonal flu mutations, but the ingenuity of man discovered how to handle this mutation and it works; people are treated again to another wonder of life.

The transistor was invented by the people of Bell Labs. This provided a new means of handling signals and reducing the power needed by radios and television and many other things. They were minute in size and more rugged and used less power. As a result, most electronic equipment became smaller and more portable. Now man could walk around with equipment and watch or listen to what was going on in the world on a "real time" basis. From this beginning came the integrated circuits and the next step up in electronics. Electronic equipment became a partner in the war against pestilence and offered unique solutions to medical procedures. The technological world was advancing as rapidly as the world's needs to fight other elements that stood in the way of man's progress.

After considerable studies and work by scientists the world over, next came answers to the riddles of man and his genetics. These wonders had been sought since man could talk and think. This search started in the nineteenth century and continued in the twentieth century. Scientists first discovered deoxyribonucleic acid (DNA) and ribonucleic acid (RNA) in the chromosomes early in the nineteenth century, but they did not consider these to be part of the heritage and secrets of life. This soon would be resolved.

It was determined that all forms of life, including plants, animals, and man, are made up of cells. After World War II, the drive to find how man inherits his various characteristics was continued in earnest. It was a drive to determine our genetic makeup, given the exciting name "the genetic code." The world of science began to search for the genetic code. Chromosomes—twenty-three pairs of them— were discovered in every cell of the human body, and scientists soon knew that they provided the source of genetics and the genetic code, but science couldn't determine how this was achieved. Researchers believed the key was in the DNA within the nucleus of the chromosomes of human cells, but needed to find how this hidden code inside this nucleus worked. In 1952, the main part of the answer came.

An American, James D. Watson, and two Englishmen, Maurice Wilkins and Francis Crick, along with Rosalind Franklin, who provided the amazing x-ray images of DNA, determined that DNA was a double helix, which is shaped like a spiral staircase, with base pairs between the rungs of the staircase, like stair steps. The strings of base pairs, like the rungs of a ladder between the double helix rungs, determine the genetic code of the person. Watson and Crick also determined how DNA works, providing—via RNA—triplets of information that leave the nucleus via messenger RNA. This sequence provides information that activates various amino acids and builds the proteins that are required by the human body from these acids. These codes and their resultant actions provide twenty of the twenty-two proteins needed by man. The other two must be supplied by consuming the proper food.

It is worth mentioning that computers became a huge technical entity around mid-century and played an important part in almost every form of activity that man was involved in. Computers, along with the appropriate programs, became the main problem-solving instruments. The evolution of the computer—from the use of vacuum tubes to transistors and eventually to integrated circuits, along with increased speed and size reduction—was probably the biggest technical achievement in the second half of the twentieth century. This involved the transition from the use of transistors to the use of integrated circuits in 1959; various types of transistors completed circuit functions, rather than the simple functions of transistors. Without the computers to do fast calculations and provide answers rapidly, many of the designs of man and of nature would have been hard to come by. The computer was to solving many problems like an enzyme was to proteins; it speeded up the answers. It also served to allow man to operate in remote places, taking man's place in environments not people-friendly, such as outer space and deep underground (when looking for oil) or deep in the oceans (when looking for anything that would advance man). When reviewing the achievements of man during the last half of the twentieth century, I find it hard to find one that didn't use the computer in some way to give refined results at super speeds. Man was on a roll with the aid of computers and microprocessors.

Man conquered "near" outer space as space vehicles were designed, and man made his first adventures around the Earth in these unique space craft in the late 1950s. Then man made the trip to outer space, beginning space flights in the late 1950s. The United States sent man to the moon and back in 1968. It was exciting to see Earth from a distance; and it looked like we had thought it would. Here was this wondrous planet that I have written about. It appeared as a handsome figure when viewed from the moon. Here man stood on the moon that had been created early in the life of Earth when a collision of some space debris hit Earth early in its life.

It's worth mentioning that man had found how to capture some of the energy from the sun with an invention called the solar cell. It was this invention that now provided energy to the space vehicles, with their clear view of the sun. Man found that the vacuum of space was ideal to fan out the solar cell array in a sail-like extension from the space vehicle to soak up the sun; without being concerned about wind blowing against the energy cells. The vacuum of outer space provides man with no source of oxygen for his needs, and so these are supplied by the manufacture of oxygen using the power of the solar cell. All the advances in reducing the size and increasing the capabilities of electronics were utilized throughout the space vehicle.

In the early 1980s came good and bad news for mankind. The good news was in the form of small computers using microprocessors that evolved into the personal computer (PC) marketplace. The size of computers decreased while their computer power increased; and this evolution resulted in a large part of the world's population having personal computers to use as they so chose. The bad news was the arrival of the HIV virus and the resultant AIDS, which was a sentence to death. It was later determined that the virus was brought into the country in 1969 from the island of Haiti, although it's origin was determined to be Africa. I have covered this extensively in prior sections of this book. Men and women the world over work on solutions for those that have the HIV virus to prevent the development of AIDS and the death that follows. Where at one time HIV would turn into full-blown AIDS in several years, the medical profession has increased the life span of those with HIV and delayed AIDS for twenty or so years.

Over the 1980s, 1990s, and on into the new century, the personal computer shrank in size per function performed and gained higher speeds and new programs for solving problems, as well providing huge storage capacity. These small computers, about one-hundredth the size of the large computers of the 1950s, have more memory than the huge computers of the 1970 variety. Many new companies were started around the world using the PC format with Microsoft's software. Intel was the biggest supplier of the microchips for the microprocessor; Microsoft supplied the software. Apple Computer was the biggest competitor with the PC, with its unique software and hardware. The biggest PC supplier was Dell Computer in Texas, but Hewlett Packard passed them in 2006.

The peripheral gear for the computer, including the printer, the fax machine (which allowed one to send printed material electronically to anywhere in the world), and the copier allowed the home computer person to do most of the functions required by many industries and transfer the information via the computer or the fax. The home now essentially had more computing power and peripheral capability then the industrial computers of the 1970s and early 1980s.

These small computers and their capabilities allowed the space vehicles to be functional and to monitor their space capability at all times. Communication from these vehicles was carried out by the onboard computers, and the space vehicle was controlled in many cases by Earth-stationed computers that provided information to the onboard computers. Man really had conquered how to function away from the mother planet.

At the end of the 80s or in the early 90s, a means of using the home computer to communicate around the work was invented: the Internet and the World Wide Web. This brought communication to another level, which exceeded the telephone in many cases. One of the biggest advantages of this means of communication was during massive emergency situations such as earthquakes and tsunamis. One could send an e-mail to the emergency area, and they didn't have to respond to it like they do with a telephone. The message would be downloaded on the receiving end, and the e-mail could be addressed at the convenience of those in the disaster area or on a priority basis. Administrators of hospitals could review the list of download messages and select which ones were more important. This capability allowed them to not have to answer all phone calls, some of which were not critical. It also provided the sender the knowledge that he or she had sent the message and that sooner or later it would be answered. This was much better than hearing a busy signal on a telephone and having to hang up and keep trying later. I have given one example, but there are millions of other examples.

The books I have written, including this one, use all of these capabilities, which allow me to look up data in minutes that would require days or weeks if I had to go to libraries and search out the information. The Internet and World Wide Web gave me access to information that no encyclopedia could provide and most libraries do not have at their disposal. With this advance, the world became another level smaller, because one could communicate with almost any place in the world just by sitting down at home on the PC and using the Internet, the fax machine, or the cell phone, and do it inexpensively.

Cell phones, which allowed a person to talk to anyone around the world, arrived in the 1980s. These cell phones began to methodically shrink in size and expand in capability. In many cases they allowed the capability of seeing the other person, perhaps thousands of miles away, on an LCD display while talking to them. Perhaps the biggest impact they had was in countries like China, India, Malaysia, and other countries in the far East without the telephone lines and power lines that existed in the Western worlds. Their job—to keep up with the progress in the West—was a monstrous one when one considers the work they had to do to provide this asset. Then came wireless cell phones, and these countries could put off the monstrous task of supplying the infrastructure for basic communication needs. Now all they had to do was build cell phone centers at strategic locations, and before you knew it they were in business and communicating with the rest of the world. Several billion people were turned on to advanced communication. People the world over became walking pieces of communication equipment. Soon cell phones became more sophisticated. People carried not only telephones but had direct communication with the Internet and its vast means of communication and information, supplying answers to questions that one had to previously look through an encyclopedia to find.

Meanwhile in the 1990s new approaches to cameras for the consumer became a big item. These cameras used solid state CCD (Charge Coupled Device) memories for storing the picture instead of film; later flash memories would invade this field. Digital cameras became smaller, with greater capability, and could be carried in pockets or purses. Stick (or thumb) memories became a big item in the first years of the twenty-first century. Small products called stick memories were packaged in a plastic or metal package that was about a quarter-inch thick, half an inch wide, and three or four inches long, and they held memories that were bigger than the entire memories of the big computers of the 90s. They became the chief means for transferring information from one computer and could be carried from one place to another or used to store electronic records of such things as pictures, books, and anything that could be provided by the PC. All of these technologies were the benefactors of the digital process, which had begun to take over the functions of analog devices in the 1960s. I was one of the first inventors of the silicon integrated circuit, later called the chip, and did much work in the analog and digital worlds of integrated circuits. As the twentieth century came to a close, television sets began to be introduced in a digital mode. It proved easier to design circuits for a specific function and easier, eventually, to receive the information. The way was now open to design systems that were completely digital.

Early in the 2000s, companies like Apple began delivering, in one small, compact size comparable to a pack of cigarettes, a combination cell phone, camera, an extension to one's computer, access to music, access to movies, access to any video, access to the stock market, and, probably more importantly, allowed the user to communicate with the Internet. There are other functions that I am not aware of. All these forms of communication—the cell phone, the computer, the Internet, the fax machine, the printer, the solid state camera, the television, the advanced transmission lines, and many other electronic wonders—allowed the world to become quite close. It was nothing to transmit business information or entertainment from one's home to others thousands of miles away via these new, fast, sharper, simpler, and broader means of information, as if they were in the next room. This is just the beginning.

Why the Technical Entities?

Why did I shift my discussion to these technical entities? I want the reader to realize there were advances in other things besides medicine and gaining knowledge about man's genetic make-up. Also, technical innovations became the backbone of the medical industry in finding solutions to diseases. I want the reader to have a feel for the vast knowledge that man has created to provide a more international means of communicating to the people around the world and to focus vast resources to the culmination of finding the genetic code and the stem cell. One could now swallow a camera that was very small; as it made its way through the body, it gave the viewer a complete view on a screen of the trail of this small electronic wizard, from the throat to the ejection at the end of the trip. Medical people could now see what went on in the body, from the mouth all the way through the digestive system and to completion. They could definitely find the problem and more definitely find the solution to medical problem that related to the path of this electronic wizard. There were now magnetic resonant indicators (MRIs) that scanned the body using this system, bit by bit. From the scan, computers and other electronics converted this data into a three-dimensional picture of whatever part of the body the doctors choose to review. One could see brain images as no other piece of equipment could show them—in three dimensions. There were now ultrasonic scans that would allow the doctors to view the functions inside the body just by moving this small (about the size of a man's fist) instrument across the part of the body they wanted to scan. This instrument is noninvasive, inexpensive for the patient, and easy for the doctor's assistants to run as they view in real time whatever they want to scan; you find the results within several minutes. They can review the functioning of a person's blood flow through the carotid arteries in the neck and see if there are any impediments to the flow. Ultrasound makes it easy to check for kidney stones, carotid artery blockage issues, aortic aneurisms, and other organ functions of the body. Women have their breasts checked for breast cancer through the use of mammograms that provide a picture of the internal parts of the breast. This allows for early detection and early medical involvement in eliminating these tumors.

One of the most outstanding features of the progress made in surgical methods relates to the fact that many operations can now be performed without making major incisions in the body. Small, unique, and precise equipment allows operations to be performed through very small incisions that allow specialized equipment to enter the area to perform surgery. New blood tests were developed which could check a man's PSA, which is an indication if prostate cancer is a problem. New equipment could perform a colonoscopy via the rectum to determine if he or she has polyps, which are growths that could be cancerous or the start of cancer. Polyps can then be removed with the same piece of equipment. Various new portable equipment are available that are inexpensive and provide a means for a person to monitor his or her blood pressure. Many different blood pressure medicines were developed by the pharmaceutical companies to treat individuals for hypertension. Individuals could monitor their own blood pressure quite easily on an hour by hour basis, if necessary, to determine whether the new medicine was performing its required function.

Radiation and chemotherapy were now the methods of choice for attacking cancer. The chemotherapy that is now being developed is designed to work on a given organ of the body. This customized and focused approach to attack a given type of cancer is being developed by small and large pharmaceutical companies the world over. Year by year, they develop new synthetic compounds to ward off the various cancers, sometimes focused by the use of a virus that can penetrate the given cells in the targeted organ and carry these chemicals into the desired area. I've written about my feelings on the use of our experience with DNA, RNA, stem cells, and AIDS and which genes control which portion or portions of the body. We are beginning to see how the human body itself has been evolving through evolutionary methods to better protect the body. We used to believe evolution took thousands of years, but are beginning to see that it happens in hundreds of years, and maybe faster. We will find out as we keep gaining knowledge on the wonders of life. (I hope you noticed that I changed the singular word. I think of it as a wonder, but it's probably wonders.)

So, now you see why I included some information about electronics. I wanted to be sure that you were aware of man's battles against the silent killers that we call microbes and how it is being assisted by the smallest of electronics, which we call microcircuits or chips. Man has come a long way since I started writing about his appearance on Earth. To think that life was started by some DNA or RNA that became DNA about a half million years ago and evolved into man, which makes life more a wonder. Pre-historic man came without any built-in weapons to fight for his survival besides a keen mind. He has used this keen mind to make him the "head of the food chain," so to speak. Just twenty-three hundred years ago, the world was populated by three hundred million humans. The Earth's population was 1.2 billion people one hundred and fifty years ago, and now it is 6.7 billion people; all of which speaks for man's ability to survive. Of course, Earth had much to do with it. It evolved into a better place to live through its acquisition of the various needs for man's survival. And then there's the sun, which made it possible for these transformations to take place. It was fun writing about how the sun adopted this planet as its own and helped to sculpture it into the place we now know. It was fun writing about the success of man (and woman) through the many cycles of nature's attacks on us humans. Mother Nature is the only thing that has come close to closing the book on man. However, as the years proceeded and man's learning curve brought new knowledge to the forefront, man has learned some ways to overcome the challenges of Mother Nature. It seems that the biggest threat to man is man himself.

CONCLUSION

I named the book *The Wonder of Life* because I felt it was a wonder that man has survived and can look back and see the obstacles he has overcome and the knowledge he has gained; not only about the world, but about himself and how his internal system works. It's a wonder how the puzzle pieces were put together and developed by man as time proceeded. Initially I was writing about the tough times man lived through and how he survived them, then all of a sudden there was an shift in my writing to man's advancements. It was like man went from a defensive battle to an offensive one. This major change probably occurred during the middle of the 1800s, when the microscope allowed man to see the little things we couldn't see without it. Here was a shift in the battle—if we could see it, we could defeat it. This offensive battle continued with the development of tools that bioscientists and medical doctors could use to improve their success rates and improve detailed operations. This offensive approach was clearly evident as man refined the elements that came together to provide him a glance at DNA and the details that made it work. This became the human genome, spread like a map before us, that we could now start analyzing, sticking a pin (not really, but it acted like this) in the various gene sites to see which ones affected which parts of our human system. We now had a road map, where a generation ago we were blindfolded.

It's interesting when you consider that we have just arrived on this road map of the human genome. We have inched up on it. Like all road maps, the more you use them the more real they become. I can imagine the impact of the human genome on the world of scientists and doctors of all types. I believe with the aid of the genome and the use of computers the world over that we will find a rapid way to map the specific genomes of the individuals with certain diseases and see what is common in their genome. From this, medical science will discover how to affect a given gene to resolve a given issue. This will transform from a research methodology on individuals to resolving man's everyday general ills. The "back and forth" method of reviewing genomes and relating information about others with certain unique capabilities to findings will lead back to the genome in search of additional complementary genes that help to solve a given problem.

We will work that genetic code for more information that will lead us to things one cannot predict at this time. There are plenty of predictions, and many of them will be proven true. I am talking about what we don't know and can't predict at this time. With every finding comes many surprises. The good news is that man has learned to document his findings so the surprises have a road map underway. In addition, the computer is both the method of documentation and key to solving problems. One of my engineers said to me about thirty years ago, "Computers can only do what you program them to do. They are basically dumb." To which I answered, "You are right to a certain degree, but as you use the computer and it brings back answers, it also shows you what is not the answer. This allows one to think about the right answer. When this is applied to the computer, a new solution arrives, and it does so rapidly. So, as dumb as it is, it makes the user smarter. Therefore the result is one of gained intelligence that one could not have without the computer."

I believe the human genome will eventually be placed on a computer with a proper program that will allow real time active intervention. You will be able to change one gene slightly, and the computer will feed back information about how that affects other genes. This will allow interactive play between the scientists and the simulated genome in the computer. As this type of action and reaction occurs, it will teach the scientist what affects what within this genome. The initial attempts at this will not work as smoothly as one would like, but it gives the user and programmer some answers that lead to improved models, and it does it rapidly. This will evolve into a magnificent tool for the solution of many medical problems. One must realize when he is using a computer that it contains the inputs from many people including many engineers, many programmers, many computer scientists, many mathematicians, many scientists, many bioscientists plus your own input as you use it. So, you are not working with a dumb machine, you are working with the best of the best.

I have shown the similarities between the HIV virus and the DNA/RNA workings, and I believe there will be dramatic results on curing HIV and AIDS within ten years. AIDS is only one of many retroviruses that attack the human system. A solution to any one of the retroviruses will result in feedback to solve other ones. The ability to program skin cells to be omnipotent or pluripotent leads me to believe that a similar action will occur with HIV and AIDS. Since the HIV virus inserts itself into the DNA (much like the RNA injects itself inside the nucleus to be programmed by the DNA) and causes the rewriting of the person's DNA such that each cell in the body eventually has this new DNA with this devilish new program, I believe that in the not too distant future we will find a way to reprogram the infected DNA and remove the retrovirus signature. We have to find a way to write the HIV virus's program to make it null and void. If this can be caught early in the cycle of the infection by the HIV virus, we should be able to erase it. There is no doubt that once a person has AIDS, the problem is much tougher. That would involve erasing every cell in the human body. Since it takes years for HIV to progress to AIDS, it may take that long to undo it. However, I think not. There must be one cell in the human body that has the "chief DNA" in it and when we find it we will make one change and the whole body will change its DNA.

I believe this review of history does a good job of showing the reader how man's technology did a great job of finding out how to deal with the silent and unseen bearer of disease and death. This battle with bacteria and viruses has been a long one but man has persevered. The battle went from one of being a passive finder of the silent and unseen to one of an active one where man has been able to provide an even better picture and is now pre-empting some before the fact. The better understanding of the genome and where the genes do their job will bring even more positive action in the near future. Stem cells will allow us to repair parts of our body that malfunction and life should be extended well beyond the present length. We can now see the unseen and it is no longer silent.

I hope this review of the tough times that man has endured will make it easier for the reader to understand what it takes to continue this journey and keep improving it. When you consider work on the genome occurred over about sixty years, it didn't take long once we got a glimpse of how the genetic code works. It took us a couple thousand years to get to that point. I am sure there is tons more to learn, but it will be an exciting adventure.

After completing this book, I thought maybe I should have called it *The Wonders of Life,* since it is obvious that a plural is involved when considering life. Life is wondrous, even when it's tough. The good news is that it is only tough when living through it, but it's a piece of cake when you look back. That's what I am doing now. Are you?

John Durbin Husher

REFERENCES AND CREDITS

1. http://en.wikipedia.org/wiki/Earth
2. http://www.indiana.edu/~geol105/images/gaia_chapter_3/earth_differentiation.htm
3. http://academic.brooklyn.cny.edu/physics/sobel/Nucphys/sun.html
4. En.wikipedia.org/wiki/Photosynthesis;R.E.Blankenship.okfirst.ocs.ou.edu/train/meteorology/EnergyBudget2.html
5. Space.com/searchforlife/life_origins_001205.html.En.wikipedia.org/wiki/Photosynthesis," Blackwell Science (2002).
6. Geolor.com/geoteach/How_Did_Earths_Atmosphere-Evolve_geoteach
7. physicalgeograpy.net/fundamentals/7j.html
8. physicalgeography.net/fundamental/7j.html
9. Global Heat Balance: Introduction to Heat Fluxes
10. okfirst.ocs.ou.edu/train/meteorology/EnergyBudget2.html
11. Arizona Cooperative Extension, College of Agriculture, Tucson, Ar.
12. En.wikipedia.org/wide/Cambrian; Stephen Jay Gould, Wonderful Life; the Burgess Shale and the Nature of Life (New York: Norton, 1989
13. ATP is considered to be the fuel for human and animal growth.
14. En.wikipedia.org/wiki/Oxygen; Neil A. Campbell and Jane B. Reece, Biology, 7th ed. (San Francisco; Stanford University Press, 2005).
15. En.wikipedia.org/wiki/Oxygen; Neil A. Campbell and Jane B. Reece, Biology, 7th ed. (San Francisco: Stanford University Press, 2005);

G.B. Dalrymple, The Age of the Earth (San Francisco: Stanford University Press, 1991).
16. climatesci.colorado.edu/2007/04/05/evaporation-is-equal-to-precipitation-on...7/26/2007
17. http://en.wikipedia.org/wiki/Aristotle
18. http://en.wikipedia.org/wiki/Alexander_the_Great
19. http;//en.wikipedia.org/wiki/Roman_Empire
20. http:://en.wikipedia.org/wiki/History_of_Christianity
21. http://en.wikipedia.org/wiki/Black_Death
22. http://en.wikipedia.org/wiki/Cholera
23. http://en.wikipedia.org/wiki/Anthrax
24. http://dermatology.about.com/cs/smallpox/a/smallpoxhx.htm
25. http://en.wikipedia.org/wiki/Spanish_flu
26. http://en.wikipedia.org/wiki/Printing_press
27. Microbe Hunters by Paul De Kruif, Introduction copyright 1996 by Harcourt, Inc. A Harvest Book Harcourt, Inc.
28. http://www.ucmp.berkeley.edu/history/hooke.html
29. http://inventors.about.com/od/mstartinventions/a/microscope.htm
30. http://en.wikipedia.org/wiki/Ilya_Ilyich_Mechnikov
31. http://en.wikipedia.org/wiki/Oxygen
32. http://en.wikipedia.org/wiki/Theobald_Smith
33. http://www.1911encyclopedia.org/Sir_David_Bruce
34. http://nobelprize.org/nobel_prizes/medicine/laureates/1902/ross-bio.html
35. http://www.mcatmaster.com/medicine&war/yellowfever.htm
36. http://www.britannica.com/eb/article-9032103/Paul-Ehrlich
37. http://en.wikipedia.org/wiki/Joseph_Lister
38. http://www.emc.maricopa.edu/faculty/farabee/BIOBK/BioBookgenintro.html
39. http://en.wikipedia.org/wiki/Charles_Darwin
40. http://www.haciendapub.com/faria5html
41. The Demon Under the Microscope, by Thomas Hager, published by Harmony Books, an imprint of the Crown Publishing Group, a division of Random House, Inc., New York in 2006
42. http://en.wikipedia.org/wiki/Sulfonamide_(medicine)

43. http://inventors.about.com/od/pstartinventions/a/Penicillin.htm
44. The Mold in Dr. Florey's Coat by Eric Lax, published by Henry Holt and company 2004
45. http://en.cellsalive.com/pen.htm
46. http://en.wikipedia.org/wiki/Gram-negative
47. Splendid Solution: Jonas Salk and the conquest of polio/Jeffrey Kluger, published by The Berkley Publishing Group, The Penguin Group
48. http://homepage.smc.edu/hgp/history.htm
49. http://en.wikipedia.org/wiki/Amino_acid
50. The Genetic Code by Isaac Asimov published by The New American Library, Inc. 1962
51. http://en.wikipedia.org/wiki/DNA
52. The Double Helix by James D.Watson, published by TOUCHSTONE, First Touchstone Edition 2001
53. How Did We Find Out About DNA? By Isaac Asimov, published by Walker and Company, New York 1985
54. http://www.estrellamountain.edu/faculty/farabhee/biobk/BioBookPROTS Yn.html
55. http://en.wikipedia.org/wiki/Chromosome
56. http://en.wikipedia.org/wiki/Human_Genome_Project
57. http://en.wikipedia.org/wiki/Genetic _code
58. http://en.wikipedia.org/wiki/Retrovirus
59. http://en.wikipedia.org/wiki/AIDS
60. http://stemcell.nih.gov/info/basics/basics1.asp
61. http://en.wikipedia.org/wiki/HIV
62. http://en.wikipedia.org/wiki/Base_pair
63. http://en.wikipedia.org/wiki/Cel_(biology)
64. Internet article titled Temperature by John Baez.)
65. Robert Koch Biography; *Nobel Lectures, Physiology or Medicine 1901-1921*, Elsevier Publishing Company, Amsterdam, 1967
66. www.bio-**medicine**.org/tag/**SARS**/ - 29k
67. *Nature Medicine* published an article in September 2006, authored by Menno de Jong,
68. en.wikipedia.org/wiki/**Ebola** - 125k

69. en.wikipedia.org/wiki/**HIV** - 261k
70. en.wikipedia.org/wiki/History_of_the_**alphabet** - 115k
71. en.wikipedia.org/wiki/Gregor_**Mendel** - 51k
72, users.adelphia.net/~lubehawk/BioHELP!/**mendel**.htm - 96k
73. en.wikipedia.org/wiki/**Mendelian**_inheritance - 44k
74. en.wikipedia.org/wiki/**Inception**_of_**Darwin**'s_**theory** - 91k
75. en.wikipedia.org/wiki/The_**Origin**_of_**Species** - 157k
76. en.wikipedia.org/wiki/**Oliver_Wendell_Holmes**,_Sr. - 42k
77. content.nejm.org/cgi/content/full/343/8/587
78. en.wikipedia.org/wiki/Gerhard_**Domagk** - 35k
79. www.chemsoc.org/timeline/pages/1928.html - 36k
80. en.wikipedia.org/wiki/**Legionella** - 53k
81. en.wikipedia.org/wiki/Acetic_**acid_bacteria** - 23k
82. medic.med.uth.tmc.edu/path/00001497.htm - 3k
83. en.wikipedia.org/wiki/**Penicillin** - 79k
84. www.geocities.com/Athens/Ithaca/2155/**history**.htm - 6k
85. www.eyewitnesstohistory.com/plague.htm - 29k
86. www3.baylor.edu/~Charles_Kemp/**typhus**.htm - 7k
87. www.ideafinder.com/history/inventions/print**press**.htm - 61k
88. **Hunt**-for-**Chromosomal**-Errors-Which-Cause-Genetic-Diseases-11203-1/ -
89. deHaseth P, Helmann J (1995). "Open complex formation by Escherichia coli RNA polymerase: the mechanism of polymerase-induced strand separation of double helical DNA".
90. from Purves et al., *Life: The Science of Biology*, 4th Edition, by Sinauer Associates (www.sinauer.com) and WH Freeman (www.whfreeman.com). Used with permission. 91. Image from Purves et al., *Life: The Science of Biology*, 4th Edition, by Sinauer Associates (www.sinauer.com) and WH Freeman (www.whfreeman.com). Used with permission
92. http://en.wikipedia.org/wiki/Bone_marrow_transplant.

INDEX

A

AIDS xi, 53, 54, 136, 205, 207, 208, 210, 211, 212, 213, 214, 215, 216, 217, 246, 249, 250, 254, 255, 263, 268, 273
Alexander the Great 38, 39, 60
Alphabet x, 34, 58, 59, 60, 61, 62, 63, 178, 184, 257
Amino Acid cycle 187
Amino Acids 157
Anthrax 47, 49, 50, 73, 76, 100
anticodon 184, 187, 192
Aristotle 37, 38, 39, 57

B

Base Pair 166, 167, 175, 176
Bedside fever and deaths 111
Bone Marrow transplant 222, 223, 224, 251
Bruce, David 81

C

Calories 11, 12, 13, 14, 25
Cambrian Explosion 19, 26, 33
Chargaff, Erwin 169, 172
chart 192
Cholera 48

Christianity 41, 42, 43
chromosomes xi, 89, 90, 91, 138, 141, 142, 143, 144, 145, 146, 147, 148, 149, 150, 151, 152, 158, 165, 176, 178, 180, 194, 196, 198, 199, 202, 210, 221, 233, 248, 261
codon 184, 187, 189, 191, 192, 194, 250
Colebrook, Leonard 111, 112

D

Darwin, Charles 86, 92, 96
differentiation 2, 3, 4, 5, 27, 97, 228, 230, 232, 233, 234, 236, 239, 240, 242, 243, 244
DNA deoxyribonucleic acid 6, 165, 166, 168, 183, 261
Domagk, Gerhard 103, 104, 105, 119
Double Helix 170
Dr. Walter Reed 82

E

Earth's energy budget 13
Ebola 54
Ehrlich, Paul 83, 105
Einstein, Albert 259
Embryonic stem cells xi, 223, 225,

227, 229, 230, 231, 232, 233, 234, 235, 241, 242, 244, 246, 247, 250, 251, 254
Embryonic stem cell testing 232
Eukaryotes 122, 140, 141, 146, 178, 180
Evolution theory 92

F

Famine in Europe 45, 46, 47, 50
Florey, Howard Walter 124
Francis Harry Crick 170
Franklin, Rosalind Elsie 170

G

Gallo, Dr. Robert 206
Genome from one bacteria to another 203
Genotype specificity 143
Gram-positive and gram-negative 128
Gutenberg 56, 57

H

Hematopoietic stem cell 222, 223
History of Adult Stem Cells xii, 225, 227, 229, 235, 236, 237, 238, 239, 240, 241, 242, 245, 254
HIV xi, 54, 205, 206, 207, 208, 209, 210, 211, 212, 213, 214, 215, 216, 217, 249, 250, 251, 254, 263, 273
HIV and AIDS are hard to get 215
Hoagland, Mahlon Bush 184
Holmes, Oliver Wendell 98
Human Genome ix, xi, 194, 198, 200, 201, 203, 213, 245, 271, 272
Human hygiene 98
Human stem cells for use in the testing of drugs 243
Hunt, Thomas 88, 89, 138
Hydrogen bonds 166, 167, 171, 174, 175, 176

Hydrologic cycle 14, 16

I

Infection 54, 102

J

Jet stream 12

K

Khorana, Har Gobind 184, 187
Koch 50, 75, 76, 77, 80, 83, 257

L

Levene 165
Lister, Joseph 84

M

Man on earth 64
Matthaei, Heinrich 189
Mendel and genetics 86, 87, 88, 89, 90, 92, 98, 138, 146, 200
Mendel inheritance law 90
Messenger RNA mRNA 168, 182, 183, 184, 185, 186, 187, 193, 206, 261
Metchnikoff and the phagocytes 77
Meteor collision 25, 262
Microscope x, 63, 64, 65, 66, 67, 68, 69, 70, 71, 72, 75, 76, 78, 83, 102, 105, 110, 122, 128, 131, 140, 146, 156, 157, 179, 209, 220, 233, 257, 271

N

Nirenberg 183, 184, 187, 189
Nucleoproteins 151, 152, 154
Nucleoside 177
Nucleotide 23, 166, 167, 168, 172,

174, 177, 182, 183, 184, 187, 201, 243
Number of genes 194, 195

O

Organics, Proteins, and Nucleic Acid 150
Oxygen buildup 22
Oxytocin 161

P

Palade, George 179
paper chromatography 160
Pasteur 71, 72, 73, 74, 77, 78, 80, 84, 85, 116, 117, 253, 257
Pauling, Linus Carl 169
Penicillin 122, 123, 124, 125, 126, 127, 128, 129, 130, 259
Photosynthesis 8, 33
Plasticity of Adult Stem Cells 236
Polio 130
Polio vaccine 260
Polynucleotide 177
Precipitation 6, 10, 11, 12, 14, 15, 16, 17, 18
Present atmosphere composition 10
Printing Press 56
Prokaryotes 122, 140, 141, 146, 180
Proliferation 228
Prontosil 113, 114, 115, 116, 117, 120, 121
Protein synthesis 168, 189

R

Rain fall 18
Recent man 29
Replication 53, 147, 148, 172, 174, 175, 176, 199, 210
Reprogrammed human skin cells 246
Retrovirus xi, 196, 206, 207, 208, 209, 210, 214, 246, 247, 248, 249, 250, 254, 273

Ribosomes 168, 179, 180, 182, 184
RNA ribonucleic acid 6, 165, 167, 183, 261
Roman Empire 39, 40, 41, 60
Ross, Ronald 81

S

Salk, Jonas 130, 136, 260
Silent deaths 43
Smallpox 50
Smith, Theobald 80
Spallanzani 70, 71, 72
Spanish Flu 52
Staphylococcus and streptococcus 259
Stem Cells 218
Stem Cell summary 254
Sulfonamide 110
Sun's daily energy 262

T

Tobacco-mosaic virus 151
Transcription 184
Transfer RNA tRNA 184, 186, 187
Translation of RNA code 189

U

Unique Properties of Stem Cells 228
Unspecialized. Stem cells 228

V

Vasopressin 161
Venter, Craig 198, 200, 203
Vigneaud, Vincent 161

W

Watson, James Dewey 170
Wilkins, Maurice Hugh Frederick 170

www.ingramcontent.com/pod-product-compliance
Lightning Source LLC
Chambersburg PA
CBHW021423070526
44577CB00001B/30